GRAMMAR MENTOR

plus 4

GRAMMAR MENTOR JOY plus 4

지은이   교재개발연구소

발행처   Pearson Education

판매처   inkedu(inkbooks)

전 화   (02) 455-9620(주문 및 고객지원)

팩 스   (02) 455-9619

등 록   제13-579호

Longman

그래머
멘토
조이
플러스
넷

GRAMMAR
MENTOR

JOY

plus 4

Preface

선택이 중요합니다!

인생에 수많은 선택이 있듯이 많은 시간 함께할 영어 공부의 시작에도 수많은 선택이 있습니다. 오늘 여러분의 선택이 앞으로의 여러분의 영어실력을 좌우합니다. Grammar Mentor Joy 시리즈는 현장 경험이 풍부한 선생님들과 이전 학습자들의 의견을 충분히 수렴하여 여러분의 선택에 후회가 없도록 하였습니다.

효율적인 학습이 필요한 때입니다!

학습의 시간은 유한합니다. 중요한 것은 그 시간을 얼마나 효율적으로 사용하는지입니다. Grammar Mentor Joy 시리즈는 우선 튼튼한 기초를 다지기 위해서 단계별 Syllabus를 현행 교과과정과 연계할 수 있도록 맞춤 설계하여 학습자들이 효율적으로 학습할 수 있도록 하였습니다. 또한 기존의 기계적 반복 학습 문제에서 벗어나 학습자들이 능동적 학습을 유도할 수 있도록 사고력 향상이 필요한 문제와 난이도를 조정하였습니다.

중학 기초 문법을 대비하는 교재입니다!

Grammar Mentor Joy 시리즈는 확고한 목표를 가지고 있습니다. 그것은 중학교 문법을 완벽하게 준비하는 것입니다. Grammar Mentor Joy 시리즈에서는 문법 기초를 확고하게 다루고 있기 때문에 중학교 문법은 새로운 것이 아닌 Grammar Mentor Joy 시리즈의 연장선에 지나지 않습니다. 또한 가장 힘들 수 있는 어휘 학습에 있어서도 반복적인 문제 풀이를 통해서 자연스럽게 기초 어휘를 학습하도록 하였습니다.

마지막으로 어떤 기초 교재보다도 처음 영어 문법을 시작하는 학습자들에게 더없이 완벽한 선택이 될 수 있다고 자신합니다. 이 교재를 통해서 영어가 학습자들의 평생 걸림돌이 아닌 자신감이 될 수 있기를 바랍니다. 감사합니다.

Guide to *Grammar Mentor Joy Plus Series*

❶ 단계별 학습을 통한 맞춤식 문법 학습

 – 각 Chapter별 Unit에는 세부 설명과 Warm-up, Start up, Check up & Writing, Level Up, Actual Test, Review Test, Achievement Test, 마지막으로 실전모의 테스트로 구성되어 있습니다.

❷ 서술형 문제를 위한 체계적인 학습

 – Check up & Writing에서는 서술형 문제에 대비할 수 있도록 하고 있습니다.

❸ 단순 암기식 공부가 아닌 사고력이 필요한 문제 풀이 학습

 – 단순 패턴 드릴 문제가 아닌 이전 문제들을 함께 섞어 제시하고 있어 사고력 향상이 도움이 되도록 하였습니다.

❹ 반복적인 학습을 통해 문제 풀이 능력을 향상시킴

 – 세분화된 Step으로 반복 학습이 가능합니다.

❺ 맞춤식 어휘와 문장을 통한 체계적인 학습

 – 학습한 어휘와 문장을 반복적으로 제시하고 있어 무의식적으로 습득이 가능합니다.

❻ 중학 기초 문법을 대비하는 문법 학습

 – 중학 문법에서 다루는 기초 문법을 모두 다루고 있습니다.

❼ 반복적인 문제풀이를 통한 기초 어휘 학습

 – Chapter별 제공되는 단어장에는 자주 쓰는 어휘들을 체계적으로 제시하고 있습니다.

Syllabus

Grammar Mentor Joy Plus 시리즈는 전체 4권으로 구성되어 있습니다. 각 Level이 각각 6개의 Chapter 총 6주의 학습 시간으로 구성되어 있는데, 특히 Chapter 3과 Chapter 6은 Review와 Achievement Test로 반복 복습할 수 있도록 구성되어 있습니다. 부가적으로 단어장과 전 시리즈가 끝난 후 실전 모의고사 테스트 3회도 제공되고 있습니다.

Level	Month	Week	Chapter	Unit	Homework
1	1st	1	1 be동사	Unit 01 be동사의 현재형과 과거형	*각 Chapter별 단어 퀴즈 제공 *각 Chapter별 드릴 문제 제공 *각 Chapter별 모의 테스트지 제공
				Unit 02 be동사의 부정문과 의문문	
				Unit 03 There is / There are	
		2	2 일반동사	Unit 01 일반동사의 현재형	
				Unit 02 일반동사의 과거형	
				Unit 03 일반동사의 부정문	
				Unit 04 일반동사의 의문문	
		3	3 시제	Unit 01 진행 시제	
				Unit 02 현재완료 시제	
			Review/Achievement Test		
		4	4 조동사 I	Unit 01 can과 be able to	
				Unit 02 may, must	
				Unit 03 have to, should	
	2nd	5	5 조동사 II	Unit 01 will, be going to	
				Unit 02 would like to, had better, used to	
		6	6 문장의 형태	Unit 01 1형식, 2형식 문장	
				Unit 02 3형식, 4형식 문장	
				Unit 03 5형식 문장	
			Review/Achievement Test		
2		1	1 명사	Unit 01 셀 수 있는 명사	*각 Chapter별 단어 퀴즈 제공 *각Chapter별 드릴 문제 제공 *각 Chapter별 모의 테스트지 제공
				Unit 02 셀 수 없는 명사	
				Unit 03 명사의 격	
		2	2 관사	Unit 01 부정관사 a, an	
				Unit 02 정관사 the와 관사를 쓰지 않는 경우	
		3	3 대명사 I	Unit 01 인칭대명사	
				Unit 02 지시대명사와 비인칭 주어 it	
				Unit 03 재귀대명사	
			Review/Achievement Test		
	3rd	4	4 대명사 II	Unit 01 부정대명사 I	
				Unit 02 부정대명사 II	
				Unit 03 부정대명사 III	
		5	5 형용사와 부사	Unit 01 형용사	
				Unit 02 부사	
		6	6 비교	Unit 01 비교급, 최상급 만드는 법	
				Unit 02 원급, 비교급, 최상급	
				Unit 03 비교 구문을 이용한 표현	
			Review/Achievement Test		

Level	Month	Week	Chapter	Unit	Homework
3	4th	1	1 to부정사	Unit 01 to부정사의 명사적 쓰임	*각 Chapter별 단어 퀴즈 제공
				Unit 02 to부정사의 형용사적 쓰임	
				Unit 03 to부정사의 부사적 쓰임	
				Unit 04 to부정사의 관용 표현	
		2	2 동명사	Unit 01 동명사의 쓰임	
				Unit 02 동명사를 이용한 표현	
				Unit 03 동사 + 동명사 / 동사 + to부정사	
		3	3 분사	Unit 01 현재분사	
				Unit 02 과거분사	*각 Chapter별 드릴 문제 제공
				Unit 03 분사구문	
			Review/Achievement Test		
		4	4 수동태	Unit 01 능동태와 수동태	
				Unit 02 수동태의 여러 가지 형태 Ⅰ	
				Unit 03 수동태의 여러 가지 형태 Ⅱ	*각 Chapter별 모의테스트지 제공
				Unit 04 주의해야 할 수동태	
	5th	5	5 전치사	Unit 01 시간 전치사	
				Unit 02 장소 전치사	
				Unit 03 방향 전치사	
		6	6 접속사	Unit 01 등위 접속사	
				Unit 02 시간, 이유, 결과 접속사	
				Unit 03 조건, 양보 접속사, 상관접속사	
			Review/Achievement Test		
4	6th	1	1 가정법	Unit 01 가정법 과거	
				Unit 02 가정법 과거 완료	
				Unit 03 I wish 가정법	
		2	2 관계대명사 Ⅰ	Unit 01 관계대명사	*각 Chapter별 단어 퀴즈 제공
				Unit 02 관계대명사 – 목적격, 소유격	
				Unit 03 관계대명사 that, what	
		3	3 관계대명사 Ⅱ	Unit 01 관계대명사 생략과 계속적 용법	
				Unit 02 관계부사	
			Review/Achievement Test		*각 Chapter별 드릴 문제 제공
		4	4 여러 가지 문장 Ⅰ	Unit 01 의문사가 있는 의문문 Ⅰ	
				Unit 02 의문사가 있는 의문문 Ⅱ	
				Unit 03 명령문과 제안문	*각 Chapter별 모의테스트지 제공
		5	5 여러 가지 문장 Ⅱ	Unit 01 부가의문문	
				Unit 02 간접의문문, 선택의문문	
				Unit 03 감탄문	*최종 3회의 실전모의고사 테스트지 제공
		6	6 시제의 일치 및 화법	Unit 01 수의 일치	
				Unit 02 시제 일치	
				Unit 03 간접 화법	
			Review/Achievement Test		

Construction

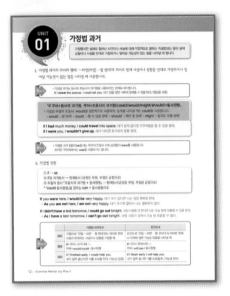

Unit
각 Chapter를 Unit으로 나누어 보다 심층적이고 체계적으로 학습할 수 있도록 했습니다.

Warm-up
본격적인 학습에 앞서 Unit의 기본적인 내용을 점검하는 단계입니다.

Start up
각 Unit에서 다루고 있는 문법의 기본적인 내용들을 점검할 수 있도록 했습니다.

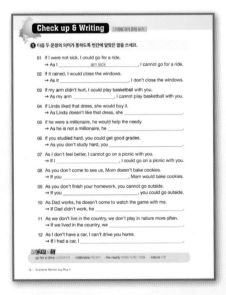

Check up & Writing
서술형 문제에 대비하는 단계로 단순 단어의 나열이 아닌, 사고력이 요하는 문제들로 구성되어 있습니다

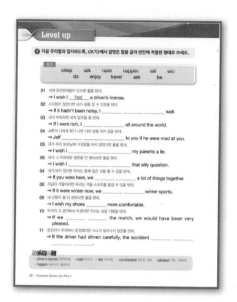

Level up

각 Chapter의 내용을 최종 점검하는 단계로 각 Unit의 내용들을 기초로 한 문제들로 구성되어 있습니다.

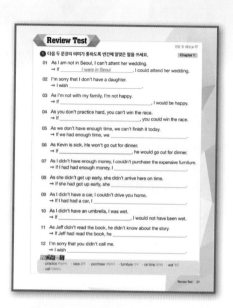

Review Test

Chapter 3개마다 구성되어 있으며, 앞서 배운 기본적인 내용들을 다시 한 번 풀어 보도록 구성했습니다.

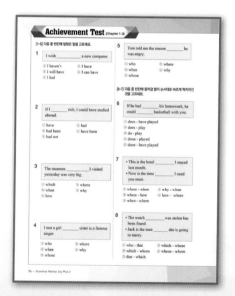

Achievement Test

Chapter 3개마다 구성되어 있으며, 5지선다형 문제와 서술형 문제로 구성되어 있어 실전 내신문제에 대비하도록 했습니다.

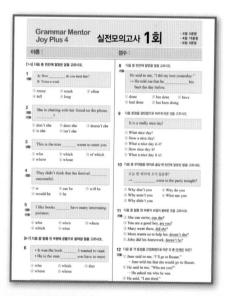

실전모의고사

총 3회로 구성되어있으며 각 level의 모든 내용을 5지선다형 문제와 서술형 문제로 구성하여 여러분들이 최종적으로 학습한 내용을 점검 할 수 있도록 했습니다.

Contents

Grammar Mentor Joy Plus 1	Grammar Mentor Joy Plus 2	Grammar Mentor Joy Plus 3
Chapter 1 be 동사	Chapter 1 명사	Chapter 1 to 부정사
Chapter 2 일반동사	Chapter 2 관사	Chapter 2 동명사
Chapter 3 시제	Chapter 3 대명사 I	Chapter 3 분사
Chapter 4 조동사 I	Chapter 4 대명사 II	Chapter 4 수동태
Chapter 5 조동사 II	Chapter 5 형용사와 부사	Chapter 5 전치사
Chapter 6 문장의 형태	Chapter 6 비교	Chapter 6 접속사

Chapter 1

가정법

UNIT 01

가정법 과거

가정법이란 실제로 일어난 사건이나 사실에 대해 직접적으로 말하는 직설법과는 달리 실제 상황이나 사실을 반대로 가정하거나 일어날 가능성이 없는 일을 나타낼 때 씁니다.

1. 가정법 과거의 의미와 형태: '~하면[라면] …할 텐데'의 의미로 현재 사실이나 상황을 반대로 가정하거나 일어날 가능성이 없는 일을 나타낼 때 사용합니다.

Plus 1
- 가정법 과거는 동사와 조동사의 과거형을 사용하지만, 현재로 해석합니다.
  If I **knew** the answer, I **could tell** you. 내가 답을 알면 너에게 말해줄 수 있을 텐데. (정답을 모름)

「**if 주어+동사의 과거형, 주어+조동사의 과거형(could/would/might/should)+동사원형**」
- 가정법 주절의 조동사: would를 일반적으로 사용하며, 능력을 나타낼 때는 could를 사용합니다.
- would '~할 텐데' - could '~할 수 있을 텐데' - should '~해야 할 텐데' - might '~할지도 모를 텐데'

If I **had** much money, I **could travel** into space. 내가 돈이 많다면 우주여행을 할 수 있을 텐데.
If I **were** you, I **wouldn't give up**. 내가 너라면 포기하지 않을 텐데.

Plus 2
- 가정법 과거 if절의 be동사는 주어의 인칭과 수에 상관없이 **were**를 사용합니다.
  하지만 구어체에서는 **was**를 사용하기도 합니다.

---

2. 직설법 전환

① if → as
② if절 과거동사 → 현재동사 (긍정은 부정, 부정은 긍정으로)
③ 주절의 동사 『조동사의 과거형 + 동사원형』 → 현재동사(긍정은 부정, 부정은 긍정으로)
* 「could 동사원형」일 경우는 can + 동사원형으로

If you **were** here, I **would be** very happy. 네가 여기 있다면 나는 정말 행복할 텐데.
→ **As** you **are not** here, I **am not** very happy. 네가 여기에 없어서 나는 행복하지 않다.

If I **didn't have** a test tomorrow, I **could go out** tonight. 내일 시험을 안 본다면 나는 오늘 밤에 외출할 수 있을 텐데.
→ **As** I **have** a test tomorrow, I **can't go out** tonight. 내일 시험이 있어서 오늘 밤 외출할 수 없다.

	가정법 과거의 if	조건의 if
의미	가정의 if: '만일 ~라면 …할 텐데'라는 의미로 현재 사실과 반대되는 사실이나 상황을 가정할 때	조건의 if: '만일 ~라면 …할 것이다'의 의미로 현재나 미래에 실현 가능성 있음을 나타낼 때
형태	If+주어+과거시제 ~, 주어+would/could+동사원형	If+주어+현재시제 ~, 주어+will/can+동사원형
의미	If I finished early, I would help you. 내가 일찍 끝난다면 너를 도와줄 텐데. (가능성 없음)	If I finish early, I will help you. 내가 일찍 끝나면 너를 도와줄게. (가능성 50%)

Warm up

정답 및 해설 p.2

● 다음 우리말과 같은 뜻이 되도록, 괄호 안에서 알맞은 것을 고르세요.

01 If I ((finish) / finished) early, I will help you.
내가 일찍 끝나면 너를 도와줄게.

If I (finish / finished) early, I would help you.
내가 일찍 끝난다면 너를 도와줄 텐데.

02 If you (teach / taught) me, I could do good work.
네가 나를 가르쳐 준다면 나는 일을 잘할 수 있을 텐데.

If you (teach / taught) me, I can do good work.
네가 나를 가르쳐 주면 나는 일을 잘할 수 있을 거야.

03 If we (leave / left) now, we can catch the early train.
우리가 지금 떠나면 우리는 새벽 기차를 탈 수 있을 거야.

If we (leave / left) now, we could catch the early train.
우리가 지금 떠난다면 우리는 새벽 기차를 탈 수 있을 텐데.

04 If I (meet / met) Timothy, I will ask him about that.
내가 Timothy를 만나면 그것에 대해 물어볼 거야.

If I (meet / met) Timothy, I would ask him about that.
내가 Timothy를 만난다면 그것에 대해 물어볼 텐데.

05 If he (invite / invited) me, I will go to the party.
그가 나를 초대하면 나는 그 파티에 갈 거야.

If he (invite / invited) me, I would go to the party.
그가 나를 초대한다면 나는 그 파티에 갈 텐데.

06 If it (is / were) sunny, we will go for a swim.
날씨가 화창하면 우리는 수영하러 갈 거야.

If it (is / were) sunny, we would go for a swim.
날씨가 화창하다면 우리는 수영하러 갈 텐데.

07 If they (hurry / hurried), they wouldn't miss the flight.
그들이 서두른다면 그들은 비행기를 놓치지 않을 텐데.

If they (hurry / hurried), they will not miss the flight.
그들이 서두르면 그들은 비행기를 놓치지 않을 거야.

08 If you (take / took) a taxi, you will arrive on time.
네가 택시를 타면 너는 제시간에 도착할 거야.

If you (take / took) a taxi, you would arrive on time.
네가 택시를 탄다면 너는 제시간에 도착할 텐데.

WORDS

• do good work 일을 잘하다   • go for a swim 수영하러 가다   • hurry 서두르다   • flight 비행기; 비행
• on time 제시간에   • miss 놓치다

1 다음 괄호 안에서 알맞은 것을 고르세요.

01 If I (know / (knew)) his phone number, I would call him.

02 If I (am / were) you, I would tell the truth.

03 If I (have / had) a lot of money, I would buy a nice house.

04 If you (are / were) here, I would be happy.

05 If I (have / had) time, I could read more books.

06 If he (am / were) not busy, he would go with you.

07 If it (snow / snowed) a lot, my brother and I could make a snowman.

08 If it (rains / rained), we will not go for a walk.

09 If you clear the table, I (will / would) do the dishes.

10 If Charles liked basketball, he (will / would) join our club.

11 If you take the subway, you (won't / wouldn't) be late.

12 If he knew my e-mail address, he (will / would) send me an e-mail.

13 If he were nicer, he (can make / could make) a lot of friends.

14 If Dad came home early, he (will cook / would cook) dinner.

15 If I went to London, I (will visit / would visit) the London Eye first.

- **truth** 사실, 진실 · **snowman** 눈사람 · **go for a walk** 산책가다 · **join** 참여하다, 가입하다 · **club** 동호회, 클럽
- **the London Eye** 런던아이

❷ 다음 주어진 단어를 이용하여 문장을 완성하세요.

01 If I ____knew____ (know) a good restaurant, I would take you there.

02 If it _____ (be) Sunday today, we wouldn't go to school.

03 What would you do if you _____ (win) first prize in the contest?

04 If I _____ _____ (be/not) sick, I could go camping with my friends.

05 If Robin _____ (read) the book, he could pass the literature test.

06 What would you say if he _____ (ask) that question?

07 If I traveled to Paris, I _____ _____ (will/visit) the Louvre Museum.

08 If she _____ (have) courage, she would make a decision by herself.

09 If I were 20 years old, I _____ _____ (can/watch) the movie.

10 If you were in my shoes, what _____ you _____ (will/do)?

11 If I were not tired, I _____ _____ (can/go) shopping with you.

12 If she had a camera, she _____ _____ (will/lend) it to you.

13 If Jamie wore a coat, she _____ _____ _____ (will/not/feel) cold.

14 If it were windy, the kite _____ _____ (will/fly) high.

15 If they practiced hard, they _____ _____ (can/win) the game.

WORDS

· literature 문학   · courage 용기   · decision 결정, 결심   · make a decision 결심하다   · by oneself 혼자, 스스로
· be in one's shoes ~의 입장에 처하다   · lend 빌려주다   · practice 연습하다

1 다음 두 문장의 의미가 통하도록 빈칸에 알맞은 말을 쓰세요.

01 If I were not sick, I could go for a ride.
→ As I _____ am sick _____, I cannot go for a ride.

02 If it rained, I would close the windows.
→ As it _____, I don't close the windows.

03 If my arm didn't hurt, I could play basketball with you.
→ As my arm _____, I cannot play basketball with you.

04 If Linda liked that dress, she would buy it.
→ As Linda doesn't like that dress, she _____.

05 If he were a millionaire, he would help the needy.
→ As he is not a millionaire, he _____.

06 If you studied hard, you could get good grades.
→ As you don't study hard, you _____.

07 As I don't feel better, I cannot go on a picnic with you.
→ If I _____, I could go on a picnic with you.

08 As you don't come to see us, Mom doesn't bake cookies.
→ If you _____, Mom would bake cookies.

09 As you don't finish your homework, you cannot go outside.
→ If you _____, you could go outside.

10 As Dad works, he doesn't come to watch the game with me.
→ If Dad didn't work, he _____.

11 As we don't live in the country, we don't play in nature more often.
→ If we lived in the country, we _____.

12 As I don't have a car, I can't drive you home.
→ If I had a car, I _____.

• go for a drive 드라이브가다 • millionaire 백만장자 • the needy 어려운[가난한] 사람들 • nature 자연

❷ 다음 우리말과 일치하도록, 주어진 단어를 이용하여 문장을 완성하세요.

01 내가 내 차를 판다면 3천 달러를 받을 수 있을 텐데. (sell, get)

→ If I _____ sold my car _____, I _____ could get _____ $3,000.

02 그녀의 친구들이 온다면 그녀가 행복할 텐데. (happy, como)

→ She _____ if her friends _____.

03 네가 자외선 차단제를 사용한다면 햇볕에 타지 않을 텐데. (use, get)

→ If you _____ sunscreen, you _____ sunburned.

04 내가 너라면 그 제안을 받아드릴 텐데. (be, accept)

→ If I _____, I _____ the offer.

05 그가 부자라면 그는 그 자동차를 살 수 있을 텐데. (be, rich, buy)

→ If he _____, he _____ the car.

06 그들이 그 사실을 듣는다면 놀랄 텐데. (hear, the truth, be, surprised)

→ If they _____, they _____.

07 눈이 오지 않는다면 차를 타고 출근할 텐데. (be, snowy, drive to work)

→ If it _____, I _____.

08 그녀에게 친구가 많다면 그녀는 외롭지 않을 텐데. (have, a lot of friends, not, feel)

→ If she _____, she _____ lonely.

09 네가 더 오래 머무른다면 내가 저녁을 해줄 텐데. (stay, longer, cook, dinner)

→ If you _____, I _____ for you.

10 내가 운전하는 법을 안다면 자동차로 세계 곳곳을 여행할 텐데. (know, travel)

→ If I _____ how to drive, I _____ across the world by car.

11 그가 영어를 잘 한다면 그는 그 면접을 통과할 수 있을 텐데. (speak, pass)

→ If he _____ well, he _____ the interview.

12 내가 Jason을 안다면 너에게 그를 소개해줄 텐데. (know, Jason, introduce)

→ If I _____, I _____ him to you.

WORDS

• sell 팔다   • sunscreen 자외선 차단제   • get sunburned 햇볕에 타다   • accept 받아들이다   • offer 제안
• surprised 놀란   • drive to work 차로 출근하다   • lonely 외로운   • interview 면접, 인터뷰   • introduce 소개하다

UNIT 02 가정법 과거완료

가정법 과거는 현재 상황이나 사실을 가정할 때 쓰지만, 가정법 과거완료는 과거의 상황이나 사실에 반대되는 내용을 가정할 때 사용합니다.

1. 의미와 형태: '~했으면[였더라면] …했을 텐데'의 의미로 과거 사실에 반대되는 상황이나 사실을 가정할 때 사용합니다.

「if 주어+과거완료(had+p.p.), 주어+조동사의 과거형(could/would/might/should) have+p.p.」

If I **had had** much money, I **could have traveled** into space.
내가 돈이 많았다면 우주여행을 할 수 있었을 텐데.
If it **had rained**, we **couldn't have enjoyed** the trip.
비가 왔다면 우리는 여행을 즐기지 못했을 텐데.
If he **had studied** hard, he **would have passed** the test.
그가 공부를 열심히 했더라면, 그는 시험에 통과했을 텐데.

Plus
• 가정법 과거완료는 완료형을 사용하지만, 과거로 해석합니다.
If I **had been** there, I **would have helped** you.
내가 거기 있었더라면 내가 너를 도와줬을 텐데.

2. 직설법 전환

① if → as
② if절 과거완료 → 과거동사 (긍정은 부정, 부정은 긍정으로)
③ 주절의 동사 『조동사의 괴거형+ have p.p.』 → 과거동사(긍정은 부정, 부정은 긍정으로)
★ 『could have p.p.』일 경우는 could+동사원형으로

If I **had arrived** earlier, I **could have met** Watney.
내가 일찍 도착했다면 Watney를 만날 수 있었을 텐데.
→ As I **didn't arrive** earlier, I **couldn't meet** Watney.
내가 일찍 도착하지 않아서 Watney를 만날 수 없었다.

If he **hadn't come**, she **would have been** disappointed.
그가 오지 않았다면 그녀가 실망했을 텐데.
→ As he **came**, she **wasn't** disappointed.
그가 와서 그녀는 실망하지 않았다.

Warm up

정답 및 해설 p.

● 다음 우리말과 일치하도록, 괄호 안에서 알맞은 것을 고르세요.

01 If you (left / (had left)) early, you could have taken the train.
네가 일찍 떠났더라면 너는 그 기차를 탈 수 있었을 텐데.

If you (left / had left) early, you could take the train.
네가 일찍 떠난다면 너는 그 기차를 탈 수 있을 텐데.

02 If you (came / had come) with me, I would go to the party.
네가 나와 함께 간다면 나는 그 파티에 갈 텐데.

If you (came / had come) with me, I would have gone to the party.
네가 나와 함께 갔다면 나는 그 파티에 갔을 텐데.

03 If I (had / had had) a library card, I would borrow some books.
나에게 도서관 카드가 있다면 책을 좀 빌릴 텐데.

If I (had / had had) a library card, I would have borrowed some books.
나에게 도서관 카드가 있었다면 책을 좀 빌렸을 텐데.

04 If she (knew / had known) my address, she would send me a postcard
그녀가 내 주소를 안다면 나에게 엽서를 보낼 텐데.

If she (knew / had known) my address, she would have sent me
postcard.
그녀가 내 주소를 알았다면 나에게 엽서를 보냈을 텐데.

05 If it were rainy, I would (stay / have stayed) home.
비가 온다면 집에 있을 텐데.

If it had been rainy yesterday, I would (stay / have stayed) home.
어제 비가 왔다면 집에 있었을 텐데.

06 If they had had more money, they could (buy / have bought) the house.
그들이 돈이 더 많았다면 그 집을 살 수 있었을 텐데.

If they had more money, they could (buy / have bought) the house.
그들이 돈이 더 많다면 그 집을 살 수 있을 텐데.

07 If we won the game, we would (be / had been) very happy.
우리가 그 경기에서 이긴다면 정말 행복할 텐데.

If we had won the game, we would (be / have been) very happy.
우리가 그 경기에서 이겼다면 정말 행복했을 텐데.

08 If I had not been tired, I would (go / have gone) for a walk.
나는 피곤하지 않았다면 산책을 갔을 텐데.

If I were not tired, I would (go / have gone) for a walk.
나는 피곤하지 않다면 산책을 갈 텐데.

WORDS

• borrow 빌리다　• address 주소　• postcard 엽서

❶ 다음 괄호 안에서 알맞은 것을 고르세요.

01 If it (were /(had been)) sunny, we would have gone on a picnic.

02 If I (were / had been) her, I wouldn't have believed Jason.

03 If you (spoken / had spoken) clearly, we could have understood you.

04 If I (known / had known) the truth, I would have forgiven you.

05 If you (took / had taken) my advice, you could have done better.

06 If you (believed / had believed) in yourself, you could have succeeded.

07 If the train had arrived on time, I wouldn't (be / have been) late for work.

08 If Tim hadn't liked you, he wouldn't (take / have taken) you out for lunch.

09 If Sam hadn't cheated, he wouldn't (fail / have failed) in the final exam.

10 If I had heard the phone ring, I would (answer / have answered) the phone.

11 If I hadn't been sick, I would (have gone / had gone) to your party.

12 If he had had more time, he could (finish / have finished) his homework.

13 If you had asked me, I would (told / have told) you about him.

14 If I had gotten good grades, Dad would (buy / have bought) me a new computer.

15 If you had driven carefully, you wouldn't (had / have had) a car accident.

WORDS

· clearly 명확하게, 또렷하게　· understand 이해하다　· forgive 용서하다　· succeed 성공하다　· yourself 너 자신
· cheat 속이다, (시험에서) 부정행위를 하다　· accident 사고

2 다음 주어진 단어를 이용하여 문장을 완성하세요.

01 If I ___had___ ___taken___ (take) the subway, I wouldn't have been late.

02 If he _____ _____ (know) everything, he wouldn't have gotten angry with you.

03 If Mom _____ _____ (hear) the news, she would have been very happy.

04 If you _____ _____ (be) wise, you wouldn't have done such a thing.

05 If they _____ _____ (hurry), they could have caught the bus.

06 If my sister _____ _____ (not/tell) me, I would have forgotten my dad's birthday.

07 If I _____ _____ (listen) carefully to the teacher, I wouldn't have spoiled the experiment.

08 If it hadn't rained, we _____ _____ _____ (can/play) outside.

09 If the police had arrived earlier, they _____ _____ _____ (will/catch) the thief.

10 If you had been quiet, the baby _____ _____ _____ (will/not wake) up.

11 If Beck had brought his camera, he _____ _____ _____ (could/take) nice pictures.

12 If you had bought fresh vegetables, you _____ _____ _____ (can/make) a salad.

WORDS

· forget 잊다   · spoil 망치다   · experiment 실험   · play outside 밖에서 놀다   · thief 도둑   · vegetable 채소

Check up & Writing   가정법 과거완료 문장 쓰기

① 다음 두 문장의 의미가 통하도록 빈칸에 알맞은 말을 쓰세요.

01 If it had rained, the crops wouldn't have died.
→ As it _____ didn't rain _____, the crops died.

02 If I hadn't known what to do, I would have asked my mother.
→ As I _____, I didn't ask my mother.

03 If I had bought the book, I could have lent it to you.
→ As I _____, I couldn't lend it to you.

04 As the movie wasn't interesting, Nick didn't stay up late.
→ If the movie _____, Nick would have stayed up late.

05 As my brother didn't go to the doctor, he didn't feel much better.
→ If my brother _____, he would have felt much better.

06 As Rachel didn't work hard, she could not become a top student.
→ If Rachel _____, she could have become a top student.

07 If I had felt better, I could have gone to the movies with you.
→ As I didn't feel better, I _____.

08 If you hadn't told me, I would have been in trouble.
→ As you told me, I _____.

09 If Jim had prepared for the test, he wouldn't have failed it.
→ As Jim didn't prepare for the test, he _____.

10 As the weather was not okay, the ferry couldn't leave on time.
→ If the weather had been okay, the ferry _____.

11 As they didn't take her to the hospital earlier, she was not alive.
→ If they had taken her to the hospital earlier, she _____.

12 As you didn't lock the door, the thief broke into our house.
→ If you had locked the door, the thief _____.

· crop 농작물   · stay up late 늦게까지 깨어 있다   · be in trouble 곤경에 처하다   · alive 살아 있는   · break into 침입하다

❷ 다음 우리말과 일치하도록, 주어진 단어를 이용하여 문장을 완성하세요.

01 내가 너의 전화번호를 알았다면 너에게 전화했을 텐데. (know, call)

➡ If I ___had known___ your phone number, I ___would have called___ you

02 네가 Eric을 만났다면 너는 그를 정말 좋아했을 텐데. (meet, like)

➡ If you _____, you _____ him very much

03 그들에게 지도가 있었다면 그들은 길을 잃지 않았을 텐데. (have, be lost)

➡ If they _____ a map, they _____

04 Max가 골을 넣지 않았다면 우리는 경기에서 이기지 못했을 텐데. (score, win)

➡ If Max _____ a goal, we _____ the game.

05 내가 사실을 얘기했다면 우리 부모님은 화를 내지 않았을 텐데. (tell, get angry)

➡ If I _____ the truth, my parents _____

06 그가 노래를 잘했다면 더 인기가 있었을 텐데. (sing, be more popular)

➡ If he _____ well, he _____.

07 내가 너였다면 그에게 무례하게 대하지 않았을 텐데. (be, be rude)

➡ If I _____ you, I _____ to him.

08 Jennifer가 열심히 공부했다면 그 시험에 통과할 수 있었을 텐데. (study hard, pass)

➡ If Jennifer _____, she _____ the test.

09 그녀가 울지 않았다면 나는 그녀의 사과를 받지 않았을 텐데. (cry, accept)

➡ If she _____, I _____ her apology.

10 내가 그때 키가 더 컸다면 나는 농구부에 가입할 수 있었을 텐데. (be taller, join)

➡ If I _____ taller then, I _____ the basketball team.

11 내 여동생이 내 드레스를 입지 않았다면 나는 그녀와 싸우지 않았을 텐데. (wear, fight)

➡ If my sister _____ my dress, I _____ with her.

12 내가 바쁘지 않았다면 너를 방문했을 텐데. (be busy, visit)

➡ If I _____, I _____ you.

WORDS

· be lost 길을 잃다 · score 골을 넣다, 득점을 올리다 · goal 골 · popular 인기 있는 · rude 무례한 · apology 사과
· accept 받아들이다

UNIT 03

I wish 가정법

I wish 가정법 과거는 현재의 이룰 수 없는 소망을 나타낼 때 쓰고, I wish 가정법 과거완료는 과거의 이루지 못한 소망이나 과거 일에 대한 후회를 나타낼 때 씁니다.

1. I wish 가정법 과거

① 의미와 형태: '~라면 좋을 텐데'의 의미로 현재의 이룰 수 없는 소망을 나타낼 때 사용합니다.

『I wish+주어+동사의 과거형』(★be동사의 경우 were를 사용해요.)

I wish it **were** Sunday today. 오늘이 일요일이면 좋을 텐데.
I wish I **didn't like** her. 내가 그녀를 좋아하지 않으면 좋을 텐데.

② 직설법 전환

① I wish → I'm sorry that으로
② that절 과거동사 → 현재동사 (긍정은 부정, 부정은 긍정으로)
★ 『could+동사원형』일 경우는 can 동사원형으로

I **wish** I **had** much time. 나에게 시간이 많으면 좋을 텐데.
→ I**'m sorry that** I don't have much time. 유감스럽지만 나는 시간이 많지 않다.

I **wish** you **were** here with us. 네가 우리와 함께 여기 있으면 좋을 텐데.
→ I**'m sorry that** you **are not** here with us. 너가 이곳에 우리와 함께하지 못해 유감이다.

2. I wish 가정법 과거완료

① 의미와 형태: '~했더라면 좋을 텐데'의 의미로 과거의 이루지 못한 소망이나 과거 일에 대한 후회를 나타 낼 때 사용합니다.

『I wish+주어+had+p.p.』

I wish it **had been** Sunday yesterday. 어제가 일요일이었으면 좋을 텐데.
I wish I **hadn't liked** her. 내가 그녀를 좋아하지 않았더라면 좋을 텐데.

② 직설법 전환

① I wish → I'm sorry that으로
② that절 had+p.p. → 과거동사 (긍정은 부정, 부정은 긍정으로)

I **wish** you **had called** me. 네가 나에게 전화해 줬으면 좋을 텐데.
→ I**'m sorry that** you **didn't call** me. 나에게 전화하지 않아서 유감이다.

I **wish** it **hadn't been** so late. 너무 늦지 않았더라면 좋을 텐데.
→ I**'m sorry that** it **was** so late. 너무 늦어서 유감이다.

Warm up

정답 및 해설 p.4

● 다음 괄호 안에서 알맞은 말을 고르세요.

01 I wish it (snowed /(had snowed)) a lot.
눈이 많이 내렸다면 좋을 텐데.

I wish it ((snowed)/ had snowed) a lot now.
지금 눈이 많이 내리면 좋을 텐데.

02 I wish I (had / had had) more time to talk you.
너와 이야기를 나눌 시간이 더 많으면 좋을 텐데.

I wish I (had / had had) more time to talk you last night.
어젯밤 너와 이야기를 나눌 시간이 더 많았다면 좋을 텐데.

03 I wish her new book (sold / had sold) well.
그녀의 새 책이 잘 팔리면 좋을 텐데.

I wish her new book (sold / had sold) well.
그녀의 새 책이 잘 팔렸다면 좋을 텐데.

04 I wish there (were / had been) no homework today.
오늘 숙제가 없으면 좋을 텐데.

I wish there (were / had been) no homework yesterday.
어제 숙제가 없었다면 좋을 텐데.

05 I wish he (took / had taken) the opportunity last year.
그가 작년에 그 기회를 잡았더라면 좋을 텐데.

I wish he (took / had taken) the opportunity without hesitation.
그가 망설임 없이 그 기회를 잡으면 좋을 텐데.

06 I wish I (went / had gone) shopping with you.
너와 함께 쇼핑하러 가면 좋을 텐데.

I wish I (went / had gone) shopping with you.
너와 함께 쇼핑하러 갔었다면 좋을 텐데.

07 I wish the weather (were / had been) nicer.
날씨가 더 좋았었으면 좋을 텐데.

I wish the weather (were / had been) nicer.
날씨가 더 좋으면 좋을 텐데.

· opportunity 기회   · hesitation 주저, 망설임

1 다음 괄호 안에서 알맞은 것을 고르세요.

01 I wish I (have / had) someone to help me now.

02 I wish I (can go / could go) with you.

03 I wish I (didn't hurt / hadn't hurt) her feelings last night.

04 I wish I (worked / had worked) hard when I was young.

05 I wish I (took / had taken) the ballet lessons last year.

06 I wish Jim (likes / liked) hiking, but he doesn't like it.

07 I have a stomachache now. I wish I (didn't eat / hadn't eaten) so much.

08 It is raining heavily. I wish I (had / had had) an umbrella with me now.

09 I think we've been lost. I wish I (know / knew) where we are.

10 I'm out of town now. I wish you (visited / had visited) me yesterday.

11 I'm too short to apply for a basketball team. I wish I (am / were) taller.

12 All my friends are good at skiing, and I envy them. I wish I (can ski / could ski) well.

13 Emma and Rachel saw a movie star at the mall yesterday. I wish I (went / had gone) there, too.

14 This chicken soup tastes awful. I wish you (followed / had followed) the recipe when you cooked.

15 The movie was a lot of fun. I wish you (watch / had watched) it with us last night.

WORDS
• hurt 상하게 하다   • feeling 느낌, 기분   • hiking 하이킹, 도보 여행   • out of town 출장 중인   • apply for ~에 지원하다
• envy 부러워하다   • mall 쇼핑 몰   • awful 끔찍한, 지독한   • recipe 요리법   • follow 따르다, 뒤를 잇다
• stomachache 복통

❷ 다음 우리말과 일치하도록, 주어진 단어를 이용하여 문장을 완성하세요.

01 I wish Christine _____ liked _____ me. (like)
Christine이 나를 좋아하면 좋을 텐데.

02 I wish I _____ more money. (earn)
내가 돈을 더 많이 벌면 좋을 텐데.

03 I wish I _____ Chinese well. (speak)
내가 중국어를 잘하면 좋을 텐데.

04 I wish I _____ on vacation now. (be)
내가 지금 휴가 중이라면 좋을 텐데.

05 I wish I _____ well. (can / dance)
나는 내가 춤을 잘 추면 좋을 텐데.

06 I wish I _____ of that idea yesterday. (think)
내가 어제 그 아이디어를 생각해냈으면 좋을 텐데.

07 I wish I _____ a lot of foreign friends. (have)
나에게 많은 외국인 친구가 있으면 좋을 텐데.

08 I wish I _____ her the truth. (not / tell)
그녀에게 그 사실을 말하지 않았다면 좋을 텐데.

09 I wish you _____ how to play the drums. (know)
네가 드럼을 치는 법을 알면 좋을 텐데.

10 I wish I _____ the work earlier yesterday. (finish)
내가 어제 그 일을 더 일찍 끝마쳤다면 좋을 텐데.

11 I wish my car _____. (not / break down)
내 차가 고장 나지 않았다면 좋을 텐데.

12 I wish they _____ themselves at the festival. (enjoy)
그들이 축제에서 즐거운 시간을 보냈다면 좋을 텐데.

13 I wish I _____ to the teacher during the class. (listen)
내가 수업 시간에 선생님 말에 귀 기울였다면 좋을 텐데.

14 I wish I _____ a fight with my brother yesterday. (have / not)
내가 어제 동생과 싸우지 않았다면 좋을 텐데.

WORDS

• earn (돈을) 벌다　• break down 고장 나다　• enjoy oneself 즐거운 시간을 보내다　• during ~동안　• have a fight 싸우다

1 다음 두 문장의 의미가 통하도록 빈칸에 알맞은 말을 쓰세요.

01 I wish I didn't work late.

→ I'm sorry that I _____ work late _____.

02 I wish she didn't like him.

→ I'm sorry that she _____.

03 I wish I wore warmer clothes.

→ I'm sorry I _____.

04 I wish she hadn't changed her mind.

→ I'm sorry that she _____.

05 I wish you called me often.

→ I'm sorry that you _____.

06 I wish I had more free time.

→ I'm sorry that I _____.

07 I wish I had heard the news earlier.

→ I'm sorry that I _____.

08 I wish I hadn't forgotten my mom's birthday.

→ I'm sorry that I _____.

09 I wish I hadn't spent all of my pocket money.

→ I'm sorry that I _____.

10 I wish I had caught a big fish in the lake.

→ I'm sorry that I _____.

11 I wish I hadn't asked that rude question to her.

→ I'm sorry I _____.

12 I wish my parents were here with me now.

→ I'm sorry that my parents _____.

· work late 늦게까지 일하다   · warm 따뜻한   · clothes 옷   · change one's mind 마음을 바꾸다
· pocket money 용돈

❷ 다음 우리말과 일치하도록, 주어진 단어를 이용하여 문장을 완성하세요.

01 오늘은 덥지 않으면 좋을 텐데. (hot, it, not, be)

➡ I wish _____ it were not hot _____ today.

02 시내에 공원이 많으면 좋을 텐데. (be, a lot of, there, parks)

➡ We wish _____ in town.

03 내가 그 약속을 지켰더라면 좋을 텐데. (I, kept, have, the promise)

➡ I wish _____.

04 5년 전에 그 집을 샀다면 좋을 텐데. (the house, I, bought, have)

➡ I wish _____ five years ago.

05 그 영화가 지루하지 않으면 좋을 텐데. (be, boring, the movie, not)

➡ I wish _____.

06 내가 그녀를 위해 무언가 할 수 있으면 좋을 텐데. (something, I, do, can)

➡ I wish _____ for her.

07 내가 남자 형제 또는 여자 형제가 있으면 좋을 텐데. (have, a sister, I, or a brother)

➡ I wish _____.

08 버스에 스마트폰을 두고 내리지 않았더라면 좋을 텐데. (leave, I, hadn't, smartphone, my)

➡ I wish _____ on the bus.

09 내 부모님이 나를 자랑스럽게 여겼다면 좋을 텐데. (had, proud, my parents, be)

➡ I wish _____ of me.

10 Susan이 자신의 꿈을 포기하지 않았다면 좋을 텐데. (give up, her dream, Susan, hadn't)

➡ I wish _____.

11 그때 그녀가 나에게 돈을 좀 빌려줬다면 좋을 텐데. (she, have, lent, me, some money)

➡ I wish _____ then.

12 우리 어머니가 나에게 컴퓨터를 사주면 좋을 텐데. (my mother, me, a computer, buy)

➡ I wish _____.

WORDS

- promise 약속 - keep a promise 약속을 지키다 - boring 지루한 - be proud of ~을 자랑스럽게 여기다
- give up 포기하다

1 다음 우리말과 일치하도록, 〈보기〉에서 알맞은 말을 골라 빈칸에 적절한 형태로 쓰세요.

보기

sleep	talk	have	happen	tell	win
do	enjoy	travel	ask	be	

01 내게 운전면허증이 있으면 좋을 텐데.

→ I wish I ___had___ a driver's license.

02 시끄럽지 않았다면 내가 잠을 잘 수 있었을 텐데.

→ If it hadn't been noisy, I _____ _____ _____ well.

03 내가 부자라면 세계 일주를 할 텐데.

→ If I were rich, I _____ _____ all around the world.

04 Jeff가 너에게 화가 나면 너와 말을 하지 않을 텐데.

→ Jeff _____ _____ _____ to you if he were mad at you.

05 내가 우리 부모님께 거짓말을 하지 않았다면 좋을 텐데.

→ I wish I _____ _____ _____ my parents a lie.

06 내가 그 어리석은 질문을 안 했더라면 좋을 텐데.

→ I wish I _____ _____ _____ that silly question.

07 네가 여기 있다면 우리는 함께 많은 것을 할 수 있을 텐데.

→ If you were here, we _____ _____ a lot of things together.

08 지금이 겨울이라면 우리는 겨울 스포츠를 즐길 수 있을 텐데.

→ If it were winter now, we _____ _____ winter sports.

09 내 신발이 좀 더 편하다면 좋을 텐데.

→ I wish my shoes _____ more comfortable.

10 우리가 그 경기에서 이겼다면 우리는 정말 기뻤을 텐데.

→ If we _____ _____ the match, we would have been very pleased.

11 운전자가 주의해서 운전했다면 사고가 일어나지 않았을 텐데.

→ If the driver had driven carefully, the accident _____ _____ _____ _____.

WORDS

• driver's license 운전면허증 • mad 화가 난 • silly 어리석은 • comfortable 편안한, 편한 • pleased 기쁜, 기뻐하는
• happen 일어나다, 발생하다

❷ 다음 밑줄 친 부분을 바르게 고쳐 문장을 다시 쓰세요.

01 I wish Brian <u>is</u> my boyfriend.

➡ _____I wish Brian were my boyfriend._____

02 If he marrled her, he <u>wlll</u> be very happy.

➡ _____

03 I wish I <u>live</u> in Paris when I was young.

➡ _____

04 If I were young, I would <u>have worked</u> hard.

➡ _____

05 If I <u>would have</u> a car, I would drive you home.

➡ _____

06 If I <u>speak</u> English fluently, I could get the job.

➡ _____

07 I wish I <u>didn't lose</u> my smartphone yesterday.

➡ _____

08 If I made more mistakes, Dad <u>will be</u> angry.

➡ _____

09 If I had had a ladder, I <u>could fixed</u> the roof.

➡ _____

10 If it <u>is</u> not so late, I could go grocery shopping.

➡ _____

11 I miss my friend, Carrie. I wish she <u>comes</u> to see me now.

➡ _____

12 If the weather had been better, we <u>have gone</u> hiking.

➡ _____

WORDS

· fluently 유창하게   · ladder 사다리   · fix 고치다, 수리하다   · grocery   · shopping 장보기

❸ 다음 우리말과 일치하도록, <보기>에서 알맞은 말을 골라 빈칸에 적절한 형태로 쓰세요.

보기

He gets up early.　　　I eat breakfast.　　　He is more careful.
I will refuse the offer.　You don't drink the milk.　She will win the race.
I am a superhero.　　　I can take a break now.　　He apologizes to me.
They spent more time with me.

01 내가 아침을 먹었다면 좋을 텐데.

➡ I wish _____I had eaten breakfast_____.

02 내가 Steve라면 그 제안을 거절할 텐데.

➡ If I were Steve, _____.

03 그녀가 열심히 연습했다면 그 경주에서 이겼을 텐데.

➡ If she had practiced hard, _____.

04 그가 일찍 일어나면 나와 같이 조깅하러 갈텐데.

➡ If _____, he could go jogging with me.

05 나는 정말 피곤하다. 내가 지금 쉴 수 있으면 좋을 텐데.

➡ I'm very tired. I wish I _____.

06 그가 나에게 사과를 했다면 나는 그를 용서했을 것이다.

➡ If _____, I would have forgiven him.

07 내가 슈퍼영웅이라면 어려움에 처한 사람들을 도울 수 있을 텐데.

➡ If _____, I could help people in trouble.

08 네가 그 우유를 마시지 않았더라면 좋을 텐데.

➡ I wish _____.

09 그가 더 주의했다면 그 사고는 일어나지 않았을 텐데.

➡ If _____, that accident wouldn't have happened.

10 내가 어렸을 때 우리 부모님은 항상 바빴다. 그들이 나와 좀 더 많은 시간을 보냈더라면 좋을 텐데.

➡ My parents were always busy when I was young. I wish _____

_____.

WORDS

• refuse 거절하다　• superhero 슈퍼영웅　• take a break 쉬다　• apologize 사과하다　• go bad 상하다, 썩다

④ 다음 우리말과 일치하도록, 주어진 단어를 이용하여 문장을 완성하세요.

01 그녀가 돈이 있다면 그 케이크를 살 수 있을텐데. (money, buy the cake)

➜ If she _____had money_____, she _____could buy the cake_____.

02 우리 할머니가 살아계시면 좋을 텐데. (alive)

➜ I _____.

03 내 남동생이 더 예의 바르면 좋을 텐데. (polite, more, my brother)

➜ I _____.

04 내가 어제 밤을 새지 않았더라면 좋을 텐데. (stay up, all night)

➜ I _____ yesterday.

05 내가 작년에 휴가로 하와이에 갔더라면 좋을 텐데. (go on a vacation)

➜ I _____ to Hawaii last year.

06 당신이 나를 도와주지 않았다면 성공할 수 없었을 텐데. (help, me, succeed)

➜ If you _____, I _____.

07 길에서 10달러 지폐를 줍는다면 무엇을 하겠니? (do, find)

➜ What _____ if you _____ $10 bill on the street?

08 키가 더 크다면 그는 우리 농구 팀에서 경기할 수 있을 텐데. (play, taller)

➜ If he _____, he _____ in our basketball team.

09 Greg가 그 영화에 출연했다면 유명해졌을 텐데. (star, famous)

➜ If Greg _____ in the movie, he _____.

10 날씨가 화창하면 우리는 학교까지 걸어갈 텐데. (sunny, be, walk)

➜ If _____, we _____ to school.

11 내가 시간이 더 있었다면 그 그림을 완성했을 텐데. (more time, have, complete)

➜ If I _____, I _____ the painting.

12 내가 공부를 열심히 했다면 더 좋은 점수를 받을 수 있었을 텐데. (study, hard, get better grades)

➜ If I _____, I _____.

WORDS

• polite 예의 바른 • stay up all night 밤을 새다 • succeed 성공하다 • star 주연을 맡다 • complete 완성하다

Actual Test

[1–4] 다음 빈칸에 들어갈 말로 알맞은 것을 고르시오.

1

> If I were you, I _____ tell him the truth.

① tell   ② told   ③ telling
④ will tell   ⑤ would tell

1
주절의 동사가 과거형입
니다.

2

> If I _____ home early, I could have met my uncle.

① came   ② have come   ③ had come
④ would come   ⑤ would have come

2
주절의 동사가 「조동사의
과거형+have p.p.」형태
입니다.

3

> I'm so busy preparing for the final exam.
> I wish I _____ a rest.

① take   ② took   ③ taken
④ have taken   ⑤ had taken

3
prepare 준비하다
final exam 기말고사
현재의 소망에 대해 이야
기하고 있습니다.

4

> I wish I _____ how to swim when I was young.

① learn   ② learned   ③ have learned
④ had learned   ⑤ would have learned

4
과거의 소망에 대해 이야
기하고 있습니다.

[5–6] 다음 빈칸에 들어갈 말이 순서대로 알맞게 짝지어진 것을 고르시오.

5

> A: I left my wallet at home. Can you lend me some money?
> B: If I _____ money, I _____ you some.

① have – lend
② have – have lent
③ had – had lent
④ had – would lend
⑤ had – would have lent

6

> A: Why didn't you come to the party last night?
> B: I had to take care of my brother.
>   If my parents _____ at home, I _____ there.

① were – would go
② were – would have gone
③ had been – would go
④ had been – would had gone
⑤ had been – would have gone

[7–8] 다음 우리말을 영어로 바르게 옮긴 것을 고르시오.

7

> 내가 그 문제의 답을 알면 좋을 텐데.

① I wish I know the answer to the question.
② I wish I knew the answer to the question.
③ I wish I had known the answer to the question.
④ I wish I didn't know the answer to the question.
⑤ I wish I doesn't know the answer to the question.

8

> 내게 우산이 있었다면 너와 같이 썼을 텐데.

① If I have an umbrella, I will share it with you.
② If I had an umbrella, I would share it with you.
③ If I had had an umbrella, I wouldn't share it with you.
④ If I had had an umbrella, I would have shared it with you.
⑤ If I had had an umbrella, I wouldn't have shared it with you.

[9–10] 다음 문장을 가정법으로 바르게 고친 것을 고르시오.

Note

9

> As my phone was broken, I couldn't call you last night.

① If my phone is broken, I couldn't call you last night.
② If my phone were not broken, I could call you last night.
③ If my phone were not broken, I couldn't call you last night.
④ If my phone had been broken, I couldn't have called you last night.
⑤ If my phone hadn't been broken, I could have called you last night.

10

> I'm sorry that she heard the rumor.

① I wish she hears the rumor.
② I wish she didn't hear the rumor.
③ I wish she hadn't heard the rumor.
④ I wish she have heard the rumor.
⑤ I wish she haven't heard the rumor.

10
rumor 소문

[11–12] 다음 밑줄 친 부분이 잘못된 것을 고르세요.

11
① If I spoke English, I <u>can make</u> lots of foreign friends.
② If we <u>had tried</u> our best, we could have won the match.
③ I wish my grandparents <u>lived</u> with me.
④ I wish I <u>hadn't made</u> that stupid mistake.
⑤ If I had a car, I <u>could pick</u> you up at the airport.

11
foreign 외국의 외국인의
match 경기
near 가까이
stupid 멍청한, 어리석은

12
① I wish he <u>were</u> healthier.
② I wish I <u>didn't lose</u> my camera yesterday.
③ If it <u>didn't rain</u>, we would go on a picnic.
④ What would you have said if you <u>had been</u> in my situation?
⑤ If you <u>had stepped</u> on the broken mirror, you would have gotten hurt.

12
situation 상황, 상태
step 밟다
broken 깨진, 고장 난
get hurt 다치다

13 다음 중 어법상 올바른 문장은?

① I wish it is Saturday today.

② If I were you, I wouldn't tell his secret to anyone.

③ If I had more money, I will buy you the jeans.

④ I wish you called me when you arrived at the airport.

⑤ If I finished earlier, I could have gone to the concert with
her last night.

14 다음 대화 중 자연스럽지 <u>않은</u> 것은?

① A: Do you know Jennifer's birthday?
B: If I knew it, I would tell you.

② A: We had a great time at the snow festival last week.
B: Really? I wish I had been there with you.

③ A: Sam and Tom are going for a bike ride. Why don't you go?
B: My bike is broken. I wish I had a new bike.

④ A: I failed the driving test again.
B: Sorry to hear that. If you had practiced hard, you couldn't
have passed it.

⑤ A: Have you seen Jane lately?
B: Yes, I have. If you had come to the party last night, you
would have seen her.

Note

14
pass 통과하다
lately 최근에

[15-16] 괄호 안에 주어진 단어를 알맞은 형태로 고쳐 문장을 완성하시오.

15
If he _____ me that question, I would have
been very embarrassed. (ask)

15
주절의 동사가 「조동사의
과거형+have p.p.」형태
입니다.

16
If you offer me a drink, I _____ coffee.
(have)

16
if절의 동사가 현재형입니
다.

Note

[17-18] 우리말과 일치하도록 괄호 안에 말을 이용하여 문장을 완성하시오.

17 어제 너를 도와 주었으면 좋을텐데. (help)

→ I wish _____ yesterday.

18 그가 내 친한 친구라면 그를 너에게 소개해줄 텐데. (introduce, him)

→ If he were a close friend with me, I _____
to you.

[19-20] 다음 문장을 가정법으로 바꿀 때, 빈칸에 알맞은 말을 쓰시오.

19 As I was sick, I stayed in bed all day.

→ If I _____, I _____ in
bed all day.

20 I'm sorry that I didn't buy a new car.

→ I _____.

Chapter

2

관계대명사 Ⅰ

UNIT 01 관계대명사

> 관계대명사는 두 문장에 공통으로 들어간 단어를 이용하여 한 문장으로 연결할 때 사용하는 대명사로 「접속사+대명사」의 역할을 합니다.

1. 관계대명사의 쓰임과 종류

   I know **the woman**. **She** is a doctor. 나는 그 여성을 알고 있다. 그녀는 의사이다.

   → I know <u>the woman</u> **who** is a doctor. 나는 의사인 그 여성을 알고 있다.
   　　　　선행사　　관계대명사

   1) a woman과 She는 동일인물입니다.

   2) 뒤에 나오는 명사나 대명사 대신 관계대명사를 이용하여 한 문장으로 만듭니다. (She 대신 who를 사용함)

선행사	주격 (-은·는·이·가)	소유격(-의)	목적격 (-을·를)
사람	who	whose	who(m)
사물, 동물	which		which

2. 주격 관계대명사: 주어 역할을 하는 관계대명사를 주격 관계대명사라고 하며 who, which가 있습니다. 주격 관계대명사 다음에는 동사나 조동사가 옵니다.

who	(선행사가 사람) 주어 역할을 하는 사람 대신 사용	I know **a girl**. **She** can dance well. 나는 한 소녀를 알고 있다. 그녀는 춤을 잘 춘다. → I know **a girl who** can dance well. 춤을 잘 추는 소녀를 나는 알고 있다. This is **the boy**. **He** broke the window yesterday. → This is **the boy who** broke the window yesterday. – 선행사 the boy 어제 창문을 깬 소년이 이 소년이다. *관계대명사절 시제가 과거이므로 broke 사용
which	(선행사가 사물, 동물) 주어 역할을 하는 사물, 동물대신 사용	She has **a car**. **It** looks new. → She has **a car which** looks new. 그녀는 새것처럼 보이는 자동차를 가지고 있다. I have **some coins**. **They** are very old. → I have **some coins which** are very old. 선행사 – 선행사 coins 나는 매우 오래된 동전들을 가지고 있다.

   Plus
   • 관계대명사절이란 「관계대명사+(주어)+동사」의 문장으로 앞 문장에서 사람·사물·동물에 해당하는 한 단어를 수식하여, 그 단어에 대한 추가적인 설명을 해줍니다. 이때 수식을 받는 명사를 「선행사」라고 부릅니다.
   This is the man [who helped me yesterday]. 이 사람이 어제 나를 도와준 남자이다.
   　선행사　　관계대명사절(형용사절) → 선행사 the man에 대한 추가 설명

3. 관계대명사 사용 시 주의할 점

   1) 선행사가 3인칭 단수(a bike, a man, the boy 등)이고 시제가 현재일 때 관계대명사 다음에 나오는 동사에는 –s(3인칭 현재형)를 붙여야 합니다.

   He knows <u>a man</u> who **plays** the guitar.

   2) 관계대명사 절의 동사의 수는 관계대명사의 선행사에 따라 결정됩니다.

   I saw <u>the children</u> who **were** swimming in the pool.

   – 선행사가 the children이므로 who 다음에 were가 쓰였음.

● 다음 괄호 안에 알맞은 말을 고르세요.

01 This is the museum (who / (which)) has many famous paintings.

02 She has a garden (who / which) has a lot of roses.

03 I met a man (who / which) was very strong.

04 My uncle has a cat (who / which) can dance.

05 He is the boy who (live / lives) next door.

06 She became one of the greatest scientists who (change / changed) the world.

07 He is the singer (who / which) is loved by all Koreans.

08 The boy (who / which) is talking to Cathy is my friend.

09 Graham Bell was a scientist who (invents / invented) a telephone.

10 I met a girl (who / which) knew you.

11 This is the dog (who / which) barked at me yesterday.

12 I know the girl who (is / are) wearing a red t-shirt.

13 He is the doctor (who / which) often helps poor children.

14 She has a computer (who / which) is very old.

15 I met some children (who / which) are very tall.

· rose 장미   · next door 옆집   · bark 짖다

❶ 다음 두 문장을 한 문장으로 만들 때 빈칸에 알맞은 말을 쓰세요.

01 I have a friend. He can play the violin.
→ I have a friend _____who_____ can play the violin.

02 That is the student. He is the tallest in my class.
→ That is the student _____ is the tallest in my class.

03 I have many books. They are very interesting.
→ I have many books _____ are very interesting.

04 This is the subway. It goes to City Hall.
→ This is the subway _____ goes to City Hall.

05 She was the doctor. She helped me yesterday.
→ She was the doctor _____ helped me yesterday.

06 These are scientists. They invented the first computer.
→ These are scientists _____ invented the first computer.

07 I bought a book. It was about UFOs.
→ I bought a book _____ was about UFOs.

08 We are living in the world. It is full of wonderful things.
→ We are living in the world _____ is full of wonderful things.

09 Today we will eat foods. They are good for our teeth.
→ Today we will eat foods _____ are good for our teeth.

10 People play sports. They need to drink lots of water.
→ People _____ play sports need to drink lots of water.

11 The man has my bag. He is sitting on the box.
→ The man _____ is sitting on the box has my bag.

12 The girl is my sister. She is playing the piano.
→ The girl _____ is playing the piano is my sister.

· wonderful 훌륭한   · be full of ~로 가득 차다

❷ 다음 두 문장을 한 문장으로 만들 때 빈칸에 알맞은 말을 쓰세요.

01 I know the boy. He stole your money.
→ I know the boy _____who_____ stole your money.

02 Sam yelled at the dog. It was biting his shoe.
→ Sam yelled at the dog _____ was biting his shoe.

03 I have a friend. He is good at soccer.
→ I have a friend _____ is good at soccer.

04 She often makes cookies. They taste good.
→ She often makes cookies _____ taste good.

05 I bought the house. It has three rooms.
→ I bought the house _____ has three rooms.

06 I will buy a smartphone. It was made in Korea.
→ I will buy a smartphone _____ was made in Korea.

07 He was the king. He was killed by his friend.
→ He was the king _____ was killed by his friend.

08 My father is a teacher. He is always kind to students.
→ My father is a teacher _____ is always kind to students.

09 She has a book. It has many beautiful pictures.
→ She has a book _____ has many beautiful pictures.

10 I went to the store. It sells candies.
→ I went to the store _____ sells candies.

11 Don't open the boxes. They are on the table.
→ Don't open the boxes _____ are on the table.

12 The woman looks healthy. She works out every day.
→ The woman _____ looks healthy works out every day.

WORDS

• steal 훔치다   • bite (이빨로) 물다   • yell 소리 지르다   • bite 물다   • work out 운동하다

Check up & Writing

❶ 다음 밑줄 친 부분을 바르게 고쳐 쓰세요.

01 She is the swimmer <u>which</u> broke the world record.

| who |

02 I will meet a lady who <u>work</u> at a bank.

03 The man <u>which</u> is in the living room is my uncle.

04 Jane ate the cake which <u>were</u> made by her mom.

05 I want a room <u>who</u> has an ocean view.

06 Terry is the cat <u>who</u> has black hair.

07 Sara is the girl <u>which</u> likes my brother.

08 Eric is the boy <u>which</u> can speak French.

09 He is the boy who <u>gives</u> me this candy this morning.

10 Most teachers like the students who <u>studies</u> hard.

11 He knows the boy <u>which</u> helped you yesterday.

12 This is the man <u>which</u> came from India.

13 She needs a bike which <u>have</u> three wheels.

14 We met the firefighter <u>which</u> saved your life.

15 Jack fixed the car <u>who</u> made a big noise.

· record 기록 · ocean 바다, 해양 · save 구하다 · wheel 바퀴 · noise 소음

❷ 다음 우리말과 일치하도록, 주어진 단어와 관계대명사를 이용하여 문장을 완성하세요.

01 나는 생물학에 관심 있는 학생들을 가르치고 있다. (are, in, interested, biology)
→ I am teaching the students _____who are interested in biology_____.

02 니는 서울 중심에 위치한 호텔에 머물 것이다. (be, located, in the center of)
→ I will stay in a hotel _____ Seoul.

03 그녀는 10대들에게 사랑받는 유명한 배우이다. (is, teenagers, loved, by)
→ She is a famous actress _____.

04 Laura는 내 고양이보다 큰 고양이를 가지고 있다. (is, bigger, mine, than)
→ Laura has a cat _____.

05 나는 이 음식을 만든 요리사를 만나고 싶다. (this, made, food)
→ I want to meet a cook _____.

06 벽에 걸려있는 사진을 보아라. (is, hung, the wall, on)
→ Look at the picture _____.

07 운동장을 달리고 있는 소녀는 내 여동생이다. (is, running, the ground, on)
→ The girl _____ is my sister.

08 너는 공항 가는 지하철을 타야 한다. (to, goes, the airport)
→ You have to take the subway _____.

09 내 말을 이해하는 로봇이 있다. (understand, my words, can)
→ There is a robot _____.

10 이 소년이 노래를 잘하는 소년이다. (sings, well)
→ This is the boy _____.

11 책상 위에 있는 책들은 빌릴 수 있다. (on, the table, be)
→ You can borrow the books _____.

12 그녀는 매우 뜨거운 차를 마셨다. (was, hot, very)
→ She drank the tea _____.

WORDS
· teenager 십대 · cook 요리사 · hung hang(매달리다)의 과거분사 · borrow 빌리다 · hot 뜨거운
· biology 생물학 · be located in ~에 위치해 있다

UNIT 02

관계대명사 - 목적격, 소유격

관계대명사는 역할에 따라 목적격 관계대명사와 소유격 관계대명사 등이 있습니다.

1. 목적격 관계대명사: 목적어 역할을 하는 관계대명사를 목적격 관계대명사라고 하며 who(m), which가 있습니다. 목적격 관계대명사 다음에는 「주어+타동사」가 옵니다.

who(m)	(선행사가 사람) 목적어 역할을 하는 사람 대신 사용	She is the girl. I saw her on the bus.
		 → She is the girl **who(m)** I saw on the bus.
		 1) her(목적어) 대신 whom이 왔음.
		 2) her 대신 whom이 왔으므로 관계대명사절에서 her는 제거해야 함.
		    I know the girl. He helped her.
		    → I know the girl **who(m)** he helped.

which	(선행사가 사물, 동물) 목적어 역할을 하는 사물, 동물대신 사용	I lost my bag. I bought it last week.
		 → I lost my bag **which** I bought last week.
		 1) it(목적어) 대신 which가 왔음.
		 2) it 대신 which가 왔으므로 관계대명사절에서 it은 제거해야 함.
		    The novel is interesting. Sara wrote it.
		    → The novel **which** Sara wrote is interesting.

Plus 1
- 목적격 관계대명사 who
  선행사가 사람일 때 who는 주격 관계대명사 뿐만 아니라 목적격 관계대명사로도 사용할 수 있습니다.
  I know the girl. He helped her
  → I know the girl **who** he helped.

2. 소유격 관계대명사: 소유격 역할을 하는 관계대명사를 소유격 관계대명사라고 하고 whose, of which가 있으며, "의", "~을 가진"으로 해석합니다. 소유격 관계대명사 whose 다음에는 명사가 옵니다.

whose	(선행사가 사람, 사물) 소유격 역할을 하는 사람이나 사물대신 사용	She has a dog. Its tail is very short.
		 → She has a dog **whose** tail is very short.
		 1) its(소유격) 대신 whose가 왔음.
		 2) its 대신 whose가 왔으므로 관계대명사절에서 its는 제거해야 함.
		    I have a friend. His name is David.
		    → I have a friend **whose** name is David.

Plus 2
- of which
  whose 대신 선행사가 사물일 때 of which를 사용할 수 있으며 of which 다음에는 the를 쓴다.
  → She has a dog **whose** tail is very short.
  → She has a dog **of which the** tail is very short.

Warm up

● 다음 괄호 안에서 알맞은 말을 고르세요.

01 I have a brother ((whose) / which) hobby is playing the piano.

02 She has a smartphone (whose / whom) color is white.

03 She is the girl (who / of which) I meet every day.

04 Do you know the boy (whose / whom) name is Andrew?

05 Look at the mountain (whose / whom) top is covered with snow.

06 The movie (whose / which) I saw last night was boring.

07 These are the shoes (whose / which) she wants to buy.

08 He carefully opened the door (which / whose) windows were broken.

09 She is the teacher (whom / which) my brother likes.

10 The man (whom / whose) I saw last night was Mr. Johnson.

11 The girl (who / whose) I want to meet is not here.

12 He has a dog (which / of which) the name is Bill.

13 A child (whom / whose) parents are dead is called an orphan.

14 I found the book (which / whose) cover is yellow.

15 She read the book (which / whom) he recommended.

· carefully 조심스럽게   · dead 죽은   · cover 표지   · orphan 고아   · recommend 추천하다

1 다음 두 문장을 한 문장으로 만들 때 빈칸에 알맞은 말을 쓰세요.

01 Jane likes the man. His hobby is playing the piano.

→ Jane likes the man _____whose_____ hobby is playing the piano.

02 These are the blue jeans. James bought them yesterday.

→ These are the blue jeans _____ James bought yesterday.

03 I know a boy. His father is a doctor.

→ I know a boy _____ father is a doctor.

04 Look at the cat. Its hair is white.

→ Look at the cat _____ hair is white.

05 She is the woman. I saw her on the bus.

→ She is the woman _____ I saw on the bus.

06 I like the dress. Ann is wearing it.

→ I like the dress _____ Ann is wearing.

07 I met my friend. His house was damaged by the storm.

→ I met my friend _____ house was damaged by the storm.

08 Amy gave me a picture. She painted it herself.

→ Amy gave me a picture _____ she painted herself.

09 Do you remember the girl? We met her at the library.

→ Do you remember the girl _____ we met at the library?

10 I want to live in a house. Its living room is large.

→ I want to live in a house _____ living room is large.

11 This is the table. His father made it last week.

→ This is the table _____ his father made last week.

12 There lived a princess. Her name was *Snow White*.

→ There lived a princess _____ name was *Snow White*.

WORDS

· damage 손상을 주다, 피해, 손상

② 다음 두 문장을 한 문장으로 만들 때 빈칸에 알맞은 말을 쓰세요.

01 Do you know the woman? Her husband is a pilot.
→ Do you know the woman _____whose_____ husband is a pilot?

02 This is an electric bill. I received it today.
→ This is an electric bill _____ I received today.

03 James wants to be a firefighter. His father is a soldier.
→ James _____ father is a soldier wants to be a firefighter.

04 Look at the birds. Their feathers are very colorful.
→ Look at the birds _____ feathers are very colorful.

05 Kate has a bike. He wants to sell it to me.
→ Kate has a bike _____ he wants to sell to me.

06 He is living in a small town. Its name is Jackson Valley.
→ He is living in a small town _____ name is Jackson Valley.

07 We are eating pizza. We ordered it yesterday.
→ We are eating pizza _____ we ordered yesterday.

08 She will marry the man. His job is to translate English into Korean.
→ She will marry the man _____ job is to translate English into Korean.

09 I met my friend. His brother was expelled from the school.
→ I met my friend _____ brother was expelled from the school.

10 The man over there is the dentist. I met him last week.
→ The man over there is the dentist _____ I met last week.

11 Simon became the conductor. Everyone loves him.
→ Simon became the conductor _____ everyone loves.

12 I am teaching the students. Their dream is to become astronauts.
→ I am teaching the students _____ dream is to become astronauts.

WORDS

· bill 청구서 · feather 깃털 · colorful 화려한 · translate 번역하다 · expel 추방하다, 쫓아내다 · dentist 치과의사
· conductor 지휘자 · astronaut 우주비행사

Check up & Writing

❶ 다음 밑줄 친 부분을 바르게 고쳐 쓰세요.

01 She is the girl <u>who</u> favorite subject is music.

> whose

02 He is a singer <u>which</u> my mom likes most.

03 This is the car <u>of which</u> I fixed last month.

04 The dictionary <u>whom</u> she bought yesterday was a little expensive.

05 I have several friends <u>whom</u> jobs are taxi drivers.

06 I met the girl <u>which</u> father is a musician.

07 I know the man <u>whose</u> you mentioned.

08 He is my friend <u>which</u> I can trust.

09 The copy machine <u>whom</u> we bought needs to be repaired.

10 The man <u>which</u> wife is in hospital is looking for a job.

11 Jack bought the plate <u>which</u> the color is white.

12 Kevin knows the man <u>who</u> son suffers from a headache.

13 The man <u>whose</u> she met today was very handsome.

14 He opened the door <u>whom</u> no one could open.

15 My mom is buying fruits <u>whom</u> I need for the party.

WORDS

· subject 과목　·several 몇 개의　·the other day 지난번, 일전에　·mention 언급하다　·trust 믿다, 신뢰하다
·repair 수리하다　·plate 접시　·suffer 고생하다

❷ 다음 우리말과 일치하도록, 주어진 단어와 관계대명사를 이용하여 문장을 완성하세요.

01 지붕이 눈으로 덮인 저 집을 봐라. (is covered with, roof, snow)

→ Look at the house _____ whose roof is covered with snow _____

02 나는 취미가 춤추는 것인 그 소녀를 좋아한다. (hobby, dancing, is)

→ I like the girl _____

03 지난달에 산 자동차가 고장이 났다. (I, last month, bought)

→ The car _____ has broken down

04 그는 Jack이 내게 소개해준 영어 선생님이다. (Jack, introduced)

→ He is an English teacher _____ to me

05 내 친구 Amy의 집은 해변 근처에 있다. (house, near, is, the beach)

→ Amy is my friend _____

06 너는 금발의 여성을 만났니? (hair, blond, is)

→ Did you meet the woman _____

07 이것은 냄새가 훌륭한 꽃이다. (is, smell, fantastic)

→ This is the flower _____

08 그녀는 내가 어젯밤에 남겨놓은 피자를 먹을 것이다. (left, I, last night)

→ She will eat the pizza _____

09 나는 꼬리가 긴 강아지를 좋아한다. (is, long, tail)

→ I like the puppy _____

10 나는 그가 방금 나에게 말 한 이야기를 믿을 수 없다. (he, told, has, just, me)

→ I can't believe the story _____

11 시장에서 만난 여성은 나의 선생님이다. (met, at the market, I)

→ The woman _____ is my teacher.

12 우리가 동굴에서 발견한 그 소년은 아파 보였다. (found, in the cave, we)

→ The boy _____ looked sick.

WORDS

• introduce 소개하다 • blond 금발 • fantastic 환상적인 • puppy 강아지 • believe 믿다 • cave 동굴

UNIT 03 관계대명사 that, what

that과 what은 시험에 자주 출제되는 관계대명사로 이들의 쓰임을 확실하게 이해하는 것이 중요합니다.

1. 관계대명사 that: 관계대명사 that은 소유격 관계대명사(whose)를 제외한 who, whom, which 대신 사용할 수 있으며, 특정한 수식어가 나오는 경우에는 that만 사용하는 경우도 있습니다.

선행사	주격 (-은·는·이·가)	목적격 (-을·를)
사람, 사물, 동물	that	that

1) 관계대명사 that의 쓰임: 관계대명사 that은 주격, 목적격을 대신해서 사용할 수 있습니다.

주격	Look at the cat **that[which]** is sleeping on the sofa. (선행사 – 사물) She is the girl **that[who]** can speak Chinese. (선행사 – 사람)
목적격	These are the shoes **that[which]** he bought last week. (선행사 – 사물) She is the woman **that[who(m)]** I saw at the shopping mall. (선행사 – 사람)

2) 선행사에 다음과 같은 표현이 있는 경우 that을 사용합니다.

the only = 유일한	Tom is **the only** man **that** can speak French in my office.
사람+동물	I saw **a girl and her dog that** were sitting on the bench.
최상급	He is **the tallest** man **that** I have ever met.
the first, the second 등의 서수	She was **the first** woman **that** climbed Mt. Everest.
something, anything 등의 부정대명사	You can have **anything that** is in the box.

2. 관계대명사 what: what이 관계대명사로 사용될 경우 선행사를 포함하고 있어 선행사를 따로 쓰지 않으며 「~하는 것」으로 해석합니다. 관계대명사 what이 이끄는 절은 주어, 목적어, 보어 역할을 합니다.

주어	**What I need** is your help. 내가 필요한 것은 너의 도움이다. = **The thing which[that]** I need is your help.
목적어	I remember **what you said** to me. 나는 네가 말한 것을 기억한다. = I remember **the thing which[that]** you said to me.
보어	This is not **what I want**. 이것은 내가 원하는 것이 아니다. = This is not **the thing which[that]** I want.

● 다음 괄호 안에서 알맞은 말을 고르세요.

01 That's just (what / which) I want to say.

02 You can buy anything (which / that) you want.

03 John is the only man (that / who) I can trust.

04 I'll tell you everything (that / what) I know.

05 (What / Who) he said is not true.

06 She is the girl (that / whose) can speak Japanese.

07 Choose (whose / what) you want for dinner.

08 He is the only baseball player (that / what) I know.

09 Is this (that / what) you wanted to buy?

10 Look at the boy and his dog (which / that) are running there.

11 (What / Which) you have to do is to study hard.

12 She is the first student (whose / that) came here.

13 He will give up (which / what) he has planned.

14 Do you know Jim (that / whose) father is a famous singer?

15 She is the woman (that / which) I saw on the subway.

· true 진실의   · choose 선택하다   · give up 포기하다

❶ 다음 빈칸에 that이나 what을 쓰세요.

01 She is the most honest girl _____that_____ I have ever met.

02 The picture _____ she was looking at was beautiful.

03 Don't believe _____ he said.

04 He lives in a small town _____ is known for wine.

05 He gave me _____ I really wanted.

06 _____ makes me happy is children's smile.

07 She is the woman _____ I met at the party yesterday.

08 Sara didn't eat _____ I cooked.

09 She was the first woman _____ I truly loved.

10 This is the book _____ I gave to her last week.

11 There is something _____ I'd like to ask you.

12 He is the only man _____ can save the child.

13 I don't understand _____ he has just told me.

14 The teacher _____ is from France is very handsome.

15 Wilson told me _____ I had to do.

WORDS

· be known for ~으로 알려지다/유명하다 · wine 포도주 · something 무엇, 어떤 것 · truly 진심으로
· handsome 잘생긴

② 다음 빈칸에 that이나 what을 쓰세요.

01 _____What_____ she told me was very boring.

02 This is not the thing _____ we want.

03 John will be satisfied with _____ you did.

04 Is there anything _____ you didn't understand?

05 They ate _____ I made for my brother.

06 She is the most beautiful girl _____ I've seen.

07 She lost the ring _____ he bought for her.

08 He and I decided to accept _____ she offered.

09 I just received the letter _____ he sent last week.

10 These are the smartphones _____ were made in Korea.

11 The Lost and Found Center has the bag _____ I lost yesterday.

12 The tsunami swept away people and buildings _____ were on the shore.

13 That is _____ she has wanted for a long time.

14 He was the first man _____ climbed Mt. Everest.

15 Don't tell her _____ I told you.

WORDS

Check up & Writing

① 다음 밑줄 친 부분을 바르게 고쳐 쓰세요.

01 This is <u>that</u> my wife wants to buy.

> what

02 She is the only friend <u>who</u> I can count on.

03 This is the watch <u>what</u> she is looking for.

04 The woman <u>what</u> I talked to was very kind.

05 You can have anything <u>who</u> is on the table.

06 <u>Which</u> I really want is to get a job.

07 She is the richest woman <u>whose</u> I've ever met.

08 Look at the girl and her doll <u>which</u> are on the bed.

09 Taking a shower is <u>which</u> he does after dinner.

10 He told me a story <u>whom</u> seemed real.

11 The book <u>who</u> I want to buy is sold out now.

12 It is the most exciting game <u>who</u> I've ever watched.

13 Neil Armstrong was the first man <u>whom</u> walked on the moon.

14 He will tell you something <u>what</u> makes you happy.

15 They liked the food <u>what</u> his mother made for them.

・**count on** 의지하다   ・**seem** ~처럼 보이다   ・**real** 진짜의   ・**sold out** 품절된, 매진된

❷ 다음 우리말과 일치하도록, 주어진 단어와 관계대명사를 이용하여 문장을 완성하세요.

01 그녀가 말하는 것을 믿니? (she, saying, is)

→ Do you believe _____ what she is saying _____?

02 이것이 네가 생일 선물로 원하는 거니? (want, you, your birthday, for)

→ Is this _____?

03 그녀는 자신의 딸을 치료할 수 있는 누군가를 만나기를 바랐다. (could, her daughter, cure)

→ She wanted to meet someone _____.

04 내가 정말로 필요한 것은 잠자는 것이다. (really, need, I)

→ _____ is to sleep.

05 그녀는 말하는 것과 행동하는 것이 다르다. (does, she)

→ What she says is different from _____.

06 지붕이 빨간색인 집을 보아라. (roof, red, is)

→ Look at the house _____.

07 저것이 이 지역을 흐르는 유일한 강이다. (through, this area, flows)

→ That is the only river _____.

08 그는 내게 대답하기 어려운 질문들을 했다. (hard, were, to answer)

→ He asked me questions _____.

09 Sam은 내게 어젯밤 발생한 자동차 사고에 대해 말했다. (happened, last night)

→ Sam told me about the car accident _____.

10 그녀는 내게 그녀가 프로젝트에 대해 아는 것을 말했다. (knew, the project, about, she)

→ She told me _____.

11 우리는 그가 어젯밤에 한 행동을 이해하지 못한다. (did, he. last night)

→ We don't understand _____.

12 그는 휴대 전화를 사용한 첫 번째 사람이다. (the, used, cellular phone)

→ He was the first man _____.

WORDS

• cure 치료하다　• roof 지붕　• different 다른　• flow 흐르다　• hard 어려운　• accident 사고

1 다음 괄호 안에서 알맞은 것을 고르세요.

01 You can see the man (who / which / whom) stole my car.

02 I can give you (that / which / what) you need.

03 She is the best scientist (that / what / whose) I've met.

04 Here are some pencils (whose / who / which) you can use.

05 He was a great man (who / whom / what) got over many difficulties.

06 I have two brothers (what / who / whom) are very clever.

07 James has a puppy (who / which / what) is three months old.

08 (What / Which / That) we need most now is your help.

09 Everything (that / which / what) she told you is not true.

10 Is this (that / which / what) you wrote?

11 He painted a woman (who / whom / which) was taking care of her baby.

12 Thank you for (that / which / what) you did for me.

13 This is the policeman (that / whose / whom) caught the thief.

14 (That / Which / What) she wants now is something to eat.

15 Don't forget the advice (whom / which / what) I gave you.

· steal 훔치다   · get over 극복하다   · difficulty 어려움   · clever 영리한   · advice 충고, 조언

2 다음 영어를 우리말로 쓰세요.

01 Do you know the animals which live in Australia?
→ _____너는 호주에서 사는 동물들을 알고 있니?_____

02 The bag which she lost yesterday was not expensive.
→ _____

03 What I think is different from what she thinks.
→ _____

04 Jane bought a skirt whose color is red.
→ _____

05 The baseball game that we watched on TV was exciting.
→ _____

06 Canada is the country that I want to visit next year.
→ _____

07 Susan is reading a book that is written in English.
→ _____

08 Do you know the boy whose name is Jackson?
→ _____

09 The first student that came to the gym is Mike.
→ _____

10 This is the only water that we have now.
→ _____

11 I will tell her what I saw in China.
→ _____

12 He is the teacher who teaches English to my brother.
→ _____

• Australia 호주

③ 다음 두 문장을 한 문장으로 만들 때 빈칸에 알맞은 말을 쓰세요.

01 I found the book. I lost it yesterday.
→ I found the book _which[that]_ _____I_____ lost yesterday.

02 The man is talking to Cathy. He is my father.
→ The man _____ _____ talking to Cathy is my father.

03 The doctor lives in New York. He is very busy.
→ The doctor _____ _____ in New York is very busy.

04 The girl is my sister. She is playing the violin.
→ The girl _____ _____ playing the violin is my sister.

05 The woman fell in love with him. She was a writer.
→ The woman _____ _____ in love with him was a writer.

06 Once there was a woodcutter. His wife was sick.
→ Once there was a woodcutter _____ _____ was sick.

07 I bought a car. It had no navigation system.
→ I bought a car _____ _____ no navigation system.

08 I am wearing the ring. My mother left it.
→ I am wearing the ring _____ _____ _____ left.

09 The boy broke the window. He ran away.
→ The boy _____ _____ the window ran away.

10 She has a dog. Its name is Black.
→ She has a dog _____ _____ is Black.

11 I want to visit Jeju island. It is very beautiful in spring.
→ I want to visit Jeju island _____ _____ very beautiful in spring.

12 This is the thing. He bought it last weekend.
→ This is _____ _____ bought last weekend.

WORDS

• fall in love 사랑에 빠지다 • woodcutter 나무꾼 • navigation 항해 • system 시스템 • run away 도망가다

❹ 다음 밑줄 친 부분을 바르게 고치세요.

01 The boy <u>which</u> I know well is dancing on the stage.

who(m)[that]

02 It is the most expensive watch <u>who</u> I've ever had.

03 Have you found the key <u>what</u> you lost yesterday?

04 May I eat the cookies <u>whose</u> are on the table?

05 Is this the camera <u>what</u> you gave to your brother?

06 We found a lost dog <u>which</u> legs were very short.

07 The man <u>whose</u> you saw at the park yesterday is my uncle.

08 Do your friends always believe <u>that</u> you say.

09 I remember <u>that</u> you said to me yesterday.

10 It was the only novel <u>who</u> she wrote during her life.

11 The tread mill <u>whose</u> he bought last year has broken.

12 <u>That</u> she said made them happy.

13 I like the car <u>of which</u> color is black.

14 Can I borrow the books <u>what</u> are on the shelf.

15 You can eat anything <u>who</u> is in the refrigerator.

• tread mill 런닝 머신　• shelf 선반　• refrigerator 냉장고

[1-4] 다음 중 빈칸에 알맞은 말을 고르세요.

1

We like to listen to the song _____ he sings.

① who   ② whose   ③ whom
④ what   ⑤ that

1
목적격 관계대명사의 쓰임을 알아보세요.

2

This is not _____ she wants.

① who   ② whose   ③ what
④ of which   ⑤ whom

3

He knew the man _____ car was damaged by the storm.

① that   ② whose   ③ what
④ which   ⑤ who

3
damage ~을 손상하다, 해치다
storm 폭풍

4

The only person _____ I can trust is Jane.

① that   ② whose   ③ what
④ which   ⑤ who

4
trust 믿다

[5–6] 다음 중 빈칸에 공통으로 알맞은 것을 고르세요.

Note

5
- The computer _____ is on the table is mine.
- I'm the only person _____ can help you.

① which   ② who   ③ that
④ whose   ⑤ whom

6
- This is the girl _____ name is Linda.
- Look at the car _____ tires are flat.

① which   ② who   ③ that
④ whose   ⑤ whom

7 다음 중 빈칸에 들어갈 알맞은 말을 고르세요.

May I eat the cookies that _____ on the table?

① be   ② is   ③ was
④ are   ⑤ were

8 다음 중 빈칸에 들어갈 말이 바르게 짝지어진 것을 고르세요.

- He said something _____ I could not understand.
- The teacher _____ teaches us is handsome.

① which - which   ② that - who
③ that - which   ④ whose - that
⑤ that - whom

9 다음 중 밑줄 친 부분의 쓰임이 나머지와 다른 것을 고르세요.

① <u>Who</u> do you want to meet most?

② He was a scientist <u>who</u> invented a computer.

③ I met a girl <u>who</u> knew you.

④ This is the girl <u>who</u> wants to meet you.

⑤ Do you know the girl <u>who</u> is wearing a skirt?

Note

9
의문사와 관계대명사의
쓰임을 알아보세요.

[10–1] 다음 중 우리말을 영어로 바르게 쓴 것을 고르세요.

10   저것은 작년에 내가 본 영화이다.

① I watched that movie last year.

② The movie is I watched last year.

③ That is the movie which I watched last year.

④ That is the movie who I watched last year.

⑤ That is the movie whose I watched last year.

11   나는 Sam이 내게 말한 것을 믿지 않았다.

① I didn't believe that Sam told me.

② I didn't believe which Sam told me.

③ I didn't believe whose Sam told me.

④ I didn't believe who Sam told me.

⑤ I didn't believe what Sam told me.

12 다음 중 that으로 바꾸어 쓸 수 없는 것을 고르세요.

① The man <u>whose</u> son is a pianist works at a bank.

② The shoes <u>which</u> she is wearing are mine.

③ He is the man <u>whom</u> we respect.

④ This is the computer <u>which</u> I bought yesterday.

⑤ He has a friend <u>who</u> wants to be an actor.

12
관계대명사 that의 쓰임을
알아보세요.

respect 존경하다

[13-14] 다음 중 어법상 <u>어색한</u> 것을 고르세요.

13
① The men that you introduced to me was kind.
② The food that I ate last night was very delicious.
③ The girl who learns English is very smart.
④ The castle which she looked around was wonderful.
⑤ The man that my sister loves is from HongKong.

14
① She met a boy whose father is a farmer.
② The man whom she loves likes to listen to music.
③ This is the watch that of the price is very high.
④ She has a friend whose hobby is watching movies.
⑤ Does she have the coin that I gave to her?

15 다음 중 어법상 옳은 문장을 고르세요.

① This is the car who she wants to buy.
② Is this what you wanted to buy?
③ He is the man who never do exercise.
④ Is this the bike what you bought last year?
⑤ She likes the boy whom wants to be a doctor.

16 다음 밑줄 친 부분을 바르게 고치세요.

1) The man <u>whom</u> works at a library comes from Poland.

➡ _____

2) Jackson gave me everything <u>what</u> he had.

➡ _____

[17-19] 관계대명사를 이용하여 한 문장으로 연결하세요.

17
- These are the gifts.
- I got them from him.

➡ _____

18
- This is the boy.
- He showed me the way to the park.

➡ _____

19
- The building is my office.
- Its roof is red.

➡ _____

20 다음 우리말과 일치하도록 빈칸에 알맞은 관계대명사를 쓰세요.

그는 정상이 눈으로 덮인 산을 보았다.
He saw the mountain _____ top was covered with snow.

➡ _____

관계대명사 II

관계대명사 생략과 계속적 용법

목적격 관계대명사와 「관계대명사+be동사」는 생략해서 사용할 수 있으므로 문장을 해석할 때 이러한 점들을 유의해야 합니다.

1. 목적격 관계대명사의 생략: 목적격 관계대명사 which, that, whom은 생략할 수 있습니다.

who(m)	This is the girl **(whom)** I met yesterday. This is the baby **(whom)** he saved.
which	Did you eat the cookies **(which)** he made? Did he get a job **(which)** he wanted?
that	You can eat anything **(that)** you want. Sara is the smartest student **(that)** I've ever met.

2. 「관계대명사+be동사」의 생략: 「관계대명사+be동사+현재분사[과거분사]」가 나오는 경우에 「관계대명사+be동사」는 생략할 수 있습니다.

| 「관계대명사
+be동사」의
생략 | I know the boy **who is** sleeping in your room.
→ I know the boy **sleeping** in your room.

This is the machine **which[that] was** invented by James.
→ This is the machine **invented** by James.

Do you know the man **who is** talking to Susan?
→ Do you know the man **talking** to Susan? |

3. 계속적 용법; 관계대명사의 계속적 용법은 관계대명사 앞에 ,(comma)를 사용하여 다음에 나오는 말이 앞에 나온 명사나 문장을 보충 설명하는 역할을 합니다.

| 계속적 용법 | He has two sons, **who** became teachers.
그는 아들이 두 명 있는데, 둘 다 선생님이 되었다. (아들이 두 명 있다.)
= He has two sons, **and they** became teachers.
This morning I met James, **who** is my best friend.
= This morning I met James, **and he** is my best friend. |
| 제한적 용법 | He has two sons **who** became teachers.
그는 선생님이 된 아들이 두 명 있다. (선생님이 아닌 아들이 더 있을 수 있다.) |

Plus

• 계속적 용법의 특징
계속적 용법은 일반적으로 앞에 구체적인 명사(선행사)가 나오는 것이 특징이며, 계속적 관계대명사는 의미에 따라 「접속사(and, or, but)+대명사」로 바꿔 쓸 수 있습니다. 계속적 용법의 관계대명사는 생략할 수 없습니다.
She met John, **who** just got back from his trip.
→ She met John, **and he** just got back from his trip.

Warm up

정답 및 해설 p.

● 다음 밑줄 친 부분이 생략할 수 있으면 O표, 생략할 수 없으며 X 하세요.

01 I've lost the umbrella <u>that</u> you gave me. O

02 Did you eat the pizza <u>which was</u> in the refrigerator?

03 I have a friend <u>who</u> lives in New York.

04 I love the girl <u>who is</u> dancing on the stage.

05 This is the magazine <u>that</u> she wants to subscribe to.

06 This is the ring <u>which</u> my husband gave me for our wedding anniversar

07 Did you use the perfume <u>which</u> you got from Sam?

08 That lady <u>who is</u> wearing glasses is my aunt.

09 I met a man <u>whose</u> son is an actor.

10 She is playing volleyball, <u>which</u> is her favorite sport.

11 The vending machine <u>which is</u> in the lobby has now been repaired.

12 Ben works for a company <u>that</u> makes refrigerators.

13 This is the child <u>whom</u> I saw on the train.

14 Tony has a cat <u>whose</u> fur is long.

15 The Eiffel tower, <u>which</u> is in Paris, is the tallest tower in Europe.

- umbrella 우산 · subscribe 구독하다 · anniversary 기념일 · perfume 향수 · magazine 잡지
- company 회사 · repair 수리하다 · fur 털

❶ 다음 문장에서 생략 가능한 부문을 생략하고 다시 쓰세요.

01 Do you know the girl who is under the tree?

→ _____Do you know the girl under the tree?_____

02 Jina likes that tall guy who is dancing on the stage.

→ _____

03 You can eat anything that you want.

→ _____

04 Sara is the smartest student that I've ever taught.

→ _____

05 This is the machine which James is looking for.

→ _____

06 Do you know the man who is talking to Susan?

→ _____

07 My mom likes the cookies which I make.

→ _____

08 Look at the boy and his dog that are swimming in the river.

→ _____

09 Bobby spent all the money that he had.

→ _____

10 This is the bike which my brother wants to buy.

→ _____

11 My son took the coins that I put on the table.

→ _____

12 The man who is delivering pizza is my cousin.

→ _____

WORDS

· deliver 배달하다   · invent 발명하다   · spend 사용하다, 쓰다

❷ 다음 문장에서 생략 가능한 부문을 생략하고 다시 쓰세요.

01 The man who is drinking coffee is my father.
→ _____ The man drinking coffee is my father. _____

02 I will do anything that I can do for you.
→ _____

03 This is the most interesting novel that I have ever read.
→ _____

04 There is nothing that you can do.
→ _____

05 She found the book which I lost yesterday.
→ _____

06 The dress that she is wearing looks great on her.
→ _____

07 The man whom you invited to the party is my friend.
→ _____

08 He is living in the house which is overlooking the river.
→ _____

09 The picture which was drawn by Samuel was beautiful.
→ _____

10 The pizza which I ordered two hours ago is not delivered yet.
→ _____

11 The shirt that he bought needs to be washed.
→ _____

12 She wants to buy a bag which was made in France.
→ _____

· find 발견하다   · draw 그리다(draw – drew – drawn)   · overlook (건물 등이) 내려다보다   · need 필요하다
· wash 씻다, 세탁하다

1 다음 영어를 우리말로 쓰세요.

01 I gave her everything that I had.
→ _____ 나는 내가 가졌던 모든 것을 그녀에게 줬다. _____

02 Albert Einstein, who was born in 1879, is one of the greatest scientists.
→ _____

03 I met Sam, who is my coworker.
→ _____

04 She has two daughters, who became nurses.
→ _____

05 The luggage she is carrying is very heavy.
→ _____

06 What is the language spoken in Spain?
→ _____

07 My teacher, who comes from Canada, will teach English soon.
→ _____

08 Did you read the letter written by Susan?
→ _____

09 This is the car my father bought last month.
→ _____

10 Jeff is the strongest boy I've ever seen.
→ _____

11 The girl raising her hand is learning English.
→ _____

12 Science is the subject they like most.
→ _____

WORDS
· coworker 직장동료   · carry 운반하다   · luggage 짐   · subject 과목

❷ 다음 우리말과 일치하도록, 주어진 단어를 이용하여 문장을 완성하세요.
(관계대명사를 사용하지 마세요.)

01 이것은 그녀가 나를 위해 산 셔츠이다. (she, the shirt, bought)

→ This is _____ the shirt she bought _____ for me.

02 너는 지붕 위에 서 있는 남자를 아니? (on, the roof, standing, the man)

→ Do you know _____ ?

03 이것은 내가 보고 싶지 않은 영화다. (the movie, want, to see, I, don't)

→ This is _____ .

04 그는 그녀가 많이 존경하는 선생님이다. (she, the teacher, respects a lot)

→ He is _____ .

05 Sally는 철로 만든 의자를 샀다. (a chair, steel, made of)

→ Sally bought _____ .

06 책상 위에 있는 저 책들은 네 것이 아니다. (those, on the table, books)

→ _____ are not yours.

07 소파에서 자고 있는 여성은 나의 이모이다. (on, sleeping, the woman, the couch)

→ _____ is my aunt.

08 그녀가 읽고 있는 책은 이해하기 어렵다. (she, is, the book, reading)

→ _____ is difficult to understand.

09 거리를 건너고 있는 남자를 보아라. (the street, the man, crossing)

→ Look at _____ .

10 기차에서 내리는 사람들은 관광객들이다. (getting off, the people, the train)

→ _____ are tourists.

11 우리가 마실 것이 있니? (we, anything, drink, can)

→ Is there _____ ?

12 저 나무 아래에서 자고 있는 남자를 아니? (under, the man, the tree, sleeping)

→ Do you know _____ ?

WORDS

• **respect** 존경하다 • **couch** 긴 의자, 소파 • **get off** ~에서 내리다 • **steel** 철, 강철

UNIT 02 관계부사

> 관계부사는 관계대명사와 마찬가지로 앞에 나온 명사(선행사)를 수식하는 형용사절을 이끌고 있습니다. 관계부사는 말 그대로 부사 역할을 하는 반면에, 관계대명사는 대명사 역할을 합니다.

1. 관계부사의 종류와 역할: 관계부사는 그 자체에 전치사를 포함하고 있으며, 관계부사는 「전치사+관계대명사」로 바꿔 쓸 수 있습니다.

	선행사	관계부사	전치사+관계대명사
장소	the place, Seoul, Canada, the hotel, the school 등	where	at/in/to which
시간	the time, the day, the year 등	when	at/in/on which
이유	the reason	why	for which
방법	(the way)	how	in which

2. 관계부사의 쓰임

where	This is the room.+She found the book in the room. This is the room **where** she found the book. = This is the room **in which** she found the book. 이 방이 그녀가 책을 발견한 곳이다.
when	I'll never forget the day.+I won the game on the day. I'll never forget the day **when** I won the game. = I'll never forget the day **on which** I won the game. 나는 게임에서 승리한 그날을 잊지 못 할 것이다.
why	I know the reason.+He hates you for that reason. I know the reason **why** he hates you. = I know the reason **for which** he hates you. 나는 그가 당신을 싫어하는 이유를 안다.
how	That is the way. Sam solved the math problem in the way. That is **how** Sam solved the math problem. = That is **the way** Sam solved the math problem. = That is the way **in which** Sam solved the math problem. 저것이 Sam이 수학 문제를 푼 방법이다.

 Plus
- the way와 how 둘은 함께 사용할 수 없습니다.
  That is <u>the way how</u> he solved the math problem. (X)
- reason, place, time이 선행사로 올 경우 이들 선행사를 생략할 수 있습니다.
  Do you know the reason **why** he was upset? → Do you know **why** he was upset?
  This is the place **where** he lives. → This is **where** he lives.

● 다음 괄호 안에서 알맞은 말을 고르세요.

01 This is the park (when / where / why) I met him.
이 공원이 내가 그를 만난 공원이다.

02 That is the reason (when / where / why) I likes him.
저것이 내가 그를 좋아하는 이유이다.

03 I remember the day (when / where / why) I bought my car.
나는 내가 자동차를 산 날을 기억한다.

04 Summer is the season (when / where / why) it rains a lot in Korea.
여름은 한국에 비가 많이 내리는 계절이다.

05 This is (when / how / why) she became a lawyer.
이것이 그녀가 변호사가 된 방법이다.

06 This is the company (when / where / why) I used to work.
여기가 내가 일했던 회사이다.

07 Do you know the time (when / where / why) the bus arrives here?
언제 버스가 이곳에 도착하는지 아니?

08 This is the house (when / where / why) my mom was born.
이곳이 엄마가 태어난 집이다.

09 Please let me know (when / where / how) I can use this washing machine.
내게 어떻게 이 세탁기를 사용할 수 있는지 알려주세요.

10 The city (when / where / why) she lives is famous for its nighttime views.
그녀가 사는 도시는 밤 야경으로 유명하다.

11 September 15th is the day (when / where / why) she left for London.
9월 15일은 그녀가 런던으로 떠난 날이다.

12 Do you know the reason (in which / for which) he was upset?
그가 왜 화가 났었는지 이유를 아니?

WORDS

• season 계절 • used to+동사원형 ~하곤 했다 • machine 기계 • washing machine 세탁기 • nighttime 야간, 밤
• be famous for ~으로 유명하다 • upset 화가 난

1 다음 빈칸에 알맞은 관계부사를 쓰세요.

01 November 5th is the day _____when_____ my brother was born.
11월 5일은 내 동생이 태어난 날이다.

02 I don't know the reason _____ he lied to his friends.
그가 그의 친구들에게 거짓말을 한 이유를 나는 모른다.

03 2002 is the year _____ World cup was held in Korea.
2002년은 한국에서 월드컵이 개최된 해이다.

04 She recommended a restaurant _____ I can have Italian food.
그녀는 내가 이태리 음식을 먹을 수 있는 식당을 추천 해줬다.

05 We will visit the palace _____ the king lived.
우리는 왕이 살았던 궁전을 방문할 것이다.

06 Now is the time _____ I need him most.
지금이 내가 그를 가장 필요 할 때이다.

07 This is _____ I solved the problem.
이것이 내가 문제를 푼 방법이다.

08 Tell me the reason _____ he was angry.
그가 왜 화가 났었는지 이유를 말해줘.

09 I forgot the day _____ I met her.
나는 그녀를 만났던 날을 잊었다.

10 She showed me _____ she fixed the copy machine.
그녀는 내게 복사기를 고친 방법을 보여줬다.

11 This is _____ he survived that crash.
이것이 그가 자동차 사고에서 살아남은 방법이다.

12 Please tell me the time _____ you have to leave.
당신이 떠나야 할 시간을 내게 말해주세요.

WORDS

· lie 거짓말, 거짓말하다   · recommend 추천하다   · palace 궁전   · survive 살아남다, 생존하다
· crash (자동차 충돌·항공기 추락) 사고   · leave 떠나다

❷ 다음 빈칸에 알맞은 관계부사를 쓰세요.

01 This is the place _____where_____ he lived for 10 years.
이곳이 그가 10년 동안 살았던 장소이다.

02 That's _____ she knows a lot about different cultures.
그것이 그녀가 다른 문화에 대해 많이 아는 이유이다.

03 I don't know the reason _____ he is popular in Korea.
나는 저 가수가 왜 한국에서 인기가 있는지 모르겠다.

04 This is the library _____ he studies on weekends.
이곳이 그가 주말에 공부하는 도서관이다.

05 Please tell me the time _____ she arrives here.
그녀가 이곳에 도착하는 시간을 알려주세요.

06 Sunday is the only day _____ I can meet her.
일요일이 내가 그녀를 만날 수 있는 유일한 날이다.

07 My mom never tells _____ she makes her special sauce.
엄마는 특별한 소스를 만드는 방법을 결코 말하지 않는다.

08 A computer has changed _____ we live.
컴퓨터는 우리가 살아가는 방법을 변화시켰다.

09 The reason _____ I'm calling you is to ask you a favor.
내가 너에게 전화한 이유는 너에게 부탁하기 위해서이다.

10 I sometimes visit the bank _____ my uncle works.
나는 때때로 나의 삼촌이 일하는 은행을 방문한다.

11 Spring is the season _____ a lot of flowers bloom.
봄은 많은 꽃들이 피는 계절이다.

12 Please explain to me _____ I can join the reading club.
내가 독서 모임에 가입할 수 있는 방법을 설명해 주세요.

WORDS

• place 장소   • different 다른, 차이가 나는   • favor 부탁, 찬성, 친절   • sauce 소스   • bloom 꽃이 피다
• explain 설명하다

1 다음 두 문장을 관계부사를 이용하여 한 문장으로 쓰세요.

01 That is the company. They worked there five years ago.
→ <u>That is the company where they worked five years ago.</u>

02 Wilson showed me the way. He made spaghetti in the way.
→ _____

03 I will drop by the office. My mom works in the office.
→ _____

04 He explained the reason. The car broke down for the reason.
→ _____

05 Sunday is the day. We can play computer games on the day.
→ _____

06 Do you know the hotel? The next conference will be held at the hotel.
→ _____

07 Do you know the way? He made the cake in that way.
→ _____

08 We didn't know the reason. Sally failed the driver's test for that reason.
→ _____

09 Spring is the season. We go on a picnic then.
→ _____

10 The cafe is the place. He meets his friends there every day.
→ _____

11 I will show you the point. You can start there.
→ _____

12 2010 was the year. We received a bonus in that year.
→ _____

• drop by 들르다   • point 장소, 지점   • bonus 보너스

❷ 다음 우리말과 일치하도록, 주어진 단어와 관계부사를 이용하여 문장을 완성하세요.

01 서울은 내가 태어난 도시이다. (was, I, born)
→ Seoul is the city _____<u>where I was born</u>_____ .

02 나는 Sam이 5년 동안 살았던 마을을 방문했다. (for, lived, Sam, five years)
→ I visited the village _____ .

03 다음 주 월요일이 그녀가 고등학교를 졸업하게 될 날이다.
(graduate, is going to, from, she, high school)
→ Next Monday is the day _____ .

04 우리는 마을 전체를 볼 수 있는 언덕으로 걸어갔다. (could, we, see, the whole, town)
→ We walked to the hill _____ .

05 그녀는 그를 처음 본 날을 잊지 못할 것이다. (she, first, him, saw)
→ She'll never forget the day _____ .

06 그 회사가 망한 이유가 아직 밝혀지지 않았다. (went, the company, bankrupt)
→ The reason _____ hasn't been found yet.

07 이것이 그가 그의 여가시간을 쓰는 방법이다. (free time, spends, his, he)
→ This is _____ .

08 그것이 그녀가 자신의 공연을 취소한 이유이다. (she, performance, canceled, her)
→ That's _____ .

09 지금이야 말로 우리가 결단을 내려야 할 때다. (have to, we, a decision, make)
→ Now is the time _____ .

10 그가 그곳에 도착한 시간이 오후 10시이다. (there, he, arrived)
→ It was ten p.m. _____ .

11 내가 너에게 거짓말한 이유를 말해주겠다. (lied, to, I, you)
→ I will tell you the reason _____ .

12 그는 그의 코트를 산 상점으로 돌아갔다. (bought, he, his coat)
→ He went back to the shop _____ .

WORDS

· village 마을 · whole 전체의 · bankrupt 파산한 · go bankrupt 파산하다 · yet 아직 · decision 결정
· cancel 취소하다 · performance 공연, 연주회 · free time 여가시간

Level up

1 다음 문장을 관계대명사를 이용하여 다시 쓰세요.

01 Kevin is using the laptop computer he bought last week.

→   Kevin is using the laptop computer which[that] he bought last week.

02 The doctor you want to see is very busy now.

→ _____

03 He is the student I taught English last year.

→ _____

04 This is the drawer my mom ordered on the Internet.

→ _____

05 The boys playing baseball are my friends.

→ _____

06 Do you know the language spoken in Thailand?

→ _____

07 This is the book I gave to Sam.

→ _____

08 This is the dog my sister wants to keep.

_____

09 Look at the car covered with snow.

→ _____

10 The man I met yesterday was my father.

→ _____

11 The palace we want to visit is currently under renovation.

→ _____

12 Do you know the man sleeping on the sofa?

→ _____

• Thailand 태국   • order 주문하다   • drawer 서랍장   • currently 현재   • renovation • 수선, 수리

❷ 다음 영어를 우리말로 쓰세요.

01 The house where he lived was very small.

➡ _____ 그가 살던 집은 매우 작았다. _____

02 I don't remember the day when I first met Jeniffer.

➡ _____

03 The country where the great musician was born is Germany.

➡ _____

04 Please tell me the reason why she always skips dinner.

➡ _____

05 September is the month when the new school year begins in Canada.

➡ _____

06 This is the gym where they play basketball after school.

➡ _____

07 We found the way he got to the destination.

➡ _____

08 Sunday is the day when she goes to the museum.

➡ _____

09 I will tell him the place where we are supposed to meet.

➡ _____

10 The hotel where she stayed last week was very nice.

➡ _____

11 She told me the reason why she broke up with him.

➡ _____

12 The video shows how we change a flat tire.

➡ _____

WORDS

· great 위대한 · musician 음악가 · Germany 독일 · skip 거르다 · destination 목적지
· be supposed to ～하기로 되어있다 · break up with 헤어지다 · change 교환하다 · flat 평평한 김빠진, 맥 빠진

❸ 다음 빈칸에 관계부사와 관계대명사를 쓰세요.

01 He explained ___how___ he completed it in a few days.
→ He explained the way ___in___ ___which___ he completed it in a few days.

02 This is the shop _____ my father lost his wallet.
→ This is the shop _____ _____ my father lost his wallet.

03 Christmas is the day _____ people celebrate the birth of Jesus Christ.
→ Christmas is the day _____ _____ people celebrate the birth of Jesus Christ.

04 Can I ask you the reason _____ you made that decision?
→ Can I ask you the reason _____ _____ you made that decision?

05 She went to the park _____ she first met her husband.
→ She went to the park _____ _____ she first met her husband.

06 He remembers the year _____ Paul immigrated to Canada.
→ He remembers the year _____ _____ Paul immigrated to Canada.

07 Tell me the reason _____ she was absent from school.
→ Tell me the reason _____ _____ she was absent from school.

08 They don't like the way I talk.
→ They don't like the way _____ _____ I talk.

09 March is the month _____ winter starts to turn into spring.
→ March is the month _____ _____ winter starts to turn into spring.

10 This is the company _____ I want to work after graduation.
→ This is the company _____ _____ I want to work after graduation.

WORDS

· complete 완성하다　· in a few days 며칠 후에　· celebrate 기념하다　· decision 결정　· immigrate 이민가다
· absent 결석한　· graduation 졸업　· turn into 바뀌다

■ 다음 밑줄 친 부분을 바르게 고쳐 다시 쓰세요.

01 The man <u>who</u> working in the garden is my father.

who is

02 This is the apartment <u>which</u> his parents live.

03 Please tell me the time <u>where</u> the last train will leave.

04 We'll never forget the day <u>how</u> we completed the project.

05 Do you know <u>the way how</u> he made the robot?

06 This is the reason <u>in which</u> she was upset this morning.

07 That handsome guy <u>wear</u> a black cap is my uncle.

08 English is the language <u>which</u> spoken in England.

09 This is the market <u>in where</u> we can get fruits and vegetables.

10 Do you know the date <u>why</u> Peter was born?

11 Sara clearly remember the day <u>to which</u> he left her.

12 Please tell us <u>on how</u> you mastered English.

13 The children <u>who is</u> playing on the ground are from Europe.

14 The summer <u>for which</u> I left for Toronto was really hot.

15 You should remember the reason <u>at which</u> you became a lawyer.

• clearly 분명히　• master 숙달하다　• hot 더운　• lawyer 변호사

[1–3] 다음 중 빈칸에 들어갈 말로 알맞은 것을 고르세요.

1

Tuesday is the day _____ she takes a ballet lesson.

① what   ② when   ③ how
④ which   ⑤ why

1
선행사 the day에 필요한 관계부사를 찾으세요.

2

My brother always reads books. That's _____ he knows a lot about science.

① where   ② on which   ③ how
④ which   ⑤ why

2
the reason, the place, the time 등의 선행사는 생략할 수 있습니다.

3

Tommy remembered something _____ his teacher had said.

① where   ② on which   ③ that
④ in which   ⑤ why

4

Let me explain _____ this machine works.

① that   ② on which   ③ who
④ in which   ⑤ how

4
explain 설명하다
machine 기계
work 작동하다

5 다음 중 빈칸에 알맞은 것을 고르세요.

> This is the machine _____ invented by James.

① where ② which was ③ which
④ in which ⑤ that

5
관계대명사를 생략할 수
있는 경우를 생각해보세
요.

6 다음 중 각 빈칸에 들어갈 알맞은 것을 고르세요.

> • We will visit the restaurant _____ the food is always fresh.
> • I remember the day _____ I met him for the first time.

① where - on which ② that - when
③ where - in which ④ how - that
⑤ when - where

6
for the first time 처
음으로

7 다음 중 빈칸에 공통으로 들어갈 말을 고르세요.

> • He went to the jungle _____ he could see rare animals.
> • This is the town _____ my mom grew up.

① where ② when ③ on which
④ how ⑤ whom

7
관계부사의 쓰임을 알아
보세요.
rare 드문, 진귀한
grow up 성장하다
jungle 정글

8 다음 중 밑줄 친 부분을 생략할 수 있는 것을 고르세요.

① That's the cafe at <u>which</u> she meets John on Sundays.
② She is a doctor <u>who</u> lives next door.
③ Sam is the smartest boy <u>that</u> I have ever met.
④ She's the only girl <u>who</u> has a computer.
⑤ He is the boy <u>whose</u> father is a farmer.

9 다음 중 빈칸에 알맞지 <u>않은</u> 것을 고르세요.

> This is _____ where we visited every summer.

① the beach   ② the cabin

③ the market   ④ the place

⑤ the reason

9
관계부사 where의 쓰임
을 알아보세요.

[10–11] 다음 중 빈칸에 알맞은 말을 고르세요.

10

> We are waiting for the day when the vacation begins.
> = We are waiting for the day _____ the vacation begins.

① on where   ② on which

③ in which   ④ for how

⑤ for which

11

> Do you know the man talking to Susan?
> = Do you know the man _____ talking to Susan?

① which is   ② whose

③ which are   ④ who is

⑤ whom is

11
관계대명사를 생략할 수 있
는 경우를 생각해 보세요.

12 다음 중 밑줄 친 when의 쓰임이 <u>다른</u> 것을 고르세요.

① August is the month <u>when</u> many people go on holiday.

② He was having dinner <u>when</u> I read a book.

③ Do you remember the time <u>when</u> they arrived here.

④ Sunday is the only day <u>when</u> we can relax.

⑤ I'm waiting for the day <u>when</u> all my pain goes away.

12
접속사와 관계사의 쓰임을
구별해 보세요.
fail 실패하다
pain 고통
go away 가다, 없어지다

13 다음 우리말을 영어로 바르게 쓴 것을 고르세요.

> Johnson 씨는 나무로 만들어진 집에 살았다.

① Mr. Johnson lived in a house that made of wood.
② Mr. Johnson lived in a house which made of wood.
③ Mr. Johnson is living in a house which is made of wood.
④ Mr. Johnson was living in a house made of wood.
⑤ Mr. Johnson lived in a house made of wood.

Note

13
[관계대명사+be동사]는 생략할 수 있다.

14 다음 중 <u>어색한</u> 문장을 고르세요.

① Jeff is the strongest boy I've ever seen.
② That is the way how he solved the math problem.
③ The picture she was looking at was beautiful.
④ That is the town in which I was born.
⑤ This is the lake where he goes fishing.

14
lake 호수

15 다음 중 올바른 문장을 고르세요.

① This is the river which they swim every day.
② She showed me the watch she bought yesterday.
③ The church which she goes on Sunday is near here.
④ I will stay at the hotel where is located near the beach.
⑤ The swimming pool when I often swim is small.

15
목적격 관계대명사는 생략할 수 있습니다.

16 다음 빈칸에 알맞은 말을 쓰세요.

> The gym _____ we were supposed to play basketball is closed.

➡ _____

16
be supposed to
~하기로 하다

17 다음 두 문장을 관계부사를 이용하여한 문장으로 완성하시오.

> We climbed to the top of the mountain.
> We could see the whole city of Seoul there.

➡ _____

_____

17
선행사가 the mountain
입니다.
climb 등산하다
whole 전체의

18 다음 영어를 관계대명사를 생략하고 다시 쓰세요.

1) | Do you know the man who is washing a car?

➡ _____

2) | This is the book which was written by John Grisham.

➡ _____

19 다음 문장에서 v 표시된 부분에 생략된 관계대명사와 be동사를 쓰세요.

1) | Look at the girl^vplaying tennis.

➡ _____

2) | Baseball is the sport^vI like most.

➡ _____

19
관계대명사를 생략할 수
있는 경우를 생각해보세
요.

20 다음 잘못된 곳을 찾아 바르게 고치세요.

> I will visit the museum in where I can see many famous
> paintings.

➡ _____

20
famous 유명한
painting 그림

Review Test

1 다음 두 문장의 의미가 통하도록 빈칸에 알맞은 말을 쓰세요.　　　　Chapter 1

01 As I am not in Seoul, I can't attend her wedding.
→ If _____I were in Seoul_____, I could attend her wedding.

02 I'm sorry that I don't have a daughter.
→ I wish _____.

03 As I'm not with my family, I'm not happy.
→ If _____, I would be happy.

04 As you don't practice hard, you can't win the race.
→ If _____, you could win the race.

05 As we don't have enough time, we can't finish it today.
→ If we had enough time, we _____.

06 As Kevin is sick, He won't go out for dinner.
→ If _____, he would go out for dinner.

07 As I didn't have enough money, I couldn't purchase the expensive furniture.
→ If I had had enough money, I _____.

08 As she didn't get up early, she didn't arrive here on time.
→ If she had got up early, she _____.

09 As I didn't have a car, I couldn't drive you home.
→ If I had had a car, I _____.

10 As I didn't have an umbrella, I was wet.
→ If _____, I would not have been wet.

11 As Jeff didn't read the book, he didn't know about the story.
→ If Jeff had read the book, he _____.

12 I'm sorry that you didn't call me.
→ I wish _____.

WORDS

· **practice** 연습하다　· **race** 경주　· **purchase** 구입하다　· **furniture** 가구　· **on time** 정각에　· **wet** 젖은
· **call** 전화하다

2 다음 두 문장의 의미가 통하도록 빈칸에 알맞은 말을 쓰세요.　　　Chapter 1

01 I wish I were rich.

→ I'm sorry _____ I am not rich _____.

02 I wish I had passed the test.

→ I'm sorry that _____.

03 I wish I could speak Japanese.

→ I'm so sorry _____.

04 I'm so sorry I didn't accept her advice then.

→ I wish _____.

05 I'm so sorry we didn't take the taxi last night.

→ I wish _____.

06 I wish I could help you.

→ I'm sorry _____.

07 If I were rich, I could buy a car.

→ As _____, I cannot buy a car.

08 I wish I were as tall as you.

→ I'm sorry _____.

09 As you didn't ask me, I didn't help you.

→ If _____, I _____.

10 If the train had not arrived late, I could have got there on time.

→ As the train arrived late, I _____.

11 As Mike was not in the office, he didn't answer the phone.

→ If _____, he _____.

12 As he didn't do well in the exam, his mother was not happy.

→ If _____, his mother _____.

· accept 받아들이다　· take (교통수단·도로 등을) 타다　· advice 충고　· then 그때　· answer 대답하다

❸ 다음 빈칸에 알맞은 관계대명사를 쓰세요.

01 The man ___who(m)[that]___ I met last week is standing there.

02 She broke the vase _____ color was white.

03 She sent me the pictures _____ she took during the vacation.

04 She has a daughter _____ works at a hospital.

05 This is not _____ I ordered.

06 She has to give up _____ she has planned.

07 I told him _____ I knew about the project.

08 A woman _____ husband has died is a widow.

09 I met a girl _____ hobby is drawing cartoons.

10 I met the old lady _____ used to work at the animal shelter.

11 Alice bought the shoes _____ were on sale.

12 This is the computer _____ she wants to buy.

13 I want to talk to the man _____ is in charge of advertising.

14 Is there anything _____ you want to buy?

15 He is the first student _____ got a perfect score in chemistry.

WORDS

· widow 과부 · cartoon 만화 · shelter 대피처 · on sale 할인 중인 · in charge of ~에 책임이 있는
· advertising 광고 · perfect 완벽한 · chemistry 화학

4 다음 영어를 우리말로 쓰세요. Chapter 2

01 I introduced to him a writer who came from Japan.

→ _____나는 그에게 일본에서 온 작가를 소개 했다._____

02 Amy is looking for a ring which she lost yesterday.

→ _____

03 The boy who is crying over there is my brother.

→ _____

04 The man who sent me a cake works at a library.

→ _____

05 Mike will fix the computer which you haven't used for a long time.

→ _____

06 I can't find the student who can speak Chinese.

→ _____

5 다음 문장을 관계대명사를 생략해서 다시 쓰세요. Chapter 2

01 This is the lamp which I bought at the store yesterday.

→ _____This is the lamp I bought at the store yesterday._____

02 I received a letter which was written in English

→ _____

03 There were a lot of students who were studying in the library.

→ _____

04 The painting which is on the wall is very fantastic.

→ _____

05 These are the books which are useful for students.

→ _____

06 Look at the boy who is sleeping under the tree.

→ _____

WORDS

· introduce 소개하다   · for a long time 오랫동안   · receive 받다   · useful 유용한   · on the wall 벽에

6 다음 보기에서 알맞은 말을 골라 빈칸에 쓰세요. (중복 사용 가능) Chapter 3

> 보기
>
> the way   where   in which   on which   when   for which   why

01 This is the cafe ____where____ I met him.

02 That is the reason _____ _____ she left me.

03 This is the town _____ _____ I spent my childhood.

04 Monday is the day _____ he is very busy.

05 This is the way _____ _____ he stole the car.

06 2010 is the year _____ she came to Canada as a refugee.

07 Sunday is the day _____ _____ he goes fishing with his friends.

08 Do you remember the day _____ she brought us to the party?

09 You will learn _____ _____ in which they work and live together.

10 Do you know the reason _____ the game was delayed?

11 November is the time _____ the entrance exam season starts.

12 That is the island _____ they hid the treasure.

WORDS

• childhood 어린 시절 • steal 훔치다 • refugee 난민, 피난민 • bring 데려오다 • together 함께 • delay 연기하다
• entrance 입구, 입장, 입학 • hid hide (숨기다)의 과거형 • treasure 보물

Achievement Test (Chapter 1-3)

[1–5] 다음 중 빈칸에 알맞은 말을 고르세요.

1

> I wish _____ a new computer.

① I haven't
② I have
③ I will have
④ I can have
⑤ I had

2

> If I _____ rich, I could have studied abroad.

① have
② had
③ had been
④ have been
⑤ had not

3

> The museum _____ I visited yesterday was very big.

① which
② where
③ when
④ why
⑤ how

4

> I met a girl _____ sister is a famous singer.

① who
② where
③ when
④ why
⑤ whose

5

> Tom told me the reason _____ he was angry.

① who
② where
③ when
④ why
⑤ whose

[6–7] 다음 중 빈칸에 들어갈 말이 순서대로 바르게 짝지어진 것을 고르세요.

6

> If he had _____ his homework, he could _____ basketball with you.

① does - have played
② does - play
③ do - play
④ done - played
⑤ done - have played

7

> • This is the hotel _____ I stayed last month.
> • Now is the time _____ I need you most.

① where - when
② why - when
③ where - how
④ how - where
⑤ when - where

8

> • The watch _____ was stolen has been found.
> • Jack is the man _____ she is going to marry.

① who - that
② which - whose
③ which - whom
④ whose - whom
⑤ that - which

9 다음 중 보기의 의미와 같은 문장을 고르세요.

> I wish I had a lot of money.

① I'm sorry that I don't have a lot of money.
② I'm sorry that I have a lot of money.
③ I'm afraid that I didn't have a lot of money.
④ I'm afraid that I wasn't have a lot of money.
⑤ I'm sorry that I haven't have a lot of money.

10 다음 중 빈칸에 들어갈 수 <u>없는</u> 것을 고르세요.

> They really liked _____ where they went last Sunday.

① the shopping mall   ② the restaurant
③ the moment   ④ the museum
⑤ the cafe

[11-13] 다음 중 두 문장이 의미가 같도록 빈칸에 알맞은 말을 고르세요.

11

> This is the thing which he wants to buy.
> = This is _____ he wants to buy.

① who   ② what
③ when   ④ why
⑤ whose

12

> Sunday is the day when he is free.
> = Sunday is the day _____ he is free.

① in which   ② on which
③ on when   ④ for which
⑤ on that

13

> I am sorry I can't speak English.
> = I wish I _____ speak English.

① can   ② will
③ don't   ④ didn't
⑤ could

[14-15] 다음 중 보기의 문장과 의미가 같은 것을 고르세요.

14

> If I had enough money, I could buy a new car.

① As I have enough money, I can buy a new car.
② As I have enough money, I can't buy a new car.
③ As I don't have enough money, I can't buy a new car.
④ As I don't have enough money, I could have bought a new car.
⑤ As I didn't have enough money, I could have bought a new car.

15

> If Paul had worn a seatbelt, he would not have broken his leg.

① As Paul doesn't wear a seatbelt, he broke his leg.
② As Paul didn't wear a seatbelt, he broke his leg.
③ As Paul wore a seatbelt, he broke his leg.
④ As Paul wore a seatbelt, he didn't break his leg.
⑤ As Paul didn't wear a seatbelt, he would break his leg.

16 다음 중 밑줄 친 부분을 생략할 수 없는 것을 고르세요.

① The bed which I bought yesterday was very expensive.
② The woman whom he saw yesterday is my aunt.
③ The boy who broke the window ran away.
④ The box that he is carrying is very heavy.
⑤ Have you seen the picture that Tom drew?

17 다음 중 빈칸에 들어갈 말이 나머지와 다른 것을 고르세요.

① Do you understand _____ I am trying to say?
② This is _____ I bought yesterday.
③ _____ he said is not true.
④ You can have _____ you want.
⑤ Angie, _____ car had broken down, was angry.

18 다음 중 두 문장을 하나로 연결할 빈칸에 들어갈 말을 고르세요.

The boy is my brother. He is playing the piano.
→ The boy _____ playing the piano is my brother.

① who   ② that are
③ which is   ④ who is
⑤ whom was

19 다음 중 보기의 밑줄 친 부분과 의미가 다른 것을 고르세요.

What makes me happy is children's smile.

① What she really needs is love.
② He gave me what I really wanted
③ What he says is true.
④ She didn`t eat what l cooked.
⑤ Tell me what your name is.

[20-22] 다음 중 어법상 어색한 문장을 고르세요.

20 ① I gave him all the coins whom I had.
② Everything that he said was true.
③ The woman that he fell in love with left him.
④ I know the man who is sitting on the bench.
⑤ The boys who are playing soccer are my friends.

21 ① I have a friend who can dance very well.
② This is the girl which lives next door.
③ This is the boy who came from America.
④ A farmer is a person who works on the farm.
⑤ A computer is a thing which is useful for everybody.

22 ① This is the way we found the lost girl.
② This is the house in which he lives.
③ Visit the museum which you can see many paintings.
④ This is the gym where he works out.
⑤ Seoul is the city where we can see many tall buildings.

23 다음 중 밑줄 친 that의 쓰임이 다른 것을 고르세요.

① I'm sure <u>that</u> she will pass the test.
② Winter is the season <u>that</u> comes after fall.
③ He has the dog <u>that</u> has brown eyes.
④ She has the bird <u>that</u> has big wings.
⑤ This is the robot <u>that</u> can clean the house.

24 다음 빈칸에 알맞은 관계부사를 쓰세요.

1) | I know the place _____ the next meeting will be held. |

→ _____

2) | She'll never forget the day _____ she first dated him. |

→ _____

[25–26] 다음 두 문장의 의미가 같도록 문장을 완성하시오.

25 | I am sorry that I am not a bird.
 = I wish I _____. |

→ _____

26 | As I woke him up early, he didn't miss the train.
 = If I had not waken him up early, he _____ the train. |

→ _____

27 다음 우리말과 의미가 같도록 문장을 완성하시오.

| 내가 만약 너라면 나는 거짓말을 하지 않을 텐데.
 → If I were you, I _____
 (tell a lie) |

→ _____

28 다음 영어를 우리말로 쓰세요.

| If I had enough money, I could buy a new computer. |

→ _____

29 다음 잘못된 부분을 바르게 고치세요.

1) | I know a boy who father is a doctor. |

→ _____

2) | The girl whom is standing under the tree is my sister. |

→ _____

30 다음 빈칸에 공통으로 들어갈 관계부사를 쓰세요.

| • This is the restaurant _____ he eats dinner every day.
 • This is the cafe _____ I met your father for the first time.
 • Do you remember the town _____ you grew up? |

→ _____

Chapter 4

여러 가지 문장 Ⅰ

UNIT 01

의문사가 있는 의문문 Ⅰ

의문사란 누가, 언제, 어디서, 무엇을, 어떻게, 왜 등을 묻는 것이 의문사입니다. 의문사로 시작하는 의문문은 Yes나 No로 대답하지 않습니다.

1. 의문사 의문문의 형태

Who	누가, 누구 (주어에 대한 정보나 동작의 주체를 물을 때 사용한다. 때로는 whom 대신 사용하기도 한다.)	What	무엇(사물의 이름을 물을 때, 사람의 직업이나 신분을 물을 때 사용)
Whose	누구의 것 (사물의 소유자 등을 물을 때 사용)	Which	어느 것 (주로 둘 중의 선택을 물을 때 사용)

2. 의문사+be동사+주어 ~? – be동사가 있을 때 사용합니다.

Who	**Who** is that boy? - He is my cousin.	What	**What** is this? - It is a cat.
Whose	**Whose** is this? - It's mine.	Which	**Which** is bigger, this table or that desk? - This table is bigger.

3. 의문사+do[does/did]+주어+동사원형 ~? – 일반동사가 있을 때 사용합니다.

Who	**Who(m)** do you want to speak with? -I want to speak with Tom.	What	**What** do you do after school? -I often play basketball.
Which	**Which** do you like better, soccer or baseball? -I like soccer better.		

Plus 1
- what은 특정하지 않은 것을 물어보는 의문문에 사용되는 반면, which는 특정한 그룹 안에서 어느 하나를 물어보는 선택의문문에 사용됩니다.
  What did you drink? 너는 무엇을 마셨니?
  Which did you drink, water or milk? 너는 어떤 것을 마셨니, 물 아니면 우유?

Plus 2
- what, which, whose 다음에 명사를 써서 사용할 수도 있습니다.
  Which **book** is cheaper, this one or that one? 이책과 저책 중 어느 것이 저렴하니?
  Whose **book** is this? 이것은 누구의 책이니?   What **sport** do you like? 무슨 운동 좋아하니?

4. who가 주어 역할을 할 때 – who는 3인칭 단수 역할을 한다.

Who+동사 ~?	**Who is** singing a song?	**Who knows** her?
Who+조동사 ~?	**Who can** speak Chinese?	

Warm up

● 다음 괄호 안에서 알맞은 말을 고르세요.

01 ((Who is) / Whose is) that boy?
저 소년은 누구니?

02 (What is / What did) you eat at the restaurant?
그 식당에서 뭘 먹었니?

03 (Whose is / Whose does) this computer?
이 컴퓨터는 누구의 것이니?

04 (What / Which) is your father doing now?
네 아버지는 지금 뭐하시니?

05 (Which do / Which is) you like better, soccer or baseball?
축구와 야구 중 어느 것을 더 좋아하니?

06 (What do / Which do) you usually do after dinner?
저녁식사 후 보통 무엇을 하니?

07 (What did / What does) she send to the man last week?
그녀는 지난주 그 남자에게 무엇을 보냈니?

08 (Who will / Who do) play the piano at the party?
누가 음악회에서 피아노를 연주할 거니?

09 (Who / What) subject do you like?
너는 무슨 과목을 좋아하니?

10 (What did / What does) she do yesterday?
그녀는 어제 무엇을 했니?

11 (What / Which) ice cream do you want, vanilla or chocolate?
바닐라와 초콜릿 중 어느 아이스크림 먹을래?

12 Who (know / knows) him?
누가 그를 아나요?

· subject 과목   · vanilla 바닐라

1 다음 빈칸에 알맞은 말을 쓰세요.

01 A: ___What___ ___is___ that man eating?
B: He's eating noodles.

02 A: _____ does your father do?
B: He is a teacher.

03 A: _____ _____ she sell at the market?
B: She sells used items.

04 A: _____ do you like better, meat or vegetables?
B: I like vegetables better.

05 A: _____ is that?
B: It's mine.

06 A: _____ one would you like better, coffee or tea?
B: Coffee, please.

07 A: _____ _____ your favorite color?
B: My favorite color is red.

08 A: _____ answered the question?
B: Ted did.

09 A: _____ cat is that?
B: It's my dad's.

10 A: _____ are you doing here, John?
B: I am waiting for a bus.

11 A: _____ _____ Tony buy yesterday?
B: He bought a sofa.

12 A: _____ do you like most?
B: I like Jake most.

WORDS
• noodle 국수　• meat 고기　• vegetable 야채　• used item 중고품　• favorite 좋아하는　• answer 대답하다

❷ 다음 빈칸에 알맞은 말을 쓰세요.

01 A: _____Who_____ _____is_____ the man eating noodles?
B: He's my uncle.

02 A: _____ is his real name?
B: His real name is Samuel Johns.

03 A: _____ will have coffee?
B: Jessie will do.

04 A: _____ car is this?
B: It's my mom's.

05 A: _____ did you support in the election?
B: Mr. Clerk.

06 A: _____ color do you like more, red or orange?
B: Orange.

07 A: _____ _____ you want for Christmas?
B: I want a bike.

08 A: _____ can teach history?
B: Mrs. Johnson.

09 A: _____ is that bag?
B: It's my sister's.

10 A: _____ food is your mom making now?
B: She is making steak.

11 A: _____ _____ pick up Jane at the station?
B: I will do it.

12 A: _____ _____ you like more, this car or that car?
B: I like this car more.

WORDS

• support 지지하다, 지원하다　• election 선거　• pick up 데리러 가다

1 다음 어색한 부분을 바르게 고치세요.

01 Who take a walk after dinner?
누가 저녁식사 후 산책을 하니?

<u> take </u> ➡ <u> takes </u>

02 Whose movie do you want to see?
너는 무슨 영화를 보고 싶니?

_____ ➡ _____

03 Who smartphone is this?
이것은 누구의 스마트폰이니?

_____ ➡ _____

04 Whose is the boy standing over there?
저쪽에 서있는 소년은 누구니?

_____ ➡ _____

05 Who is he doing in the library?
그는 도서관에서 무엇을 하고 있니?

_____ ➡ _____

06 What is singing on the stage?
누가 무대에서 노래를 부르고 있니?

_____ ➡ _____

07 What do he have in his hand?
그의 손에 무엇이 있니?

_____ ➡ _____

08 What is your mother's cell phone,
this one or that one?
이것과 저것 중 어느 것이 네 엄마 휴대폰이니?

_____ ➡ _____

09 What is that?
저것은 누구의 것이니?

_____ ➡ _____

10 Who does the woman in the office?
사무실에 있는 여성은 누구니?

_____ ➡ _____

11 What is your uncle do?
네 삼촌 직업은 뭐니?

_____ ➡ _____

12 What is she waiting for?
그녀는 누구를 기다리고 있습니까?

_____ ➡ _____

WORDS

· take a walk 산책하다　　· cell phone 휴대폰

❷ 다음 우리말과 일치하도록, 문장을 완성하세요.

01 네가 좋아하는 야구 선수는 누구니?

➡ _____ Who is _____ your favorite baseball player?

02 네 아버지의 직업은 무엇이니?

➡ _____ your father's job?

03 너는 누구와 함께 살고 싶니?

➡ _____ you want to live with?

04 이것은 누구의 자동차이니?

➡ _____ is this?

05 우유와 주스 중 어떤 게 더 좋니?

➡ _____ you like better, milk or juice?

06 이것과 저것 중 어느 것이 그녀의 고양이이니?

➡ _____ her cat, this one or that one?

07 로비에 있는 저 사람들은 누구니?

➡ _____ those people in the lobby?

08 네 친구들은 공원에서 무엇을 하고 있니?

➡ _____ your friends doing at the park?

09 무엇을 찾고 있습니까?

➡ _____ you looking for?

10 '스타워즈'와 '배트맨' 중 어느 영화를 보고 싶니?

➡ _____ do you want to see, *Star wars* or *Batman*?

11 누가 일주일에 한 번 그 집을 청소하니?

➡ _____ the house once a week?

12 Sam은 보통 일요일에 무엇을 하니?

➡ _____ Sam usually do on Sunday?

WORDS

· lobby 로비   · look for ~을 찾다   · once a week 일주일에 한 번   · usually 보통

UNIT 02

의문사가 있는 의문문 II

의문사는 특정 정보를 물을 때 사용하며, Yes와 No로 대답하는 대신 특정 정보로 답을 해야 합니다.

1. 의문사 의문문의 형태

When	언제 (시간이나 때를 물을 사용한다.)	**How**	어떻게, 어떠한 (방법이나 상태를 물을 때 사용한다.)
Where	어디에 (장소나 위치를 물을 때 사용한다.)	**Why**	왜 (원인이나 이유를 물을 때 사용하며, 대답은 주로 because로 한다.)

2. 의문사+be동사+주어 ~? / 의문사+do[does/did]+주어+동사원형 ~?

When	**When** is Christmas? - It's **December 25th**. **When** do you usually get up? - I get up **at six**.
Where	**Where** is my book? - It's on your desk. **Where** do you want to visit? - I want to visit **the museum**
How	**How** is the weather in Seoul? - It's **sunny.** **How** does he go to school? - He goes to school **by bus**.
Why	**Why** is John absent today? - **Because** he got up late. **Why** did they come home late? - **Because** they missed the train.

Plus 1
- When은 경우에 따라 What time으로 쓸 수도 있습니다.
  When do you get up in the morning? 너는 아침에 언제 일어나니?
  = **What time** do you get up in the morning? 너는 아침에 몇 시에 일어나니?

3. how+형용사[부사]

How deep	「깊이」 얼마나 깊은	**How deep** is this river?
How old	「나이」 몇 살	**How old** are you?
How tall	「키, 높이」 얼마나 큰	**How tall** is that tree?
How big	「크기」 얼마나 큰	**How big** is your room?
How far	「거리」 얼마나 먼	**How far** is it from here to the station?
How long	「길이」 얼마나 긴 「기간」 얼마나 오래	**How long** is this river? **How long** are you going to stay in Korea?
How often	「빈도」 얼마나 자주	**How often** do you go to the movies?
How many+복수명사	「개수」 얼마나 많은	**How many** coins do you have?
How much+셀 수 없는 명사	「양」 얼마나 많은 「가격」 얼마	**How much** water do you need? **How much** is this car?

Plus 2
- 의문사 다음에 조동사 can, will 등이 올 수 있습니다.
  When **can** I see you? 내가 언제 너를 만날 수 있을까?
  How long **can** I borrow this book? 이 책을 얼마 동안 빌릴 수 있을까요?

Warm up

정답 및 해설 p.20

● 다음 괄호 안에서 알맞은 말을 고르세요.

01 (What / (When)) did he leave for Seoul?
그는 언제 서울로 떠났니?

02 (How / Why) do you like your coffee?
커피를 어떻게 드십니까?

03 (When is / When do) your birthday?
네 생일이 언제니?

04 (Where did / Where is) you buy the sunglasses?
그 선글라스 어디서 샀니?

05 (Where / When) can you deliver the furniture?
언제 가구를 배달해 주실 수 있나요?

06 (When did / What did) you become a doctor?
너는 언제 의사가 되었니?

07 (Where is / What is) your mom?
너의 엄마는 어디에 계시니?

08 (Where did / Where does) you put your bag?
너는 가방을 어디에 두었니?

09 (Why was / Why is) she late for school yesterday?
그녀는 왜 어제 학교에 지각했니?

10 (What / Where) can I buy roses?
장미꽃을 어디서 살 수 있나요?

11 (What / When) time do you get up in the morning?
아침에 몇 시에 일어나니?

12 (How is / How does) he go to school?
그는 학교에 어떻게 가니?

• furniture 가구   • deliver 배달하다

1 다음 빈칸에 알맞은 말을 쓰세요.

01 A: _____Why_____ _____do_____ you study English?
B: Because I want to be a diplomat.

02 A: _____ _____ Sophia go after school?
B: She goes to the swimming pool.

03 A: _____ _____ they stay during the vacation?
B: They stayed at a hotel.

04 A: _____ will he return from the business trip?
B: He will return next Tuesday.

05 A: _____ _____ you want to listen to music?
B: I want to listen to music after school.

06 A: _____ _____ I buy the concert tickets?
B: You can buy them on the Internet.

07 A: _____ _____ is this car?
B: It's twenty thousand dollars.

08 A: _____ _____ languages can you speak?
B: I can speak three languages.

09 A: _____ _____ are you going to stay here?
B: I'm going to stay here for three days.

10 A: _____ _____ do you usually go to bed?
B: At eleven.

11 A: _____ is the weather in Tokyo?
B: It's rainy.

12 A: _____ _____ is your office?
B: It's about ten minutes' walk from here.

WORDS

• diplomat 외교관 • return 돌아오다 • language 언어 • weather 날씨

❷ 다음 빈칸에 알맞은 말을 쓰세요.

01 A: _____How_____ _____old_____ are you?
B: I'm 12 years old.

02 A: _____ _____ bats are there in the box?
B: There are seven.

03 A: _____ _____ did you meet him last year?
B: About twice a month.

04 A: _____ _____ hours a day do you surf on the Internet?
B: More than 3 hours.

05 A: _____ _____ does it take from here to the top of the mountain?
B: About three hours.

06 A: _____ _____ do you take a bus to school?
B: About three times a week.

07 A: _____ _____ is the swimming pool?
B: It is two meters deep.

08 A: _____ _____ you eat lunch yesterday?
B: At the Chinese restaurant.

09 A: _____ _____ you finish the report?
B: I can finish it by tomorrow.

10 A: _____ is your mom?
B: She is fine.

11 A: _____ _____ they arrive in Korea?
B: They arrived in Korea three days ago.

12 A: _____ _____ is the tower?
B: It's 10 meters tall.

WORDS
• twice 두 번 • surf 인터넷을 서핑「검색」하다 • top 정상, 꼭대기 • take 「시간이」 걸리다 • about 대략

1 다음 빈칸에 알맞은 말을 쓰세요.

01 A: ___How___ ___often___ do you play the guitar?
    B: Once a week.

02 A: _____ _____ is your father?
    B: He is 170 centimeters.

03 A: _____ _____ is this coat?
    B: It's $300.

04 A: _____ _____ sugar does she need?
    B: She needs two bags of sugar.

05 A: _____ _____ children do you have?
    B: I have three children.

06 A: _____ _____ is your school from your house?
    B: It's about three kilometers.

07 A: _____ _____ is your sister?
    B: She is eleven years old.

08 A: _____ _____ is the bridge?
    B: It's two kilometers long.

09 A: _____ _____ is the lake?
    B: It is five feet deep.

10 A: _____ _____ he want to go?
    B: He wants to go to the theme park.

11 A: _____ _____ you late for the meeting?
    B: Because the traffic was very heavy.

12 A: _____ _____ the next train for Busan leave?
    B: It leaves at five p.m.

WORDS
· lake 호수 · leave 떠나다

❷ 다음 우리말과 일치하도록 주어진 단어를 이용하여 완성하시오.

01 너는 보통 몇 시에 저녁식사를 하니? (usually, have)

➡ _____When[What time] do you usually have_____ dinner?

02 얼마나 많은 책들이 네 가방에 있니? (there, are, books)

➡ _____ in your bag?

03 너는 얼마나 자주 수영을 하니? (go)

➡ _____ swimming?

04 스테이크 어떻게 드시나요? (like, your)

➡ _____ steak?

05 너는 밀가루가 얼마나 필요하니? (flour)

➡ _____ need?

06 그녀는 개가 몇 마리 있니? (she, dogs)

➡ _____ have?

07 그들은 왜 나의 요구를 거절했니? (my, refuse, they)

➡ _____ request?

08 너는 오늘 수업이 얼마나 있니? (classes, have)

➡ _____ today?

09 너는 얼마나 오랫동안 호주에 머물 예정이니? (be going to, stay)

➡ _____ in Australia?

10 너는 우산을 어디에 두고 왔니? (leave)

➡ _____ your umbrella?

11 그는 한국에서 왜 그렇게 인기가 있니? (popular, so)

➡ _____ in Korea?

12 여기서 지하철역까지 얼마나 멀어요? (the subway station, from)

➡ _____ here?

WORDS

• refuse 거절하다 • request 요청, 요구 • leave 두고 오다, 남기다 • so 매우 • popular 인기 있는

UNIT 03

명령문과 제안문

명령문은 상대방에게 명령, 부탁 등을 할 때 사용하고 제안문은 상대방에게 무언가를 제안할 때 사용합니다.

1. 긍정명령문: 주어를 생략하고 동사원형으로 시작하며 '~해라'라는 의미입니다.

| 일반동사원형 ~.
Be+형용사/명사 ~.(~해라) | **Run** fast. 빨리 달려라. **Be** quiet. 조용히 해라.
Be an honest person. 정직한 사람이 되어라. |

2. 부정명령문: '~하지 마라'라는 의미로 「Don't+동사원형」으로 시작합니다.

| Don't+일반동사원형 ~.
Don't be+형용사/명사 ~
(~하지 마라) | **Don't** open the door. 문을 열지 마라.
Don't be late again. 다시는 늦지 마라.
Don't be a fool. 멍청한 짓 하지 마라. |

Plus 1
• 부정의 의미를 강조하기 위해 Don't 대신 Never를 사용하기도 합니다.
Never say it again. 다시는 그 말 하지 마.

Plus 2
• 명령문에서 and, or가 사용되는 경우
and + 긍정의 결과 (그러면) : Don't eat fast food, **and** you will be healthy.
패스트푸드를 먹지마라 그러면 건강해 질것이다.
or + 부정의 결과 (그렇지 않으면) : Hurry up, **or** you'll lose your chance.
서둘러라 그렇지 않으면 너의 기회를 잃을 것이다.

3. 제안문 (같이 하는 경우)

Let's+동사원형 ~. (~하자)	**Let's play** baseball. 야구 하자. **Let's go** to the movies. 영화 보러 가자.
Let's not+동사원형 ~. (~하지 말자)	**Let's not** give up now. 지금 포기하지 말자. **Let's not** talk about it. 그것에 대해 얘기하지 말자.
Why don't we+동사원형? (~하는 것이 어때?)	**Why don't we** play tennis this Sunday? 이번 주 일요일 테니스 하는 게 어때?
How about ~ing? / What about ~ing? (~하는 것이 어때?)	**How about** playing tennis this Sunday? = **What about** playing tennis this Sunday? 이번 주 일요일 테니스 하는 게 어때? (말하는 사람도 같이 하는 경우)
Shall we+동사 원형?	**Shall we play** tennis this Sunday. 이번 주 일요일 테니스 할래?

4. 제안문 (상대방에게)

| How about ~ing? /
What about ~ing?
(~하는 것이 어때?) | **How about** playing tennis this Sunday?
= **What about** playing tennis this Sunday?
이번 주 일요일 테니스 하는 게 어때? |
| Why don't you+동사원형?
(~하는 게 어때?) | **Why don't you** go skating? 너 스키 타러 가는 게 어때?
(상대방에게 제안하는 경우) |

Warm up

● 다음 괄호 안에서 알맞은 말을 고르세요.

01 Let's (go / goes) swimming in the river.

02 How about (buy / buying) flowers for your mom?

03 (Don't / Doesn't) waste time.

04 (How about / Let's not) bother him.

05 What about (watch / watching) a movie after lunch?

06 (Don't / Do) watch TV too much.

07 (Why / Shall) we play soccer today?

08 Let's (not / don't) play computer games today.

09 Don't (do / be) late for school.

10 (How / Why) don't we take the subway?

11 Let's (talk / talks) about your problem.

12 (Don't / Let's) disappoint your parents.

13 Don't (press / presses) the red button.

14 (Why / How) don't you wear the white dress?

15 (Don't / Doesn't) sit on the grass.

• waste 낭비하다   • bother 괴롭히다   • disappoint 실망시키다   • grass 잔디

1 다음 빈칸에 알맞은 말을 보기에서 골라 쓰세요. (한번만 사용하세요.)

보기

why	let's	buying	shall	how about		
don't	not	or	be	turn off	don't be	go to

01 ____Why____ don't we take him to the concert?

02 _____ eat out with him.

03 _____ throwing a party for him?

04 How about _____ a bike for her?

05 _____ we bake him some cookies?

06 Shall we _____ the beach?

07 _____ drive too fast, please.

08 Let's _____ the lamp when we aren't using it.

09 Take the subway, _____ you'll miss the airplane.

10 _____ quiet in the library.

11 Let's _____ waste money.

12 _____ late for school.

WORDS

· eat out 외식하다   · throw a party 파티를 열다

❷ 다음 빈칸에 알맞은 말을 보기에서 골라 쓰세요. (한번만 사용하세요.)

보기

shall	or	be	recycle	meet	and	drinking
don't be	unplug	take	why don't	let's not		

01 ____Shall____ we go out for lunch?

02 Shall we _____ at the park at ten?

03 Get up early, _____ you will feel much better.

04 Study hard, _____ you will fail the final exam.

05 _____ kind to others.

06 Let's _____ bottles and newspapers.

07 _____ this medicine, and your pain will go away.

08 Let's _____ electrical equipments after we use them.

09 _____ disappointed. Cheer up!

10 _____ you join the reading club after school?

11 _____ forget the brave soldiers.

12 How about _____ some milk?

WORDS

• final exam 기말고사   • recycle 재활용하다   • cheer 환호하다, 기운이 나다   • unplug ~에서 전원을 끊다
• electrical equipments 전자장비   • equipment 장비   • disappointed 실망한   • brave 용감한

Check up & Writing

❶ 다음 문장 중 <u>어색한</u> 부분을 바르게 고치세요.

01 Study harder, and you can't get good marks.   _and_ ➡ _or_

02 Why don't you coming and play with me?   _____ ➡ _____

03 Don't throws away anything that can recycle.   _____ ➡ _____

04 What about order pizza for her?   _____ ➡ _____

05 Let's making breakfast for her.   _____ ➡ _____

06 Please, doesn't make a noise.   _____ ➡ _____

07 What about go mountain climbing next week?   _____ ➡ _____

08 Why don't you carrying this bag for me?   _____ ➡ _____

09 Do honest, and people will trust you.   _____ ➡ _____

10 How about stay in the hotel today?   _____ ➡ _____

11 Let's not gave up now.   _____ ➡ _____

12 Why doesn't we take a break for ten minutes?   _____ ➡ _____

13 Open the window, or you can get some fresh air.

    _____ ➡ _____

14 Shall we going out for a bite?   _____ ➡ _____

15 Finish your homework, and you can't watch TV.

    _____ ➡ _____

WORDS

• **throw away** 버리다　• **noise** 소음　• **carry** 들고 있다; 나르다　• **give up** 포기하다　• **bite** 소량의 음식[식사], 요기
• **trust** 신뢰하다

❷ 다음 우리말과 일치하도록, 주어진 단어를 이용하여 문장을 완성하세요.
(필요하면 단어를 추가하거나 변경 하세요.)

01 우리 영화 보기 전에 저녁 먹을래? (eat, before, dinner)

→ ___Shall___ we ___eat dinner before___ the movie?

02 정치에 대한 이야기는 하지 말자. (not, about, talk)

→ _____ politics.

03 그에게 도움을 청하는 게 어때? (we, ask for)

→ Why _____ his help?

04 너 그 계획을 바꾸는 게 어때? (change, you)

→ Why _____ the plan?

05 저녁 먹으러 나가는 게 어때? (for, go out)

→ How _____ dinner?

06 오늘 집에 머무르는 게 어때? (stay, at home)

→ What _____ today?

07 테이블 위에 있는 쿠키를 먹지 마라. (cookies, the, eat)

→ _____ on the table.

08 제시간에 이곳에 와라, 그러면 그녀를 만날 수 있을 것이다. (will, you, meet, her)

→ Come here on time, _____.

09 너무 많은 돈을 쓰지 마라. (too, spend, much)

→ _____ money.

10 서둘러라, 그렇지 않으면 통학 버스를 놓칠 것이다. (miss, will, you, the school bus)

→ Hurry up, _____.

11 네 친구들에게 잘해라. (to, nice)

→ _____ your friends.

12 부모님에게 무례하게 굴지 마라. (rude, to)

→ _____ your parents.

WORDS

• politics 정치   • ask for 요청하다   • rude 무례한

Level up

① 다음 빈칸에 알맞은 말을 쓰세요.

01 A: ___Who___ ___is___ that girl?
    B: She is my history teacher.

02 A: _____ _____ your uncle do?
    B: He is an architect.

03 A: _____ umbrella is this?
    B: It's Mike's.

04 A: _____ cake is cheaper, this one or that one?
    B: That one.

05 A: _____ animal do you like?
    B: I like a cat.

06 A: _____ _____ going to drive tomorrow?
    B: My mom.

07 A: _____ _____ your hobby?
    B: My hobby is playing the guitar.

08 A: _____ _____ the woman in the living room?
    B: She is my aunt.

09 A: _____ _____ your students doing on the ground?
    B: They are playing soccer.

10 A: _____ _____ answer his question?
    B: Anthony can do it.

11 A: _____ cat do you want to have, the black one or the white one?
    B: The black one.

12 A: _____ _____ you want to speak with?
    B: Mrs. Stacy, please.

WORDS

• architect 건축가　• cheap 저렴한　• with ~와 함께

정답 및 해설 p.2

② 다음 문장에서 <u>어색한</u> 부분을 바르게 고쳐 쓰세요.

01 A: How much chairs do you need?
    B: I need five chairs.
    <u>　much　</u> ➡ <u>　many　</u>

02 A: What is your brother so nervous?
    B: Because he has a job interview today.
    ＿＿＿＿ ➡ ＿＿＿＿

03 A: How long do you take a walk?
    B: Three times a week.
    ＿＿＿＿ ➡ ＿＿＿＿

04 A: How many water do you drink a day?
    B: I drink five bottles of water.
    ＿＿＿＿ ➡ ＿＿＿＿

05 A: Who computer is this?
    B: It's my mother's.
    ＿＿＿＿ ➡ ＿＿＿＿

06 A: How deep did you live in Seoul?
    B: For five years.
    ＿＿＿＿ ➡ ＿＿＿＿

07 A: How long is the statue over there?
    B: It's about 10 meters tall.
    ＿＿＿＿ ➡ ＿＿＿＿

08 A: How tall is it from here to the station?
    B: It's about two kilometers.
    ＿＿＿＿ ➡ ＿＿＿＿

09 A: How deep is the river?
    B: It's about 50 kilometers long.
    ＿＿＿＿ ➡ ＿＿＿＿

10 A: Who does your father do?
    B: He is a teacher.
    ＿＿＿＿ ➡ ＿＿＿＿

11 A: Where do you usually get up?
    B: I get up at six.
    ＿＿＿＿ ➡ ＿＿＿＿

12 A: What do you go to school?
    B: I go to school by bus.
    ＿＿＿＿ ➡ ＿＿＿＿

WORDS
· nervous 긴장한　· statue 동상

③ 다음 문장을 괄호안의 지시대로 바꿔 쓰세요.

01 Let's go for a bike ride this Sunday. (why로 시작)

➡ _____Why don't we go for a bike ride this Sunday?_____

02 Why don't we get together next week? (how로 시작)

➡ _____

03 Let's go to the movies. (Shall로 시작)

➡ _____

04 You should clean up the meeting room after using it. (명령문)

➡ _____

05 You should not buy such a book. (부정명령문)

➡ _____

06 Help poor people. (let's로 시작)

➡ _____

07 You should drink lots of water every day. (why를 이용한 제안문)

➡ _____

08 We should not talk about this problem next time. (let's의 부정문)

➡ _____

09 You must follow the traffic rules when you drive. (명령문)

➡ _____

10 You should be careful when you use a knife. (명령문)

➡ _____

11 Let's play soccer together. (shall로 시작)

➡ _____

12 You should not be late for school. (부정명령문)

➡ _____

WORDS

• such 그러한 • follow (충고·지시 등을) 따르다 • traffic rule 교통법규 • clean up 청소하다

④ 다음 영어를 우리말로 쓰세요.

01 Who will water the garden while you are away?

→ _____ 당신이 없는 동안 누가 정원에 물을 줄거니? _____

02 Let's talk about our favorite color.

→ _____

03 When do you go to the library?

→ _____

04 How many subjects do you learn?

→ _____

05 How long have you studied English?

→ _____

06 Where does he usually park his car?

→ _____

07 How do I get to the hotel from the airport?

→ _____

08 Why don't you help people in poor countries?

→ _____

09 Let's not use smartphones too much.

→ _____

10 How often do you talk to your parents?

→ _____

11 Please, don't be sad, my friend.

→ _____

12 How much are the shoes on display?

→ _____

· favorite 좋아하는   · subject 과목   · on display 진열 중

Actual Test

[1-4] 다음 중 빈칸에 알맞은 말을 고르세요.

1

_____ don't we go to the movies this afternoon?

① When ② Where ③ Why

④ How ⑤ What

2

Don't _____ surprised today.

① do ② is ③ does

④ be ⑤ was

3

_____ do you like better, pizza or spaghetti?

① Which ② Who ③ Whose

④ How ⑤ What

4

_____ many people are there in the gym?

① Which ② Who ③ Whose

④ How ⑤ What

Note

5   다음 중 빈칸에 공통으로 들어갈 말을 고르세요.

> • This is the house _____ I was born.
> • _____ is the library?

① where   ② which   ③ which

④ in which   ⑤ that

5

선행사가 the house인
것을 생각하세요.

[6–7] 다음 중 우리말과 의미가 같도록 빈칸에 알맞은 말을 고르세요.

6   오늘 밤 파티에 오지 않을래?

→ _____ come to the party tonight?

① Why don't you   ② Why do you

③ Why aren't you   ④ What are you

⑤ Why didn't you

7   얼마 동안 이곳에 체류하고자 하십니까?

→ _____ do you want to stay here?

① How often   ② How far   ③ How deep

④ How much   ⑤ How long

8   다음 중 두 문장이 같은 뜻이 되도록 빈칸에 알맞은 것을 고르세요.

> You look tired. How about taking a rest?
> → You look tired. Why don't you _____.

① took a rest   ② take a rest   ③ takes a rest

④ taking a rest   ⑤ to take a rest

8

take a rest 휴식하다
How about+동명사 ~?
= What about+동명사 ~?
= Shall we+동사원형 ~?
= Let's+동사원형 ~?

9 다음 중 빈칸에 알맞은 말이 바르게 짝지어진 것을 고르세요.

> • _____ dictionary is this?
> • _____ did you lose your smartphone?

① Who - How   ② What - Whom
③ Where - Where   ④ Whose - When
⑤ How - Where

Note

9
what, which, whose
다음에는 명사가 올 수
있습니다.
lose 잃다
smartphone
스마트폰

[10-12] 다음 중 대화의 대답으로 알맞은 것을 고르세요.

10
> A: _____ do you take a bus to school?
> B: About two or three times a week.

① How often   ② How far
③ How deep   ④ How much
⑤ How long

10

about 대략
three times a week
일주일에 세 번

11
> A: What does your father do?
> B: _____.

① He's reading a book.
② He goes to the beach.
③ He likes Korean food very much.
④ He is an English teacher.
⑤ He is going to visit the museum.

12
> A: _____
> B: For two hours.

① Why do you want to listen to classical music?
② When do you want to listen to classical music?
③ Where do you want to listen to classical music?
④ How often do you listen to classical music?
⑤ How long do you listen to classical music?

13 다음 중 의미가 <u>다른</u> 문장을 고르세요.

① Let's join the soccer club after school.

② Could I join the soccer club after school?

③ Shall we join the soccer club after school?

④ Why don't we join the soccer club after school?

⑤ What about joining the soccer club after school?

14 다음 중 어법상 <u>어색한</u> 것을 고르세요.

① <u>Who</u> is the woman?　　② <u>Whom</u> is your math teacher?

③ <u>What</u> does he want?　　④ <u>What</u> are those boxes?

⑤ <u>Whose</u> is this?

15 다음 중 우리말을 영어로 바르게 옮긴 것을 고르세요.

> 우리의 임무를 잊지 말자.

① Let's not forget our duty.

② Why don't we forget our duty?

③ Shall we forget our duty?

④ Why don't you forget our duty?

⑤ What about forgetting our duty?

15
duty 임무
forget 잊다

16 다음 빈칸에 들어갈 의문사를 쓰세요.

> A: _____ food do you like best?
> B: I like pizza best. How about you?
> A: I like noodles.

→ _____

16
what, which, whose
다음에는 명사가 올 수 있
습니다.
noodle 국수

17 다음 주어진 단어를 빈칸에 알맞게 쓰세요.

> A: How about _____ baseball today? (play)
> B: That sounds great.

➡ _____

18 다음 빈칸에 알맞은 의문사를 쓰세요.

18
각 의문사의 쓰임을 알아
보세요.

1) | A: _____ dog is this?
   | B: It's my dog.

2) | A: _____ did you go to the gym?
   | B: Because I practiced basketball there.

3) | A: _____ is your car, the black one or the red one?
   | B: The black one.

19 다음 우리말을 영어로 완성하시오.

19
nervous 긴장한

> 다음에는 긴장하지 마라. (nervous)

➡ _____ next time.

20 다음 어색한 부분을 찾아 바르게 고치세요.

20
2) how many와 how
   much의 쓰임을 알아
   보세요.
habit 습관

1) | Why don't you making a new habit today?

   ➡ _____

2) | How many apple do you need?

   ➡ _____

여러 가지 문장 II

UNIT 01

부가의문문

> 부가의문문은 자신이 한 말을 확인하거나 상대방에게 동의를 구할 때 평서문 뒤에 붙이는 의문문으로 '그렇지?', '그렇지 않니?'로 해석합니다.

1. 앞 문장이 긍정문일 때

앞 문장 be동사 - be동사+not+주어? (그렇지 않니?)	He **is** a teacher, **isn't he?** 그는 선생님이다, 그렇지 않니? Sara **was** very tall, **wasn't she?** Sara는 키가 매우 컸었다, 그렇지 않았니? This **is** your car, **isn't it?** 이것은 너의 자동차지, 그렇지 않니? *this와 that은 대명사 it으로 받습니다.
앞 문장이 일반동사 - don't/doesn't/ didn't+주어?(그렇지 않니?)	Jane **likes** flowers, **doesn't she?** Jane은 꽃을 좋아한다. 그렇지 않니? They **ate** pizza, **didn't they?** 그들은 피자를 먹었다, 그렇지 않니?
앞 문장이 조동사 - can't/won't+주어? (그렇지 않니?)	You **can** speak English, **can't you?** 당신은 영어를 할 수 있어, 그렇지 않니? He **will** go camping tomorrow, **won't he?** 그는 내일 캠핑을 갈 거야, 그렇지 않니?

> **Plus 1**
> • 부가의문문의 주어는 항상 대명사(she, he, you, they, we, it)만 옵니다.
> Your mom is very tall, **isn't your mom?** (x) / Your mom is very tall, **isn't she?** (o)

> **Plus 2**
> • 부정의 부가의문문은 축약형만 사용합니다.
> She is a doctor, **is not she?** (x) / She is a doctor, **isn't she?** (o)
> Jane likes apples, **does not she?** (x) / Jane likes apples, **doesn't she?** (o)

2. 앞 문장이 부정문일 때

앞 문장 be동사 - be동사+주어? (그렇지?)	He **isn't** tall, **is he?** 그는 키가 크지 않다, 그렇지? That **isn't** your car, **is it?** 저것은 너의 자동차가 아니니, 그렇지?
앞 문장이 일반동사 - do/does/did+주어? (그렇지?)	Jeff **doesn't** like apples, **does he?** Jeff는 사과를 좋아하지 않는다, 그렇지? They **didn't** eat pizza, **did they?** 그들은 피자를 먹지 않는다, 그렇지?
앞 문장이 조동사 - can/will+주어? (그렇지?)	She **can't** speak Korean, **can she?** 그녀는 한국말을 못한다, 그렇지? He **won't** go camping tomorrow, **will he?** 그는 내일 캠핑을 가지 않을 것이다, 그렇지?

3. 명령문의 부가의문문 – 앞 문장이 긍정문이든, 부정문이든 상관없이 will you?가 옵니다.

will you? (알았지?)	**Do** your homework, **will you?** 숙제를 해라, 알았지? **Don't** use my computer, **will you?** 내 컴퓨터를 사용하지 마라, 알았지?

4. 제안문과 부가의문문: Let's로 시작하는 제안문은 '~하자', '~하지 말자'의 의미로 부가의문문은 긍정이든 부정이든 상관없이 shall we?를 씁니다.

shall we? (우리 그럴래?)	**Let's** have lunch, **shall we**? 점심먹자, 그럴래? **Let's** not eat fast food, **shall we**? 패스트푸드 먹지 말자, 그럴래?

Plus 3
• 부가의문문에 대한 대답: 질문에 상관없이 긍정이면 Yes, 부정이면 No로 답합니다.
This book is funny, isn't it?   Yes, it is. 그래, 재미있어. / No, it isn't. 아니, 재미없어.

Warm up

정답 및 해설 p.24

● 다음 괄호 안에서 알맞은 말을 고르세요.

01 The woman is not your mom, ((is she) / isn't she)?

02 They weren't very heavy, (are they / were they)?

03 Don't be late for school, (shall you / will you)?

04 You changed your plan, (don't you / didn't you)?

05 He (won't / will) cheat on the test, will he?

06 He (can't / can) play baseball with a broken hand, can he?

07 Your father likes to watch baseball games, (doesn't he / does he)?

08 Andrew (is / isn't) from England, isn't he?

09 My sister can't eat spicy food, (can she / can't she)?

10 Let's play baseball today, (will you / shall we)?

WORDS

• cheat on 속이다, 부정행위를 하다   • spicy 매운

❶ 다음 빈칸에 알맞은 부가의문문을 쓰세요.

01 Don't put too much sugar in the food, _____will you_____?

02 Sara will visit you every month, _____?

03 My younger sister reads a book at night, _____?

04 She feels tired all the time, _____?

05 Brown and James work out after dinner, _____?

06 The shopping mall doesn't close on the weekend, _____?

07 They don't go to school on Saturday, _____?

08 Read a newspaper every day, _____?

09 You stayed at home yesterday, _____?

10 She found the lost purse, _____?

11 His younger brother fought with his friend, _____?

12 Your friends can drive a car, _____?

13 Your mother lived in Canada for 5 years, _____?

14 That is a good idea, _____?

15 Don't do it again, _____?

• fight 싸우다   • all the time 항상   • purse 지갑

❷ 다음 빈칸에 알맞은 부가의문문을 쓰세요.

01 He wants me to go to the party, _____ doesn't he _____?

02 This is your first visit to London, _____?

03 The new copy machine is more efficient, _____?

04 Let's go to the film festival, _____?

05 I didn't tell you about the new English teacher, _____?

06 The stairs on the third floor are too steep, _____?

07 Kelly is the most popular actress in this country, _____?

08 Don't be afraid of trying new things, _____?

09 You and Mike studied abroad, _____?

10 Those boxes are made of wood, _____?

11 He won't keep his promise, _____?

12 She has more books than I have, _____?

13 They can breathe under the water, _____?

14 Let's take a break after lunch, _____?

15 That isn't your car, _____?

• film 영화   • efficient 효율적인   • steep 가파른   • abroad 해외에서   • keep 지키다   • promise 약속
• try 시도하다, 노력하다   • breathe 숨 쉬다

1 다음 문장에서 밑줄 친 부분을 바르게 고치세요.

01 Alice and Tony like Korean food, <u>aren't they</u>?

don't they

02 This movie is very funny, <u>isn't this</u>?

03 They don't want to hear about that, <u>didn't they</u>?

04 Let's make a plan for our vacation, <u>shall you</u>?

05 The soup tastes really good, <u>don't it</u>?

06 The boys painted the wall, <u>aren't they</u>?

07 Don't think of the future, <u>shall we</u>?

08 The birds in the cage can fly, <u>can't it</u>?

09 Your favorite sport isn't soccer, <u>are you</u>?

10 His father will visit the hospital, <u>doesn't he</u>?

11 Don't keep me waiting, <u>won't you</u>?

12 His mom sells fresh vegetables at the market, <u>doesn't he</u>?

13 His face turned red with anger, <u>didn't he</u>?

14 You and your sister don't eat raw fish, <u>do they</u>?

15 The game we watched yesterday was very exciting, <u>isn't it</u>?

· taste 맛이 나다   · anger 노여움, 화   · raw fish 생선회

❷ 다음 우리말과 일치하도록, 주어진 단어를 이용하여 문장을 완성하세요.
(필요하면 단어를 추가하거나 변경 하세요.)

01 그들은 수학을 잘해, 그렇지 않니? (good at / are / math)

→ They _____ are good at math, aren't they

02 시험 성적에 대해서 걱정하지 마, 알았지? (worry about, result, the test)

→ Don't _____

03 너의 아버지는 운전을 조심스럽게 하신다, 그렇지 않니? (drives, carefully)

→ Your father _____

04 Sara는 그녀의 친구들을 돕지 않는다, 그렇지? (help, doesn't, her, friends)

→ Sara _____

05 Tom과 Jane은 고전 음악을 듣지 않았다, 그렇지? (didn't, classical music, listen to)

→ Tom and Jane _____

06 태양은 서쪽으로 진다, 그렇지 않니? (in, goes down, the west)

→ The sun _____

07 산책하러 가자, 그럴래? (for, a walk, go)

→ Let's _____?

08 너와 Tom은 물이 전혀 없다, 그렇지? (have, any, don't, water)

→ You and Tom _____?

09 내 아버지는 이번 주말 한가할 것이다, 그렇지 않니? (free, be, this weekend, will)

→ My father _____?

10 저 책들은 아이들에게 매우 유용하다, 그렇지 않니? (very, are, for children, useful)

→ Those books _____?

11 오늘은 택시를 타지 말자, 그럴래? (a taxi, take, not, today)

→ Let's _____?

12 그 경찰관은 어제 그 도둑을 잡았다, 그렇지 않니? (yesterday, the thief, caught)

→ The policeman _____?

WORDS

• result 결과   • carefully 조심스럽게   • go down (해·달이) 지다, 넘어지다   • free 한가한   • useful 유용한
• caught catch(잡다)의 과거형

UNIT 02

간접의문문 / 선택의문문

의문문의 다양한 형태를 습득하는 것이 중요합니다. 특히 간접의문문은 시험에 자주 등장하므로 간접의문문의 형태를 완전히 이해하는 게 중요합니다.

직접의문문 - What did he want?
간접의문문 - Do you know **what he wanted?**
　　　　　　　　　　　　(명사절 - 목적어 역할)

---

1. 간접의문문: 간접의문문이란 어떤 질문을 직접적으로 언급하지 않고, 의문문이 문장의 일부가 되어 있을 때를 말하며, 일반적으로 의문사가 이끄는 명사절이 주절의 목적어로 쓰인 경우를 말합니다.

2. 의문사가 있는 경우: 「의문사+주어+동사」의 어순

의문사+주어+동사	Do you know?+Where is Mike? → Do you know **where Mike is**? 　　　　　　　　(의문사) (주어) (동사) Do you know?+What does she like? → Do you know **what she likes**? *간접의문문 동사는 시제에 따라 변화며 3인칭 단수 현재일 경우 동사에 s나 es를 붙여야 합니다.

Plus 1　• 간접의문문에서 의문사가 주어로 쓰인 경우에는 직접의문문의 어순과 동일하게 씁니다.
Do you know? + **Who** broke the window? → Do you know **who broke the window**?

3. 의문사가 없는 경우: 의문사가 없는 경우 '~인지를' 의미하는 if, whether를 사용하여 문장을 연결합니다.

if[whether]+주어+동사	I don't know.+Can he come to the party? → I don't know **if[whether] he can come to the party**. I am not sure.+Can she do it? → I am not sure **if[whether] she can do it**.

Plus 2　• 의문사가 없는 간접의문문은 wonder, don't know, doubt, not sure 등과 같이 의구심을 나타내는 동사와 함께 사용합니다. 이 때 사용하는 if[whether]는 간접의문문을 이끌며 '~인지 어떤지'의 의미를 가지고 있습니다.

4. think, believe, guess, suppose 등의 동사가 나오는 경우: 「의문사+do you think[believe, guess]+주어+동사」의 형태를 취합니다.

의문사+do you think[believe, guess]+주어+동사	Do you think?+Why was she sad? → **Why** do you think she **was** sad? Do you believe?+When <u>did</u> he finish the report? → **When** do you believe he **finished** the report? *시제가 과거(did)를 나타내므로 간접의문문의 동사도 과거형(finished)이 되어 합니다.

5. 선택의문문: 선택의문문이란 or를 사용하여 둘 중 하나를 선택하는 의문문으로 Yes나 No로 대답할 수 없습니다.

> A: Is she a doctor **or** a nurse?
> A: Who broke the window, you **or** Jake?
> A: Which car is yours, this one **or** that one?
>
> B: She is a doctor.
> B: Jake did.
> B: This one.

Warm up

정답 및 해설 p.25

● 다음 괄호 안에서 알맞은 말을 고르세요.

01 ((What do you think) / Do you think what) he wants?

02 Do you know what (his name is / is his name)?

03 I am not sure (if / who) she can pass the test.

04 Please tell me (why he was / why was he) late for the meeting.

05 When do you believe (will he / he will) come to the party?

06 (Where do you know / Do you know where) Mike is?

07 Who closed the window, you (and / or) Jake?

08 (Where do you think / Do you think where) he lives?

09 Why do you (know / think) she quit the job?

10 I wonder (where she live / where she lives).

· sure 확신하는   · quit 그만두다

① 다음 직접의문문을 간접의문문으로 바꾸어 쓰세요.

01 Who is a doctor?
➡ ___Who___ do you think _____is a doctor_____ ?

02 What is his favorite color?
➡ Do you know _____ ?

03 Can he play the flute?
➡ I am not sure _____ .

04 Was he at the shopping mall yesterday?
➡ Do you know _____ ?

05 When did she eat dinner?
➡ When do you think _____ ?

06 How tall is the tree?
➡ I wonder _____ ?

07 Where did she have lunch?
➡ Please tell me _____ ?

08 Why do they go to the beach?
➡ _____ do you think _____ ?

09 Where did you lose your cell phone?
➡ _____ do you guess you _____ ?

10 Does he have a laptop computer?
➡ I don't know _____ .

11 Why do you learn English?
➡ Please tell me _____ .

12 Is there a bookstore near your house?
➡ Can you tell me _____ ?

WORDS

· favorite 좋아하는　· wonder 궁금해 하다　· lose 잃다　· guess 추측하다　· bookstore 서점

❷ 다음 직접의문문을 간접의문문으로 바꾸어 쓰세요.

01 What is his phone number?
→ Do you know _____ what his phone number is _____ ?

02 What does that mean?
→ Can you tell me _____ ?

03 Is she a math teacher?
→ I wonder _____ .

04 Who won the race?
→ _____ do you think _____ ?

05 How can I get to the airport?
→ Can you tell me _____ ?

06 Can she ride a bike?
→ Do you know _____ ?

07 What is she making?
→ _____ do you think _____ ?

08 When did he take the pill?
→ _____ do you believe _____ ?

09 Is there a shopping mall near here?
→ Can you tell me _____ ?

10 Where is she going now?
→ Do you know _____ ?

11 How old is her uncle?
→ I wonder _____ ?

12 Why did Susan get up early today?
→ _____ do you think _____ ?

• mean 의미하다   • race 경주   • airport 공항   • pill 알약

Check up & Writing 간접의문문과 선택의문문 점검하기

1 다음 두 문장을 간접의문문을 이용하여 한 문장으로 바꾸어 쓰세요.

01 Do you know? What is Mike's hobby?
→ _____Do you know what Mike's hobby is?_____

02 Do you know? Does she like apples?
→ _____

03 Do you know? Where did she buy the camera?
→ _____

04 Do you know? How did he get his job?
→ _____

05 Do you know? Who does she like?
→ _____

06 Do you think? Why did she cry?
→ _____

07 Do you think? What is his job?
→ _____

08 Do you think? When did she arrive at the station?
→ _____

09 Do you think? Why did she come here?
→ _____

10 Do you think? Who does he like?
→ _____

11 Do you think? How did she open the door?
→ _____

12 Do you think? What time did she come back here?
→ _____

WORDS

• come back 돌아오다

❷ **다음 우리말과 일치하도록, 주어진 단어를 이용하여 문장을 완성하세요.**
(필요하면 단어를 추가하거나 변경 하세요.)

01 그가 어디서 그의 지갑을 찾았는지 아니? (he, his wallet, found, where)

➡ Do you know _____ where he found his wallet _____?

02 저 강이 얼마나 깊은지 궁금하다. (how, is, the river, deep)

➡ I wonder _____.

03 너는 그녀가 왜 그를 만나기를 원하는지 아니? (she, want, why, him, to meet)

➡ Do you know _____?

04 그녀가 어떻게 공원에 갔다고 생각하니? (do, you, went, think, she, how)

➡ _____ to the park?

05 그녀가 몇 시에 떠났는지 아니? (she, what time, left)

➡ Do you know _____?

06 그녀가 어제 자신의 차를 세차했는지 궁금하다. (she, yesterday washed, her, car, if)

➡ I wonder _____.

07 그가 좋아하는 운동이 뭐라고 생각하니? (favorite, is, his, sport)

➡ What do you think _____?

08 그를 화나게 만든 것이 뭐라고 생각하니? (made, angry, him)

➡ What do you think _____?

09 나는 Jane이 좀 더 머물 수 있는지 모른다. (Jane, a little longer, can, stay, if)

➡ I don't know _____.

10 너는 Amy가 나를 위해 무엇을 샀는지 아니? (what, bought, me, for, Amy)

➡ Do you know _____?

11 우리는 누가 그림들을 훔쳤는지 모른다. (stole, who, the pictures)

➡ We don't know _____.

12 나는 그가 문제를 어떻게 해결할지 궁금하다. (he, how, solve, the problem, is going to)

➡ I wonder _____.

WORDS

• wallet 지갑　　• a little longer 좀 더 오래　　• solve 해결하다

UNIT 03 감탄문

감탄문이란 기쁨, 슬픔, 놀라움 등의 감정을 표현하는 문장입니다.

1. 평서문과 감탄문: 평서문에서 really나 very 등의 부사가 감탄문에서 what이나 how로 바뀝니다.

> It is a very exciting story.
> → **What an exciting story it is!**
> (명사 story 강조)

> The book is very interesting.
> → **How interesting the book is!**
> (형용사 interesting 강조)

2. What으로 시작하는 감탄문: what으로 시작하는 감탄문은 명사가 포함된 어구를 강조할 때 사용하여 「What+a/an+형용사+명사(+주어+동사)!」의 형태를 취하며, '매우 ~하구나!'라는 의미입니다.

> **What+a/an+형용사+명사 (+주어+동사)! (정말[매우] ~하구나!)**

> It is a very nice car.
> → **What a nice car** it is! 그것은 정말 멋진 자동차이구나!
> He is a great musician.
> → **What a great musician** he is! 그는 정말 훌륭한 음악가 이구나!

Plus 1
> • 명사가 있는 감탄문에서 명사가 복수 일 경우에는 a(an)를 명사 앞에 붙이지 않습니다.
> **What nice horses** they are! 그들은 매우 멋진 말들이구나!

Plus 2
> • 단수 명사를 수식하는 형용사가 모음 발음으로 시작하면 형용사 앞에 an을 씁니다.
> **What an** interesting book (this is)! 이것은 정말 흥미로운 책이구나!

3. How로 시작하는 감탄문: how로 시작하는 감탄문은 형용사나 부사를 강조할 때 사용하여 「How+형용사/부사(+주어+동사)!」의 형태를 취하며, '매우 ~하구나!'라는 의미입니다.

> **How+형용사/부사(+주어+동사)! (정말 「매우」 ~하구나!)**

> He is very tall.
> → **How tall** he is! 그는 정말 키가 크구나!
> She is very beautiful.
> → **How beautiful** she is. 그녀가 정말 아름답구나!

Plus 3
> • 뒤의 주어와 동사는 종종 생략 된다.
> **What a strong boy** (he is)!   **How tall** (he is)!

4. 감탄문 전환: What으로 시작하는 감탄문을 How로 시작하는 감탄문으로 바꿀 수 있습니다.

> **What** a smart boy he is! → **How** smart the boy is!
> **What** brave soldiers they are! → **How** brave the soldiers are!

● 다음 괄호 안에서 알맞은 말을 고르세요.

01 (What / (How)) high he jumps!

02 (What / How) a fast train it is!

03 (What / How) a wonderful day!

04 (What / How) an old car that is!

05 (What / How) a nice idea it is!

06 What a wonderful trip (it is / they are)!

07 What (a kind / kind) boy my brother is!

08 (What / How) kind you are!

09 What (a nice / nice) girls they are!

10 (What / How) greedy she is!

11 (What / How) a beautiful mountain it is!

12 (What / How) a nice party!

13 What (a beautiful / beautiful) roses!

14 (What / How) big the animal is!

15 What a wonderful (present / presents) it is!

· greedy 욕심 많은   · present 선물

1 다음 빈칸에 알맞은 말을 쓰세요.

01 _____What_____ a beautiful garden it is!

02 _____ handsome he is!

03 _____ fast the dog can run!

04 _____ a small car you have!

05 _____ great paintings these are!

06 _____ slowly she walks!

07 _____ a lucky man Tom is!

08 _____ cute the baby is!

09 _____ sad the movie is!

10 _____ a selfish man he is!

11 _____ delicious they are!

12 _____ a lovely girl she is!

13 _____ smart students they are!

14 _____ well Jane speaks English!

15 _____ busy she is!

WORDS

• fast 빠르게 • lucky 운이 좋은 • selfish 이기적인 • lovely 사랑스러운

❷ 다음 빈칸에 알맞은 말을 쓰세요.

01 _____How_____ beautiful that full moon is!

02 _____ interesting the computer game is!

03 _____ a tall girl Mary is!

04 _____ heavily it rains!

05 _____ jealous she is!

06 _____ a nice chair she has!

07 _____ beautiful the flowers are!

08 _____ a pretty dress she has!

09 _____ an honest boy he is!

10 _____ cheerful those boys are!

11 _____ expensive shoes these are!

12 _____ hard David works!

13 _____ an amazing record it is!

14 _____ kind nurses they are!

15 _____ deep the river is!

• full moon 보름달　　• heavily 심하게, 아주 많이　　• jealous 질투심이 있는　　• cheerful 발랄한, 쾌활한　　• amazing 놀라운

Check up & Writing

① 다음 문장을 감탄문으로 바꾸세요.

01 Your room is very small.

➡ _____ How small your room is! _____

02 They are very big pants.

➡ _____

03 It was a very exciting game.

➡ _____

04 He is a really brave policeman.

➡ _____

05 This is a very long bridge.

➡ _____

06 This is a very old watch.

➡ _____

07 We had a very good time.

➡ _____

08 It is very hot.

➡ _____

09 The traffic is very heavy.

➡ _____

10 He is a really wise man.

➡ _____

11 He drives very carefully.

➡ _____

12 The test was really difficult!

➡ _____

WORDS

• brave 용감한   • bridge 다리   • heavy 심한   • wise 현명한

2 다음 우리말과 일치하도록, 주어진 단어를 이용하여 감탄문을 완성하세요.
(필요하면 단어를 추가하거나 변경 하세요.)

01 이것은 정말 큰 집이구나! (house, a large)

➡ _____ What a large house _____ this is!

02 네 방은 정말 더럽구나! (dirty, is, your room)

➡ How _____!

03 그는 정말 강한 남자구나! (man, a, strong)

➡ _____ he is!

04 그것은 정말 멋진 선물이구나! (nice, gift, a)

➡ _____ it is!

05 그는 정말 빠르게 걷는구나! (he, fast)

➡ _____ walks!

06 그것들은 정말 저렴한 옷들이구나! (cheap, they, clothes)

➡ _____ are!

07 그것은 정말 비싼 차구나! (car, expensive)

➡ _____ it is!

08 이 기계는 정말 유용하구나! (useful, machine, this)

➡ _____ is!

09 그 고양이는 정말 귀엽구나! (cute)

➡ _____ the cat is!

10 그는 매우 못생긴 개를 가지고 있구나! (dog, ugly)

➡ _____ he has!

11 사고가 매우 끔찍하구나! (terrible, the accident)

➡ _____ is!

12 그것은 매우 훌륭한 생각이구나! (excellent, idea)

➡ _____ it is!

WORDS

• **cheap** 저렴한   • **useful** 유용한   • **terrible** 끔찍한   • **accident** 사고   • **excellent** 훌륭한

Level up

1 다음 밑줄 친 부분을 바르게 고치세요.

01 You want to take a rest, <u>do you</u>?

don't you

02 You and Sara like popcorn, <u>aren't you</u>?

03 My brother and I are handsome, <u>aren't you</u>?

04 This computer is not new, <u>isn't this</u>?

05 Your mother was a teacher, <u>isn't she</u>?

06 That is your camera, <u>isn't that</u>?

07 Tom and Jack brought their food, <u>don't they</u>?

08 It rains a lot in summer, <u>don't it</u>?

09 His parents don't live in Seoul, <u>are they</u>?

10 You won't listen to the radio, <u>do you</u>?

11 Your favorite food is noodles, <u>aren't you</u>?

12 He didn't want to be a teacher, <u>does he</u>?

13 Your mother changed her mind, <u>didn't her</u>?

14 Don't make me angry, <u>shall we</u>?

15 Let's make a cake for him, <u>will you</u>?

· bring 가지고 오다   · mind 마음

❷ 다음 문장에서 <u>잘못된</u> 부분을 고쳐 문장을 다시 쓰세요.

01 Do you know where was she last night?

➡ _____Do you know where she was last night?_____

02 Can you tell me how can I get to the beach?

➡ _____

03 I wonder what she likes Korean food.

➡ _____

04 Do you know why did Mike meet Jenny yesterday?

➡ _____

05 Do you think when they are going to have dinner?

➡ _____

06 What do you think is she doing now?

➡ _____

07 Do you know will who take her to the hospital?

➡ _____

08 I wonder how old is his father.

➡ _____

09 I can't remember where did I put my glasses.

➡ _____

10 Please tell me what do you want.

➡ _____

11 Do you believe who is responsible for the accident?

➡ _____

12 Do you know how long does it take to Seoul?

➡ _____

• take 데리고 가다   • responsible 책임 있는

③ 다음 문장을 감탄문으로 바꾸세요.

01 The movie is very funny.
→ _____How funny the movie is!_____

02 She is very curious.
→ _____

03 She grows very fresh vegetables.
→ _____

04 This chair is really comfortable.
→ _____

05 Kelly speaks very fast.
→ _____

06 It is a very wonderful story.
→ _____

07 She has a very pretty doll.
→ _____

08 They are very scary movies.
→ _____

09 The music is very fantastic.
→ _____

10 It is very cold today.
→ _____

11 Jack has a really creative idea.
→ _____

12 This is a very old truck.
→ _____

WORDS

· funny 재미있는 · grow 재배하다 · curious 호기심이 있는 · comfortable 편안한 · scary 무서운
· fantastic 환상적인 · creative 창조적인

❹ 다음 문장에서 <u>잘못된</u> 부분을 바르게 고쳐 쓰세요.

01 Let's eat out tonight, will you?

> will you → shall we

02 How a nice car Mike has!

03 Ann usually watches TV after dinner, does she?

04 How beautiful roses they are!

05 Do you know will who attend the meeting?

06 I'm not sure what she can speak English.

07 Is it yours and your mother's?

08 What a kind teachers they are!

09 What a excellent player she is!

10 What beautiful they are!

11 Did you buy it and borrow it?

12 Can you tell me what is your dream?

13 Do you think who broke the vase?

14 Don't be rude to your teachers, do you?

15 Those puppies are not yours, aren't they?

• borrow 빌리다   • rude 무례한   • puppy 강아지

[1–4] 다음 중 빈칸에 알맞은 말을 고르세요.

Note

1

> You like dancing, _____?

① do you　　　② don't you　　　③ aren't you

④ are you　　　⑤ isn't it

1
부가의문문의 쓰임을 알아보세요.

2

> _____ pretty she is!

① What　　　② When　　　③ Where

④ Why　　　⑤ How

2
명사를 강조할 때와 형용사를 강조할 때의 쓰임을 알아보세요.

3

> Mike doesn't speak Japanese well, _____?

① did he　　　② didn't he　　　③ don't he

④ does he　　　⑤ doesn't he

4

> I am not sure _____ he can help me.

① if　　　② what　　　③ who

④ where　　　⑤ why

4
sure 확실한

Note

5 다음 중 빈칸에 들어갈 말이 바르게 짝지어진 것을 고르세요.

> • Don't swim here, _____?
> • Let's go to the concert, _____?

① do you - shall we　　② will you - will you
③ do you - do we　　④ shall we - do we
⑤ will you - shall we

5
명령문과 let's로 시작하는 문장에 쓰이는 부가의문문을 알아보세요.

6 다음 중 빈칸에 들어갈 말로 <u>어색한</u> 것을 고르세요.

> Do you know _____?

① where Sam is　　② how airplanes fly
③ where she put the key　　④ what did she want
⑤ why she went to the library

7 다음 중 대화의 빈칸에 들어갈 말로 알맞은 것을 고르세요.

> A: What did Sam buy yesterday?
> B: I don't know _____ yesterday.

① what he buy　　② what he buys
③ what did he bought　　④ what he bought
⑤ what did he buy

7
간접의문문의 어순을 알아보세요.

8 다음 중 빈칸에 알맞지 <u>않은</u> 것을 고르세요.

> How _____ they are!

① smart　　② tall　　③ lie
④ fast　　⑤ noisy

8
*How+형용사+주어+동사
*What+a+형용사+명사+주어+동사

[9–10] 다음 우리말을 영어로 바르게 쓴 것을 고르세요.

9

> 우리는 그가 그 문제에 대해 어떻게 생각하는지 모른다.

① We don't know what does he think of the problem.
② He doesn't know what we think of the problem.
③ We don't know what he thinks of the problem.
④ Do we know what does he think of the problem?
⑤ We don't know what he think of the problem.

Note

9
think of
～에 대해 생각하다

10

> 너는 누가 영화 배우를 죽였다고 믿고 있니?

① Who do you believe killed the actor?
② Whom do you believe killed the actor?
③ Do you believe who will kill the actor?
④ Do you believe who killed the actor?
⑤ Do you believe whom will kill the actor?

[11–12] 다음 중 밑줄 친 부분이 올바른 것을 고르세요.

11
① Jessica can't swim, <u>can't she</u>?
② You are very strong, <u>are you</u>?
③ It's a hot day, <u>is it</u>?
④ You came here yesterday, <u>didn't you</u>?
⑤ They can drive, <u>can they</u>?

12
① Open the window, <u>won't you</u>?
② You bought a bike, <u>don't you</u>?
③ He likes soccer, <u>doesn't he</u>?
④ You can't swim, <u>don't you</u>?
⑤ Let's play soccer, <u>shall you</u>?

12
명령문과 let's로 시작하
는 문장에 쓰이는 부가의
문문을 알아보세요.

13 다음 문장을 감탄문으로 바르게 바꾼 것을 고르세요.

> My brother is a very kind boy.

① How kind boy!
② What a kind boy my brother is!
③ How a kind boy my brother is!
④ What a very kind boy!
⑤ What kind a boy my brother is!

13
*How+형용사+주어+동사
*What+a+형용사+명사+주어+동사

14 다음 중 대화의 빈칸에 알맞은 것을 고르세요.

> A: Come with me. Let me show you the way to the museum.
> B: _____
> A: It's my pleasure.

① How kind you are!　　② How are you!
③ How about meeting Helen?　　④ Here you are.
⑤ Good for you.

14
show 안내하다, 보여주다
way 길
pleasure 기쁨

15 다음 중 빈칸에 공통으로 들어갈 말을 고르세요.

> • _____ a nice party it is!
> • _____ are you doing?

① if　　　　② what　　　　③ who
④ where　　⑤ why

15
*How+형용사+주어+동사
*What+a+형용사+명사+주어+동사

16 다음 문장을 감탄문으로 바꾸세요.

1) | This is really good cheese. |

➜ _____

2) | The food is very delicious. |

➜ _____

17 다음 문장을 바르게 고쳐 쓰세요.

> We don't know where is he.

→ _____

18 다음 빈칸에 들어갈 말을 쓰세요.

1) You didn't come to the party last night, _____?

2) Please, be quiet, _____?

3) He and Tony came together, _____?

19 다음 빈칸에 들어갈 말을 쓰세요.

1) _____ a smart dog!
2) _____ beautiful you are!

20 다음 영어를 우리말로 쓰세요.

> You didn't watch TV last night, did you?

→ _____

Note

17
간접의문문의 어순을 알
아보세요.

18
quiet 조용한
together 함께

19
*How+형용사+주어+동
사
*What+a+형용사+명사
+주어+동사

20
duty 임무
forget 잊다

Chapter 6

시제의 일치 및 화법

UNIT 01

수의 일치

수의 일치란 주어가 단수이냐 복수이냐에 따라 동사의 수를 일치시키는 것을 의미합니다.
영어를 사용할 때 반드시 수를 일치시켜야 합니다.

1. 아래 주어가 오는 경우 단수동사를 쓴다.

「every+단수명사」 또는 「each+단수명사」	**Every girl wants** to buy a smartphone. **Each child has** his own room.
-thing / -one / -body	**Something is** moving in the room. **Somebody was** knocking on the door.
이름(학문, 국가, 질병)	**Economics is** his major. **The Netherlands is** famous for tulips. *끝에 s가 붙지만 단수 취급 하는 단어: news, mathematics, politics, physics, The United States 등
to부정사, 동명사, 절	**Making cookies is** her hobby. **What she wants is** to take a rest.
「the number of+복수명사」	**The number of the tourists has** been increasing.

2. 아래 주어가 오는 경우 복수동사를 쓴다.

복수이거나 「A and B」	**The flowers** in the garden **are** beautiful. **Tom and Jane are** my friends.
「A number of+복수명사」 [많은~]	**A number of people were** killed during Korean War. 많은 사람들이 한국전쟁 동안 죽었다.
both A and B (A, B 둘 다)	**Both** she **and** I **go** to high school.

3. 상관접속사 구문이 주어일 때 동사는 B에 수를 일치시킵니다.

either A or B (A, B 둘 중 하나)	**Either** you **or** he **has** to attend the meeting. 너 또는 그 둘 중 하나는 회의에 참여해야 한다.
neither A nor B (A, B 둘 다 아닌)	**Neither** my friend **nor** I **like** baseball. 내 친구도 나도 야구를 좋아하지 않는다.
not only A but also B (A뿐만 아니라 B도)	**Not only** Tom **but also** his parents **are** very tall. Tom뿐만 아니라 그의 부모님도 키가 매우 크다.

Plus 2
• A as well B는 A에 수를 일치시킵니다.
  He as well as you **is** responsible for the accident.

● 다음 괄호 안에서 알맞은 말을 고르세요.

01 The girls in the room (is /(are)) my friends.

02 Collecting stamps (is / are) my hobby.

03 The water in these glasses (look / looks) clean.

04 Every picture (has / have) special meaning to me.

05 What he said the other day (is / are) not true.

06 Every student (wear / wears) a uniform in this school.

07 Both Smith and Amy (go /goes) to middle school.

08 A number of scientists (is / are) working at the company.

09 Politics (is / are) too hard for me to understand.

10 Each boy (has / have) a different dream.

11 Either you or Sam (has to / have to) stay at home.

12 Did you eat the pumpkin pies which (was / were) on the plate?

13 Neither Mike nor Jack (like / likes) baseball.

14 Not only Koreans but also Japanese people (eat / eats) rice.

15 The number of cars in China (has been / have been) increasing rapidly.

WORDS

• collect 모으다　• clean 깨끗한　• mean 의미하다　• pumpkin 호박　• pie 파이　• plate 접시　• politics 정치학
• different 다른　• increase 증가하다　• rapidly 빠르게

① 주어진 단어를 이용하여 빈칸에 알맞은 말을 쓰세요. (단, 현재형으로 쓰세요.)

01 What I did _____is_____ just for you. (be)

02 To play computer games _____ very exciting. (be)

03 Not only James but also his brothers _____ on a farm. (work)

04 Either she or I _____ to drive the truck. (has)

05 Both Bob and his son _____ not eat any meat. (do)

06 The information in his books _____ accurate. (be)

07 Every person in the office _____ exhausted. (look)

08 Every dish on the table _____ cooked by Mark. (be)

09 The land between the two mountains _____ yours. (be)

10 Not only he but also his children _____ afraid of a dog. (be)

11 Neither John nor his friends _____ football. (like)

12 Studying foreign languages _____ very useful. (be)

13 What he wants to buy _____ a bike. (be)

14 Tom and Jane _____ shopping every Sunday. (goes)

15 A number of bicycles _____ on the street. (be)

・information 정보　・accurate 정확한　・exhausted 지친　・be afraid of ~을 두려워하다　・foreign 외국의
・useful 유용한

❷ 주어진 단어를 이용하여 빈칸에 알맞은 말을 쓰세요. (단, 현재형으로 쓰세요.)

01 Both Sam and his sister usually ____get up____ early. (get up)

02 Every student _____ a diary every day. (keep)

03 The number of emigrants _____ decreasing. (be)

04 A number of obese children _____ going to join the camp. (be)

05 Tom and Jane _____ to take a trip to Europe. (plan)

06 Look at the boys who _____ dancing on the street. (be)

07 The news about the politician _____ not true. (be)

08 Mathematics _____ one of my favorite subjects. (be)

09 Either Jack or Edward _____ been to France before. (have)

10 The passenger on the train _____ some water. (want)

11 Taking care of patients _____ my job. (be)

12 Somebody _____ knocking on the door now. (be)

13 Something _____ wrong with my computer. (be)

14 Each country _____ its own traditional culture. (have)

15 All the houses _____ been destroyed by the storm. (has)

・emigrant 이민자 ・decrease 줄어들다 ・obese 비만의, 뚱뚱한 ・politician 정치인 ・passenger 승객
・patient 환자 ・knock 두드리다 ・wrong 잘못된 ・traditional 전통적인 ・storm 폭풍

❶ 다음 밑줄 친 부분을 바르게 고치세요.

01 The socks in the drawer <u>is</u> my father's. | are

02 Jack as well as his friends <u>learn</u> English.

03 A number of rumors about her <u>is</u> spreading over the country.

04 Can you see the cat which <u>are</u> sitting on the fence?

05 Neither Amy nor the boys <u>has</u> never been to Canada.

06 The United States <u>consist</u> of 50 states.

07 Physics <u>are</u> not popular among teenagers.

08 Cathy and Richard often <u>visits</u> the temple.

09 What I saw last night <u>are</u> his dog.

10 The number of traffic accidents <u>have</u> decreased rapidly.

11 Not only the sofa but also the chairs <u>was</u> imported from Italy.

12 All the employees at the department <u>brings</u> their lunch.

13 Every student <u>are</u> going to attend the meeting.

14 Each person <u>have</u> a different voice.

15 Drawing portraits <u>are</u> my father's job.

WORDS

· drawer 서랍 · consist 구성하다 · physics 물리학 · temple 절, 사원 · spread 퍼지다 · import 수입하다
· employee 종업원 · bring 가지고 오다 · voice 목소리 · portrait 초상화

② **다음 우리말과 일치하도록, 주어진 단어를 이용하여 문장을 완성하세요.**
(필요하면 단어를 추가하거나 변경 하세요.)

01 테마 공원에 가는 것은 매우 신난다. (be, to go, the theme park, to)
→ _____ To go to the theme park is _____ very exciting

02 바다에서 수영하는 것은 매우 재미있다. (in, swimming, the sea, be)
→ _____ a lot of fun.

03 모든 부모들은 자신의 아이들이 특별하다고 생각한다. (think, parent, that, every)
→ _____ their child is special

04 많은 학생들이 안경을 쓰고 있다. (student, a number of, be)
→ _____ wearing glasses.

05 그녀 또는 내가 책임질 것이다. (be, or, either, she, I)
→ _____ going to take the responsibility

06 내가 대학에서 공부하려고 하는 것은 경제학이다. (what, want, I, to study, be, at college)
→ _____ economics.

07 Jane과 Jessie 둘 다 다른 방에 갇혀있다. (Jane, both, be, and, Jessie)
→ _____ locked in different rooms.

08 Sam뿐만 아니라 그의 친구들도 테니스 클럽에 가입하기를 원치 않는다. (neither, Sam, his friends, want
→ _____ to join the tennis club.

09 최근에 서울의 자동차 수가 증가했다. (cars, the number, of, have, in Seoul)
→ _____ increased lately.

10 각각의 사람은 선택할 권리가 있다. (each, have, person, the right)
→ _____ to make choices.

11 엔진에 뭔가 문제가 있다. (be, wrong, something, with)
→ _____ the engine.

12 이 호텔의 모든 객실이 작년에 보수되었다. (last year, be, renovated)
→ All the rooms in this hotel _____ .

WOR D S
• theme park 테마 공원   • responsibility 책임   • lock 감금하다   • lately 최근에   • right 권리   • choice 선택
• renovate 보수하다

UNIT 02 시제의 일치

시제 일치란 주절의 동사의 시점에 따라 종속절의 동사를 현재, 과거, 과거완료 중 하나를 올바르게 선택하여 사용 하는 것을 말합니다.

1. 시제일치의 원칙

주절이 현재 – 종속절(that절)에는 모든 시제를 사용할 수 있다. (현재, 미래, 과거, 완료)	He **says** that he **will study** English. 　　주절　　　　　　종속절 He **says** that he **studies** English. He **says** that he **studied** English. He **says** that he **has been studying** English for 2 years.
주절이 과거 – 종속절에 과거시제 또는 과거완료(had p.p)가 온다.	He **said** that the pizza **was** delicious. He **said** that the pizza **had been** delicious. He **thought** that I **could** fix the computer. *주절의 동사가 과거시제일 때, that절 안에서 조동사는 would, could 등의 과거형을 사용합니다.

Plus 1
- 주절의 동사가 과거시제일 때, that절의 동사가 과거이면 주절의 동사와 같은 때 일어난 일을 나타내고, 과거완료(had p.p)이면 주절의 동사보다 먼저 일어난 일을 나타냅니다.
→ I knew that he **had visited** the museum. 나는 그가 그 박물관을 방문했었던 것을 알았다.
└→ knew보다 먼저 일어난 일

2. 주절이 현재시제에서 과거시제로 바뀌는 경우: 종속절의 시제가 현재나 미래면 과거시제로 바꾸고 과거면 과거완료시제로 바꾸어야 합니다.

종속절의 시제가 현재나 미래면 과거시제로 바꾼다.	They **say** that she **helps** the poor people. → They **said** that she **helped** the poor people.
종속절의 시제가 과거면 과거완료시제로 바꾼다.	They **think** that she **was** a teacher. → They **thought** that she **had been** a teacher.

Plus 2
- 주절이 현재시제에서 과거시제로 바뀌는 경우 종속절의 시제가 현재완료면 과거완료로 바꾼다.
He says that he **has taught** English for three years.
→ He **said** that he **had taught** English for three years.

3. 시제일치의 예외: 다음과 같은 경우에는 현재시제를 사용합니다.

that절의 내용이 불변의 진리, 과학적 사실	We **learned** that the earth **moves** around the sun. He **knew** that the earth **is** round. 그는 지구가 둥글다는 것을 알았다.
that절의 내용이 현재의 습관적이거나 반복적인 행동	He **said** that he **takes** a walk at 7 every morning. She **said** that she **practices** the violin every weekend.

Plus 3
- that절의 내용이 역사적 사실일 경우에는 항상 과거시제로 씁니다.
→ I learned that Korean war **broke** out in 1950. 나는 한국전쟁이 1950년에 발발했다고 배웠다.

Warm up

정답 및 해설 p.3

● 다음 괄호 안에서 알맞은 말을 고르세요. (둘 다 적합하면 모두 고르세요.)

01 I know that it (rains / rained) last night.

02 Jane said that she (takes / taken) a shower every morning.

03 I told him that I (have / had) volunteered at the fire station.

04 He was sure that he (can / could) come here in time.

05 Jane says that it (is / was) such a wonderful movie.

06 The book says that World War II (ends / ended) in 1945.

07 My son knew that oil (is / was) heavier than water.

08 She said that Mike (can / could) not come to the party.

09 She told Tom that she (washes / was washing) her hair every day.

10 She complained that the movie (has been / had been) boring.

11 Alice knew that her mom (will not / would not) help her.

12 We learned that Seoul (is / was) larger than Busan.

13 She said that she (practices / will practice) the violin every Saturday.

14 They told me that the moon (moves / moved) around the earth.

15 The child knew that Korea (is / was) invaded by Japan in 1592.

WORDS

• World War II 2차 세계대전   • in time (~에) 시간 맞춰[늦지 않게]   • heavy 무거운   • complain 불평하다
• around 주변   • invade 침입하다   • volunteer 자원하다

Start up   시제의 일치 확인하기

1 다음 주절의 시제를 과거로 바꿀 때 빈칸에 알맞은 말을 쓰세요.

01 She says that she loves James.
→ She said that she ___loved___ James.

02 She tells me that she will take me to the zoo.
→ She told me that she _____ _____ me to the zoo.

03 I believe that she can drive a bus.
→ I believed that she _____ _____ a bus.

04 She tells me that Tom was kind to his friends.
→ She told me that Tom _____ _____ kind to his friends.

05 My father knows that Tom has been to Canada.
→ My father knew that Tom _____ _____ to Canada.

06 My brother says that Isaac Newton discovered the law of gravity.
→ My brother said that Isaac Newton _____ the law of gravity.

07 John knows that the sun rises in the east.
→ John knew that the sun _____ in the east.

08 I am sure that you agreed to cooperate with each other.
→ I was sure that you _____ _____ to cooperate with each other.

09 Jeniffer says that she had a good time with her family.
→ Jeniffer said that she _____ _____ a good time with her family.

10 I learn that Steve Jobs was born in San Francisco.
→ I learned that Steve Jobs _____ born in San Francisco.

11 Jack says that he tried to become a doctor.
→ Jack said that he _____ _____ to become a doctor.

12 He tells me that he has cut down on salty food.
→ He told me that he _____ _____ down on salty food.

WORDS

• take 데리고 가다 • discover 발견하다 • law 법칙, 법 • gravity 중력 • cooperate 협력하다 • try 노력하다
• cut down on ~을 줄이다 • salty 짠

❷ 다음 주절의 시제를 과거로 바꿀 때 빈칸에 알맞은 말을 쓰세요.

01 Kelly is certain that everything will be OK.
→ Kelly was certain that everything ___would___ be OK.

02 They say that Joe works as a taxi driver at night.
→ They said that Joe _____ as a taxi driver at night.

03 Charlie believes that the cookies were made by his uncle.
→ Charlie believed that the cookies _____ _____ made by his uncle

04 I think that eating fast food made her fat.
→ I thought that eating fast food _____ _____ her fat.

05 They say that the shopping mall closes at 9:00 p.m.
→ They said that the shopping mall _____ at 9:00 p.m.

06 He tells me that Edison invented light bulb.
→ He told me that Edison _____ light bulb.

07 Victor says that he can lend me some money.
→ Victor said that he _____ lend me some money.

08 Mom says that she bought the white microwave.
→ Mom said that she _____ _____ the white microwave.

09 Sam says that he will stay at the hotel for a week.
→ Sam said that he _____ stay at the hotel for a week.

10 I learn that Mozart was born in 1756.
→ I learned that Mozart _____ _____ in 1756.

11 People believe that the actor has gone to America.
→ People believed that the actor _____ _____ to America.

12 I believe that he has been interested in politics.
→ I believed that he _____ _____ interested in politics.

WORDS
· certain 확신하는   · lend 빌려주다   · microwave 전자레인지

1 다음 밑줄 친 부분을 바르게 고치세요.

01 She said that the sun <u>has set</u> in the west.
그녀는 해는 서쪽으로 진다고 말했다.

sets

02 Mike believed that she <u>will</u> pass the exam.
Mike는 그녀가 시험에 통과할 것이라고 믿었다.

03 Sam told me that water <u>boiled</u> at 100 degrees.
Sam은 내게 물을 100도에서 끓는다고 말했다.

04 She told me that she <u>has seen</u> me before.
그녀는 내게 전에 나를 본 적이 있었다고 말했다.

05 The teacher told us that World War I <u>breaks out</u> in 1914.
세계 1차 대전이 1914년에 발발했다고 선생님이 말했다.

06 We learned that Beethoven <u>composes</u> "Moonlight Sonata."
우리는 베토벤이 월광 소나타를 작곡했다고 배웠다.

07 I know that Graham Bell first <u>invents</u> a telephone in 1876.
나는 Graham Bell 최초로 전화기를 발명했다는 알고 있다.

08 He says that he <u>go</u> to work by subway every day.
그는 매일 지하철로 출근한다고 말한다.

09 Do you know that Pablo Picasso <u>has been</u> born in Spain?
너는 Pablo Picasso 스페인에서 태어난 것을 알고 있니?

10 Galileo believed that the earth <u>went</u> around the sun.
Galileo는 지구가 태양 주의를 돈다고 믿었다.

11 He knew that something <u>is</u> wrong.
그는 뭔가 잘못되었다는 것을 알았다.

12 They told me that they <u>have been</u> there once.
그들은 내게 그곳에 한 번 가 본 적이 있다고 말했다.

WORDS

· boil 끓다 　· compose 작곡하다 　· once 한 번

❷ 다음 우리말과 일치하도록, 주어진 단어를 이용하여 시제에 맞게 문장을 완성하세요.

01 나는 엠파이어스테이트 빌딩이 1931년에 건설되었다는 것을 알고 있다. (built, in 1931, be)
→ I know that the Empire State Building _____ was built in 1931 _____.

02 그는 내게 그가 그녀에게 반지를 줬다고 말했다. (he, has, to her, given, a ring)
→ He told me that _____.

03 그들은 자신들의 직업에 만족한다고 말한다. (their jobs, they, be satisfied with)
→ They say that _____.

04 그는 작년에 컴퓨터 회사에서 일했다고 말한다. (a computer, work for, company, last year)
→ He says that he _____.

05 Jessie는 매일 열 시에 잔다고 말했다. (to bed, go, at 10 p.m., she)
→ Jessie said that _____ every day.

06 그는 독일이 폴란드를 1939년 침공했다는 것을 알고 있다. (Poland, Germany, in 1939, invade)
→ He knows that _____.

07 우리는 아폴로가 1969년 7월 20일 달에 착륙했다고 배웠다. (the Apollo, the moon, on, land)
→ We learned that _____ on July 20, 1969.

08 그는 지구가 달보다 크다고 말했다. (be, than, the moon, the earth, larger)
→ He said that _____.

09 Cathy는 그녀가 은행에서 15년 동안 일하고 있다고 말한다. (at, she, has, the bank, work)
→ Cathy says that _____ for 15 years.

10 그녀는 내게 전에 만난 적이 있었다고 말했다. (met, me, she, have, before)
→ She told me that _____.

11 그들은 그들이 지난달 공해 문제를 해결했다고 말한다. (solve, problem, the pollution, they)
→ They say that _____ last month.

12 Alice는 그가 좋은 점수를 받기를 희망했다. (will, good grades, get)
→ Alice hoped that he _____.

WORDS

· Poland 폴란드 · land 착륙하다 · pollution 공해, 오염 · grade 점수, 등급

UNIT 03 간접화법

간접화법이란 남의 말을 인용할 때, 현재 말하는 사람의 입장에서 인칭이나 시제 따위를 고쳐서 말하는 화법을 말합니다.

직접화법: 말한 그대로를 따옴표 (" ") 안에 나타내는 방법	Jane said, "**I'm tired.**" (I = Jane)
간접화법: 따옴표 안의 내용을 접속사(that)를 이용하여 전달자의 입장에서 말하는 방법	Jane said **that she was tired**. (she = Jane)

1. 평서문을 간접화법으로 전환하는 방법

1) 전달동사의 형태를 바꿉니다.

> say / says / said → 그대로
> say to → tell   says to → tells   said to → told

2) 콤마(,)와 따옴표(" ")를 빼고 연결어를 쓴 후, 대명사와 동사의 형태를 적절히 바꿉니다.

직접화법	1인칭 (I, we 등)	2인칭 (you 등)	3인칭 (he, she 등)
간접화법	말하는 사람	듣는 사람	그대로

3) 간접화법으로 전환 시 시간·장소부사와 지시대명사는 다음과 같이 바꿉니다.

직접화법	today	now	ago	here	this	yesterday	tomorrow
간접화법	that day	then	before	there	that	the day before	the next day

4) 시제: 전달동사가 현재형일 때는 that절 안 동사의 시제를 그대로 쓰고, 전달동사가 과거형일 때는 that절 안의 시제를 과거 또는 과거완료로 바꾸어 씁니다.

2. 간접화법 만들기

1)
> He **said**, "I feel good today." 그는 말했다, "나는 오늘 기분이 좋아."
> → He **said** that **he felt good that day**. 그는 그날 그가 기분이 좋다고 말했다.

① 전달동사 said는 그대로 씁니다.
② 콤마(,)와 따옴표(" ")를 빼고 접속사 that을 씁니다.
③ that절 안 동사의 시제를 과거로 바꾸고 주어 I를 말하는 사람 he로 바꿔야 합니다.
④ 시간부사 today는 that day로 바꿔 씁니다.

2)
> She **said to** me, "I love you." 그녀는 나에게 말한다, "나는 너를 사랑해."
> → She **told** me that **she loved me.** 그녀는 나에게 그녀가 나를 사랑한다고 말했다.

① 전달동사 said to는 told로 바꿔 씁니다.

② 콤마(,)와 따옴표(" ")를 빼고 접속사 that을 씁니다.

③ that절 안 동사의 시제를 과거로 바꾸고 주어 I를 말하는 사람 she로 바꾸며 목적어 you를 듣는 사람인 me로 바꿔 씁니다.

3)
> He **said to** me, "You were the best player." 그는 나에게 말했다, "네가 최고의 선수였어."
> · He **told** me that I **had been** the best player. 그는 나에게 내가 최고의 선수였다고 말했다.

① 전달동사 said to는 told 로 바꿔 씁니다.

② 콤마(,)와 따옴표(" ")를 빼고 접속사 that을 씁니다.

③ that절 안 동사의 시제를 과거완료 바꾸고 주어 you를 듣는 사람인 I로 바꿔 씁니다. 직접화법의 시제가 과거이면 간접화법 that절의 시제는 과거완료로 쓴다. 직접화법의 시제가 과거이므로 하나 앞선 과거완료를 쓴다.

4)
> He said to me, "I will leave tomorrow."
> → He told me that **he would leave the next day**.

※ that절 안 동사의 시제를 과거(would)로 바꾸고 주어 I를 말하는 사람 he로 바꿔 씁니다.

tomorrow는 the next day로 바꿔 씁니다.

3. 의문사가 있는 의문문의 화법 전환

1) 전달동사를 ask 로 바꿉니다.

2) 콤마와 따옴표를 없애고 「의문사+주어+동사 ~」의 순서로 씁니다. 필요한 경우 대명사와 동사의 시제를 바꾸어 써야 합니다.

> He **said to** me, "What time do you get up?"
> → He **asked** me **what time I got up**.

① said to me는 asked me로, 주어는 듣는 사람인 I로 바꿉니다.

② do/does/did는 지우고 시제에 맞춰 동사를 씁니다.

> I **said to** him, "When **did** you have lunch?"
> → I **asked** him **when he had had lunch**. → 과거인 경우 하나 앞선 과거완료를 씁니다.

4. 의문사가 없는 의문문의 화법 전환

1) 전달동사를 ask로 바꿉니다.

2) 콤마와 따옴표를 없애고 if 또는 whether를 쓴 뒤 「주어+동사 ~」의 어순으로 정리하여 씁니다. 필요한 경우 대명사와 동사의 시제를 바꾸어 써야 합니다.

> · She **said to** me, "Do you like Korean food?"
> → She **asked** me **if[whether] I liked Korean food**.
> · He **said to** me, "Did you send me flowers?"
> → He **asked** me **if[whether] I had sent him flowers**.
> * if절의 주어는 듣는 사람인 I로 목적어는 말하는 사람인 him으로 바꿉니다.

Warm up

1 다음 직접화법을 간접화법으로 바꾸어 쓸 때, 괄호 안에서 알맞은 말을 고르세요.

01 James said to me, "It is very cold today."
→ James told me that it (is / (was)) very cold that day.

02 She said to him, "I am waiting for you here."
→ She told him that (she / I) was waiting for him there.

03 Tom said to him, "I am eating pizza now."
→ Tom told him that he was eating pizza (now / then).

04 Tom said to her," I saw you crossing the street."
→ Tom told her that he (have seen / had seen) her crossing the street.

05 He said to me, "I have some coins."
→ He (told / said) me that he (has / had) some coins.

06 My mom said, "I am happy today."
→ My mom said that (she / my mom) was happy that day.

07 She said to me, "I will call you tomorrow."
→ She told me that she (will / would) call me the next day.

08 My sister said to him, "I broke your glasses."
→ My sister told him that she had broken (his / her) glasses.

09 She said, "I bought a present for James."
→ She said that she (had bought / has bought) a present for James.

10 Jessica said to me, "You look tired.
→ Jessica told me that (I / she) looked tired.

11 My teacher said to him, "You are always late for school."
→ My teacher told him that he (was / had been) always late for school.

12 He said, "I am satisfied with my job."
→ He said that he was satisfied with (my / his) job.

WORDS

· call 전화하다   · present 선물   · be satisfied with ~에 만족해하다

❷ 다음 직접화법을 간접화법으로 바꾸어 쓸 때, 괄호 안에서 알맞은 말을 고르세요.

01 He said to her, "Where do you live?"
→ He asked her where (he / (she)) lived.

02 She said to me, "What did you eat for dinner?"
→ She asked me what I (had eaten / ate) for dinner.

03 She said to him, "Are you angry?"
→ She asked him (that / if) he was angry.

04 The man said to me, "Can you speak Chinese?"
→ The man asked me if I (can / could) speak Chinese.

05 Thomson asked to me, "When is your wedding ceremony?"
→ Thomson asked me when (my / his) wedding ceremony was.

06 He said to me, "Where did you get the couch?"
→ He (told / asked) me where I (got / had got) the couch.

07 Alice said to me, "Do you have a car?"
→ Alice asked me if (I / she) had a car.

08 The boy said to his mom, "I stole the bread at the bakery."
→ The boy told his mom that he (had stolen / stole) the bread at the bakery.

09 He said to her, "Do you go fishing?"
→ He asked her If (she / he) went fishing.

10 He said to me, "Are you free tomorrow?"
→ He asked me if I was free (tomorrow / the next day).

11 She said to him, "Do you have a girlfriend?"
→ She asked him if he (has / had) a girlfriend.

12 He said to me, "How can I get to the embassy?"
→ He asked me (how / that) he could get to the embassy.

WORDS

• ceremony 의식   • bakery 빵집   • embassy 대사관

Start up

① 다음 직접화법을 간접화법으로 바꾸어 쓸 때, 빈칸에 알맞은 말을 쓰세요.

01 He said, "I am very happy."
→ He ____said____ ____that____ ____he____ was very happy.

02 They said to me, "You are beautiful."
→ They _____ _____ that _____ was beautiful.

03 She said, "I will leave tomorrow."
→ She said that _____ _____ _____ the next day.

04 He said to me, "I did my best yesterday."
→ He told me that _____ _____ _____ his best the day before.

05 She said to him, "What are you doing?"
→ She _____ _____ what _____ was doing.

06 I said to him, "You are a good student."
→ I _____ _____ that _____ was a good student.

07 Tom said to her, "Do you like music?"
→ Tom _____ her _____ she liked music.

08 He said to me, "I ate too much."
→ He told me that _____ _____ _____ too much.

09 She said to me, "I'll call you tomorrow."
→ She told me that she _____ _____ _____ the next day.

10 He said to her, "You broke the rule."
→ He told her that _____ _____ _____ the rule.

11 Mom said to me. "What are you doing?"
→ Mom _____ me what _____ was doing.

12 He said to me, "Do you like me?"
→ He _____ me _____ _____ liked him.

WORDS

· leave 떠나다   · break 어기다, 깨뜨리다   · rule 규칙

❷ 다음 직접화법을 간접화법으로 바꾸어 쓸 때, 빈칸에 알맞은 말을 쓰세요.

01 He said, "I am very tired now."
　→ He said that ＿＿＿he＿＿＿ ＿＿＿was＿＿＿ very tired ＿＿＿then＿＿＿.

02 She said to me, "I respect you."
　→ She told me that ＿＿＿＿ ＿＿＿＿ ＿＿＿＿.

03 Jane said to her, "I met Tom yesterday."
　→ Jane ＿＿＿＿ her that ＿＿＿＿ ＿＿＿＿ ＿＿＿＿ Tom the day before.

04 Jack said to me, "I will go to Busan."
　→ Jack told me that ＿＿＿＿ ＿＿＿＿ ＿＿＿＿ to Busan.

05 He said to me, "When can you finish the work?"
　→ He ＿＿＿＿ me ＿＿＿＿ ＿＿＿＿ ＿＿＿＿ finish the work.

06 His daughter said to me, "I need more water."
　→ His daughter ＿＿＿＿ me that ＿＿＿＿ ＿＿＿＿ more water.

07 He said to me, "Are you a teacher?"
　→ He ＿＿＿＿ me ＿＿＿＿ ＿＿＿＿ ＿＿＿＿ a teacher.

08 My uncle said to me, "I don't like to go to the movies."
　→ My uncle told me that ＿＿＿＿ ＿＿＿＿ ＿＿＿＿ ＿＿＿＿ go to the movies.

09 He said to me, " I visited your uncle yesterday."
　→ He told me that ＿＿＿＿ ＿＿＿＿ ＿＿＿＿ my uncle ＿＿＿＿ ＿＿＿＿ ＿＿＿＿.

10 He said, "There's nothing I can do."
　→ He ＿＿＿＿ that there was nothing ＿＿＿＿ ＿＿＿＿ do.

11 The man said to him, "Why are you here?"
　→ The man asked him why ＿＿＿＿ ＿＿＿＿ ＿＿＿＿.

12 He said to me, "I will take care of your brother."
　→ He told me that ＿＿＿＿ ＿＿＿＿ take care of ＿＿＿＿ brother.

WORDS
· then 그때　· respect 존경하다

1 다음 직접화법을 간접화법으로 바꾸어 쓰세요.

01 My mom said to me, "I have good news for you."
→ _____ My mom told me that she had good news for me. _____

02 Bill said to me, "I love your sister."
→ _____

03 I said to him, "I will help you."
→ _____

04 Sam said to me, "I will go swimming tomorrow."
→ _____

05 He said to me, "Do you like Tom?"
→ _____

06 He said to me, "I agree with you."
→ _____

07 She said to her brother, "Do you want some milk?"
→ _____

08 Paul said to me, "How are you doing at school?"
→ _____

09 He said to me, "I did my best yesterday."
→ _____

10 He said to her, "Where did you find the bag?"
→ _____

11 The doctor said to him, "Do you cough a lot?"
→ _____

12 He said to me, "Do you have a cat?"
→ _____

WORDS

・agree 동의하다　・cough 기침하다　・a lot 많이

❷ 다음 직접화법을 간접화법으로 바꾸어 쓰세요.

01 He said to her, "Who are you?"

→ _____ He asked her who she was. _____

02 She said to me, "I lost my dog yesterday."

→ _____

03 He said to me. "Why is she crying?"

→ _____

04 The man said to her, "When will the next train arrive?"

→ _____

05 My mom said to me, "You make me happy."

→ _____

06 He said to her, "Can I borrow your computer?"

→ _____

07 My teacher said to me, "Were you in the shopping mall yesterday?"

→ _____

08 James said, "I have a fever and a runny nose."

→ _____

09 The weather man said, "It will be windy tomorrow."

→ _____

10 Joe said to her, "Where did you buy this sofa?"

→ _____

11 John said to me, "Did you see the game?"

→ _____

12 She said to me, "Where are you going?"

→ _____

WORDS

· fever 열   · runny nose 콧물이 나는   · windy 바람 부는

1 주어진 단어를 이용하여 빈칸에 알맞은 말을 쓰세요. (단, 현재형으로 쓰세요.)

01 The trees in the park _____are_____ very tall. (be)

02 The birds in the cages _____ very small. (be)

03 All the people in the office _____ busy. (look)

04 Do you know the girls who _____ on the stage? (be)

05 Watching soccer games on TV _____ very exciting. (be)

06 A number of movie stars _____ in the film festival every year. (participate)

07 The number of single women _____ growing. (be)

08 Both Steve and Susan _____ to be fashion designers. (want)

09 Either Steve or his mom _____ to move the boxes. (have)

10 His parents as well as Mike _____ worried about my health. (be)

11 Neither she or Sam _____ to church on Sunday. (go)

12 To get up early _____ good for health. (be)

13 Selling used cars _____ my uncle's job. (be)

14 What I want to do _____ to go home and sleep. (be)

15 All the meat in the refrigerator _____ gone bad. (have)

WORDS

• cage 새장   • grow 증가하다, 자라다   • single 독신   • participate 참여하다   • used car 중고차
• go bad 썩다, 나빠지다

❷ 주어진 단어를 이용하여 빈칸에 알맞은 말을 쓰세요. (단, 현재형으로 쓰세요.)

01 All my friends _____are_____ invited to the opening ceremony. (be)

02 All the furniture _____ made in France. (be)

03 Studying physics _____ not what she wants. (be)

04 Every person _____ their role in the society. (has)

05 The number of the foreign students _____ been increasing. (has)

06 Eating a well-balanced food _____ very important. (be)

07 A number of languages _____ spoken in the country. (be)

08 Each team _____ six players including a goalie. (has)

09 Her classmates as well as Jane _____ going to volunteer in a day-care center. (be)

10 Neither Joe nor his friend _____ the museum. (visit)

11 The Netherlands _____ famous for windmills. (be)

12 Working as a report _____ very hard. (be)

13 All the passengers on the bus _____ students. (be)

14 The Philippines _____ made up of more than 7,000 islands. (be)

15 These are the people who _____ with me. (work)

WORDS

• windmill 풍차　• be made up of ~로 구성되다

③ 다음 문장을 간접화법으로 고치시오.

01 She said to me, "Do you like apples?"

➡ _____ She asked me if[whether] I liked apples. _____

02 She said to me, "I met Mike yesterday.

➡ _____

03 He said to me, "I loved her."

➡ _____

04 I said to her, "What did your father say about it?

➡ _____

05 He said to me, "Which movie will you see?"

➡ _____

06 John said to me, "I don't like to listen to the radio today."

➡ _____

07 My mom said to me, "Did you use my computer?"

➡ _____

08 She said to me, "Did you see John?"

➡ _____

09 She said to me, "Are you hungry now?"

➡ _____

10 She said to me, "I will meet him tomorrow."

➡ _____

11 Joe said to her, "Where did you buy this bike?"

➡ _____

12 My father said to me, "I don't understand what you say"

➡ _____

· understand 이해하다

④ 다음 문장을 직접 화법으로 바꿀 때 빈칸에 알맞은 말을 쓰세요.

01 She asked me if I knew the doctor.

→ She _____said_____ _____to_____ me, "_____Do_____ you know the doctor?"

02 She said that she was reading a book then.

→ She said, "_____ am reading a book _____."

03 Mike told me that he had a job interview the next day.

→ Mike said to me, "_____ _____ a job interview _____."

04 Eric asked her when her family was going to move to Seoul.

→ Eric said to her, "_____ is _____ family going to move to Seoul?"

05 Mr. Johnson told us he would visit the college the next day.

→ Mr. Johnson said to us, "_____ _____ visit the college _____."

06 She asked him where he had found the dog.

→ She said to him, "_____ _____ you find the dog?"

07 Amy asked me if I liked living in the city like Seoul.

→ Amy said to me, "_____ _____ _____ living in the city like Seoul?"

08 She asked them why they had been late for school the day before.

→ She said to them, "_____ _____ _____ late for school _____?"

09 The woman asked the boy what he was looking for.

→ The woman said to the boy, " What _____ _____ looking for?"

10 She asked him what he usually did on weekends.

→ She said to him, 'What _____ _____ usually _____ on weekends?"

11 She told me that she would write a letter to him the next day.

→ She _____ _____ me, "I _____ write a letter to him _____."

![WORDS]

· like ~와 같은, ~처럼　·college 대학　·look for ~을 찾다　·on weekends 주말에

[1-4] 다음 중 빈칸에 알맞은 말을 고르세요.

1

> He knows that Shakespeare _____ *Romeo and Juliet*.

① writes ② write ③ wrote
④ is writing ⑤ has written

2

> She asked me _____ I liked Korean food.

① what ② if ③ where
④ which ⑤ that

3

> _____ are watching a basketball game in the gym.

① Every student ② Each student
③ The number of students ④ Either Jack or James
⑤ Both Sam and his brother

4

> Not only the boy but also _____ like baseball.

① his friend ② his sister ③ his parents
④ Michelle ⑤ his brother

[5-8] 다음 중 문장을 간접화법으로 고칠 때 빈칸에 들어갈 알맞은 말을 고르세요.

Note

5

Tom said to her, "Do you like music?"
→ Tom asked her _____ she liked music.

① what   ② if   ③ where
④ which   ⑤ that

6

She said to me, "Where did you meet him?"
→ She asked me where _____ had met him?

① I   ② he   ③ she
④ they   ⑤ did

7

She said to me, "I'll take you to the beach tomorrow."
→ She told me that she would take me to the beach _____.

① today   ② that day
③ yesterday   ④ the day before
⑤ the next day

8

She said to him, "What did you buy?"
→ She asked him what he _____.

① buy   ② bought
③ has bought   ④ had bought
⑤ was buying

9   다음 중 빈칸에 알맞지 <u>않은</u> 것을 고르세요.

> I thought that she _____ in the river.

① swam   ② could swim   ③ was swimming
④ had swum   ⑤ has been swimming

Note

9
주절의 동사가 과거일 때
종속절의 시제를 알아보
세요.

[10–11] 다음 중 보기의 문장을 간접화법으로 바르게 전환한 것을 고르세요.

10   > He said to me, "I did my best yesterday."

① He told me that he did his best the day before.
② He told me that he has done his best the next day.
③ He told me that he had done his best yesterday.
④ He told me that he had done his best the day before.
⑤ He told me that he has done his best the day before.

10
간접화법으로 전환 시 시
제변화에 대해 알아보세
요.

11   > She said to him, "Do you have a computer?"

① She said to me that he has a computer.
② She told me that he has a computer.
③ She asked him if you had a computer.
④ She asked me if he has a computer.
⑤ She asked him if he had a computer.

12   다음 문장을 과거시제로 쓸 때 빈칸에 알맞은 것을 고르세요.

> I know that the World Cup was held in Korea and Japan in
> 2002.
> → I knew that the World Cup _____ held in Korea and
>   Japan in 2002.

① are   ② was   ③ has been
④ have been   ⑤ had been

12
hold 개최하다, 열다

[13-14] 다음 중 어법상 <u>어색한</u> 문장을 고르세요.

13 ① Either he or his mom knows where she is.
② Neither she nor you are a liar.
③ She as well as they gets up early.
④ Both he and his wife are doctors.
⑤ Every student have to attend the speech contest.

14 ① She says that she has been to America.
② Jessie says that Tim used to take a walk.
③ He said that Columbus had discovered America in 1492.
④ They thought that I ate pizza for dinner.
⑤ I promise that I will stop smoking.

15 다음 중 문장의 변환이 바르지 <u>않은</u> 것을 고르세요.

① He said, "I am very happy."
   = He said that he was very happy.
② She said to me, "You are kind to my brother."
   = She told me that I was kind to my brother.
③ Mom said to me, "What are you doing?"
   = Mom asked me what I was doing.
④ He said to me, "Do you like me?"
   = He asked me if I liked him.
⑤ David said, "I have a headache."
   = David said that he had a headache.

16 다음 빈칸에 알맞은 말을 쓰세요.

I said to him, "Do you like chocolate?"
→ I asked him _____ he liked chocolate.

→ _____

17 다음 보기의 간접화법을 직접화법으로 바꾸시오.

> The doctor asked me if I had a fever.

➔ The doctor said to me, "_____?"

18 다음 문장을 간접화법으로 전환하세요.

1) He said to her, "When did you buy this?"

   ➔ _____

2) John said to me, "Did you see the game?"

   ➔ _____

19 다음 주어진 단어를 이용하여 빈칸에 알맞은 말을 쓰세요. (현재형으로 쓰세요.)

2) Either Sam or his mom _____ to wash the dishes. (have)

2) His parents as well as Mike _____ worried about my safety. (be)

20 다음 문장을 과거시제로 쓸 때 빈칸에 알맞을 쓰세요.

1) I think that you can fix the broken watch.

   ➔ I thought that you _____ the broken watch.

2) My mom knows that Sam is my best friend.

   ➔ My mom knew that Sam _____.

Note

17
fever 열

18
간접화법으로 전환 시 시제 변화에 대해 알아보세요.

19
writer 작가
safety 안전

20
broken 고장 난

Review Test

정답 및 해설 p.34

1 다음 빈칸에 알맞은 의문사를 쓰세요.

01 A: ___What___ do they want?

B: I want a computer.

02 A: _____ is good at baseball?

B: Jason.

03 A: _____ do you feel today?

B: I feel very good.

04 A: _____ does Sam study English?

B: He studies it to be an English teacher.

05 A: _____ do you come home?

B: At 6.

06 A: _____ didn't you come to the party?

B: Because I was very busy.

07 A: _____ do you eat for breakfast?

B: I eat cereal.

08 A: _____ will pay the rent?

B: My mom will pay it.

09 A: _____ does he study so hard?

B: Because he wants to get a scholarship.

10 A: _____ does your father get up?

B: He usually gets up at 7.

11 A: _____ watch is that?

B: It's my dad's.

12 A: _____ does he live?

B: He lives in Toronto.

WORDS

• rent 임대료   • pay 지불하다   • cereal 곡물   • scholarship 장학금

2 다음 빈칸에 알맞은 의문사를 쓰세요.　　　　　　　　　　　Chapter 4

01 A: ___How___ ___many___ chairs are there in the room?
　　B: There are four.

02 A: _____ _____ do you go to the movies?
　　B: About two times a month.

03 A: _____ _____ hours a day do you read a book?
　　B: More than three hours.

04 A: _____ _____ money did you pay for the smartphone?
　　B: I paid 300 dollars for it.

05 A: _____ _____ do you plan to spend in Korea?
　　B: Five days.

3 다음 문장을 괄호 안의 지시대로 바꿔 쓰세요.　　　　　　　　　Chapter 5

01 Let's go for a walk after dinner. (why로 시작)
　　➝ ____Why don't we go for a walk after dinner?____

02 Why don't we meet at 4:00 tomorrow? (how로 시작)
　　➝ _____

03 Let's have a surprise birthday party for her. (shall로 시작)
　　➝ _____

04 You should not drive at the park. (부정 명령문)
　　➝ _____

05 Save the money for a rainy day. (let's로 시작)
　　➝ _____

06 You should eat lots of vegetables. (why를 이용한 제안문)
　　➝ _____

WORDS
• save 저금하다　• rainy day 궁할 때, 만일의 경우

④ 다음 밑줄 친 부분을 바르게 고치세요.

01 Tom and his brother don't wear glasses, <u>don't they</u>?   do they

02 His friends stayed up last night, <u>don't they</u>?

03 You can do it without my help, <u>do you</u>?

04 Your favorite subject is science, <u>aren't you</u>?

05 Your sister wants to be a singer, <u>does she</u>?

06 Your father accepted her apology, <u>doesn't he</u>?

07 That is not your dog, <u>isn't that</u>?

⑤ 다음 두 문장을 간접의문문을 이용하여 한 문장으로 바꾸어 쓰세요.

01 Do you know? What did she buy?
→ _____Do you know what she bought?_____

02 Do you think? Why is she so busy?
→ _____

03 Do you think? What is his favorite sport?
→ _____

04 Do you think? How much are the shoes?
→ _____

05 Can you tell me? What does he look like?
→ _____

06 Do you know? How big is the museum?
→ _____

WORDS
• look like ~처럼 생기다

6 다음 빈칸에 알맞은 말을 쓰세요.

Chapter 5

01 _____How_____ pretty she is!

02 _____ a nice hotel it is!

03 _____ fast she runs!

04 _____ an exciting game it was!

05 _____ fresh these vegetables are!

06 _____ an old bike he has!

07 _____ brave the soldiers are!

08 _____ a big pizza it is!

7 다음 문장을 감탄문으로 바꾸세요.

Chapter 5

01 The museum is very big.
   → _____How big the museum is!_____

02 These sneakers are very cheap.
   → _____

03 They are really kind nurses.
   → _____

04 They work very hard.
   → _____

05 These are really sweet mangos.
   → _____

06 It is a very windy day.
   → _____

WORDS

· sneaker 운동화 · sweet 달콤한 · windy 바람이 부는

8 다음 밑줄 친 부분을 바르게 고치세요. (고칠 필요 없으면 X 하세요.)   Chapter 6

01 Every student <u>have to</u> learn Korean history. | has to |

02 Both Smith and Tina want to be movie directors.

03 A number of people is attending his funeral.

04 Economics is too hard for me to understand.

05 Each uniform have a different design.

06 Either you or Sam has to fix the door.

07 Did you buy the cake which <u>were</u> on the table?

08 Not only Sam but also his friends uses chopsticks.

9 다음 직접화법을 간접화법으로 바꾸어 쓰세요.   Chapter 6

01 The boy said to me, "I don't want to eat pizza."
→ _____ The boy told me he didn't want to eat pizza. _____

02 She said to us, "You look very young."
→ _____

03 He said to her, "I like your daughter."
→ _____

04 She said to him, "Where are you?"
→ _____

05 She said to me, "Where did you park your car?"
→ _____

06 He said to her, "Who did you meet yesterday?"
→ _____

WORDS
· funeral 장례식   · park 주차하다

[1–3] 다음 중 빈칸에 들어갈 알맞은 말을 고르세요.

1

_____ much money did you spend on the shoes?

① Which   ② Who
③ Whose   ④ How
⑤ What

2

You watched TV last night, _____ ?

① are you   ② do you
③ did you   ④ didn't you
⑤ were you

3

She asked me _____ I had a girlfriend.

① what   ② if
③ where   ④ which
⑤ that

[4–5] 다음 중 대화의 빈칸에 알맞은 말을 고르세요.

4

A: _____ has she been in London?
B: She's been here for six months.

① How many   ② How much
③ How long   ④ How about
⑤ How often

5

A: _____ one do you want to buy?
B: That red one.

① Which   ② Who
③ Whose   ④ How
⑤ What

6 다음 중 빈칸에 들어갈 말로 바르게 짝지어진 것을 고르세요.

- Let's make a shopping list, _____ ?
- Mom wants me to help her, _____ ?

① will you - doesn't she
② shall we - didn't she
③ shall we - does she
④ shall we - doesn't she
⑤ do we - doesn't she

7 다음 중 밑줄 친 부분의 쓰임이 올바른 것을 고르세요.

① Cathy can swim, <u>can she</u>?
② You are a good boy, <u>are you</u>?
③ Mary went to the park, <u>did she</u>?
④ Dad wants to buy a car, <u>doesn't he</u>?
⑤ John did his homework, <u>doesn't he</u>?

8 다음 중 의미가 <u>다른</u> 문장을 고르세요.

① Why don't we go for a walk?
② How about going for a walk?
③ Did you go for a walk?
④ What about going for a walk?
⑤ Shall we go for a walk?

[9-10] 다음 중 문장을 간접화법으로 전환할 때 빈칸에 들어갈 알맞은 말을 고르세요.

9

> He said, "I will be busy tomorrow."
> → He said that _____ be busy the next day.

① he would   ② he will
③ I would   ④ I will
⑤ he would not

10

> Kevin said to me, "Have you seen the musical?"
> → Kevin asked me if I _____ the musical.

① saw   ② seen
③ has seen   ④ had seen
⑤ have seen

11 다음 중 빈칸에 알맞지 않은 것을 고르세요.

> Do you know _____?

① where Ann lives
② how he solved the problem
③ where I put the key
④ what did he want
⑤ why she cried

12 다음 중 두 문장을 하나로 바르게 연결한 것을 고르세요.

> Do you know?+Where did she meet him?

① Where do you know she meet him?
② Where do you know she meets him?
③ Where do you know she met him?
④ Do you know where she meets him?
⑤ Do you know where she met him?

13 다음 중 보기의 문장을 감탄문으로 알맞게 바꾼 것을 고르세요.

> My sister is a very kind girl.

① How kind girl!
② What a kind girl my sister is!
③ How a kind girl my sister is!
④ What a very kind girl!
⑤ What kind a girl my sister is!

14 다음 문장과 의미가 같은 것을 고르세요.

> Shall we make breakfast for her?

① Have you ever made breakfast for her?
② Why don't we make breakfast for her?
③ What does she eat for breakfast?
④ How can we make breakfast for her?
⑤ Let's not make breakfast for her.

[15–16] 다음 중 대화의 빈칸에 알맞은 것을 고르세요.

15

A: How often do you take a bus to school?

B: _____

① Let's play basketball together.
② It's not far from here.
③ It takes thirty minutes.
④ That's a good idea.
⑤ About two or three times a week.

16

A: _____

B: Next month.

① Why do you want to start working?
② Who do you want to start working with?
③ Where do you want to start working?
④ How do you want to start working?
⑤ When do you want to start working?

[17–18] 다음 중 어법상 어색한 문장을 고르세요.

17 ① Where do you think she will stay tonight?
② Who do you think he will invite?
③ I don't know why she left early.
④ What time do you think she started studying?
⑤ When do you know she fixed the door?

18 ① To get up early is good for health.
② Neither she or Sam like baseball.
③ The number of single women is growing.
④ What I want to do is to stay home.
⑤ The Netherlands is famous for tulips.

[19–20] 다음 중 우리말을 영어로 바르게 쓴 것을 고르세요.

19

넌 그녀가 무엇을 해야 한다고 생각하니?

① Do you think if she should do?
② Do you think what she should do?
③ Do you think what should she do?
④ What do you think she should do?
⑤ What do you think should she do?

20

오늘 밤 파티에 오지 않을래?

① Why don't you come to the party tonight?
② Why do you come to the party tonight?
③ Why aren't you come to the party tonight?
④ What are you come to the party tonight?
⑤ Why didn't you come to the party tonight?

21 다음 중 어법상 옳은 문장을 고르세요.

① Tom and Jane goes fishing every Sunday.
② Not only he but also I are not singers.
③ Either he or you are wrong.
④ He or you has to go there.
⑤ Both he and his wife is lawyers.

22 다음 중 대화가 어색한 것을 고르세요.

① A: Please give me a chance, will you?
   B: No problem.
② A: Where is the restroom?
   B: Go straight and turn right.
③ A: Why don't you carry this bag for me?
   B: Because the bag is too heavy.
④ A: What are you going to do?
   B: I'm going to sleep.
⑤ A: What would you like to be?
   B: I want to be an actor.

23 다음 주어진 단어를 이용하여 빈칸에 알맞을 말을 쓰세요.

> 한국의 관습에 대해 배우는 거 어때? (learn)
> How about _____ Korean customs?

➡ _____

24 다음 영어를 우리말로 쓰세요.

> Don't be nervous today.

➡ _____

25 다음 두 문장을 간접의문문을 이용하여 한 문장으로 바꾸어 쓰세요.

> Do you know?+What is he going to buy?

➡ _____

26 다음 두 문장의 의미가 같도록 빈칸에 알맞은 말을 쓰세요.

> Why don't you read a book tonight?

➡ What _____?

27 다음 우리말과 일치하도록 빈칸에 알맞은 말을 쓰세요.

> 우리 수영하러 갈래?
> _____ we go for a swim?

➡ _____

[29-30] 다음 문장을 간접화법으로 전환하세요.

28
> She said to him, "Where did you get this?"

➡ _____

29
> She said to me, "You are kind to me."

➡ _____

30 다음 중 어색한 부분을 바르게 고치세요.

> 그들뿐만 아니라 그녀도 일찍 일어난다.
> She as well as they get up early.

➡ _____

기출

① The woman _____ lives next door is a writer.

② Do you know the man _____ gave him the book?

③ A narrator is a person _____ explains what is happening in plays.

④ Do you know _____ went to the concert?

⑤ There lived a stupid prince _____ name was *Pride*.

17 다음 중 밑줄 친 부분을 생략할 수 없는 것을 고르시오.

기출

① Jenny met a boy whom she likes.

② I know the woman whom you met.

③ I met a lady who works at a shopping mall.

④ I found the bag which you lost.

⑤ She read the book which he recommended.

18 다음 중 어법상 어색한 것을 고르시오.

기출

① This is the hotel which I stayed.

② This is how I solved the problem.

③ Now is the time when I need him most.

④ Harvard University is near Boston where I live.

⑤ The machine that broke down has just been repaired.

5점

1) You watched TV last night, _____ ?

2) She doesn't like ice cream , _____ ?

1) _____   2) _____

23 의미가 같도록 다음 빈칸에 알맞은 말을 쓰시오.

5점

I'm sorry we are not rich.

= I wish _____ .

24 다음 문장을 간접화법으로 바꿀 때 빈칸에 알맞은 말을 쓰시오.

5점

Ann said, "I will leave tomorrow."

= Ann said that _____ .

25 다음 문장을 부정의문문으로 쓰시오.

5점

You are nervous.

_____

_____ come to the party tonight?

① Why don't you
② Why do you
③ Why aren't you
④ What are you
⑤ Why didn't you

11 다음 중 밑줄 친 부분의 쓰임이 올바른 것을 고르시오.

기출

① She can swim, <u>can she</u>?
② You are a good boy, <u>are you</u>?
③ Mary went there, <u>did she</u>?
④ Mom wants us to help her, <u>doesn't she</u>?
⑤ John did his homework, <u>doesn't he</u>?

12 다음 중 각 문장을 간접화법으로 바르게 옮긴 것 중 어색한 것은?

기출

① Jane said to me, "I'll go to Busan."
→ Jane told me that she would go to Busan.
② He said to me, "Who are you?"
→ He asked me who he was.
③ He said, "I am tired."
→ He said that he was tired.
④ He said to me, "Do you like Tom?"
→ He asked me if I liked Tom.
⑤ He said, "I will be busy tomorrow."
→ He said that he would be busy the next day.

1-1

They didn't think that the festival _____ successful.

3점

① is
② can be
③ will be
④ would be
⑤ be

5 I like books _____ have many interesting pictures.

3점
기출

① who
② when
③ where
④ which
⑤ what

[6~7] 다음 중 빈칸에 공통으로 들어갈 말을 고르시오.

6
• It was the book _____ I wanted to read.
• He is the man _____ you have to meet.

① who
② which
③ that
④ whom
⑤ whose

7
• _____ a nice car it is!
• _____ are you doing?

① How
② Who
③ What
④ When
⑤ Where

Grammar Mentor
Joy Plus 4

실전모의고사 1회

이름 :

점수 :

· 3점: 5문항
· 4점: 15문항
· 5점: 5문항

[1-5] 다음 중 빈칸에 알맞은 말을 고르시오.

1 3점

A: How _____ do you meet him?
B: Twice a week.

① many　　② much　　③ often
④ tall　　⑤ long

2 3점 기출

She is chatting with her friend on the phone, _____ ?

① don't she　　② does she　　③ doesn't she
④ is she　　⑤ isn't she

3 3점

This is the man _____ wants to meet you.

① who　　② which　　③ of which
④ where　　⑤ whose

8 기출

다음 중 빈칸에 알맞은 말을 고르시오.

He said to me, "I did my best yesterday."
→ He told me that he _____ his best the day before.

① done　　② has done　　③ have
④ had done　　⑤ has been doing

9 다음 문장을 감탄문으로 바르게 바꾼 것을 고르시오.

It is a really nice day!

① What nice day!
② How a nice day!
③ What a nice day is it!
④ How nice day it!
⑤ What a nice day it is!

10 다음 중 우리말을 영어로 옮길 때 빈칸에 알맞은 말로 고르

13 다음 문장을 명령문으로 바꿀 때 빈칸에 알맞은 말을 고르시오.

> You are a good student.
> → _____ a good student.

① Do ② Don't ③ Are
④ Let's ⑤ Be

14 다음 중 빈칸에 알맞은 말을 고르시오.

> We are waiting for the day when the war will end.
> = We are waiting for the day _____ the war will end.

① on where ② on which ③ in which
④ for how ⑤ for which

15 다음 밑줄 친 부분의 쓰임이 나머지와 다른 것을 고르시오.

① Who do you respect most?
② She was a scientist who invented the machine.
③ I met a girl who knew you.
④ This is the man who wants to meet you.
⑤ I mean the girl who is wearing a skirt.

19 다음 중 보기의 의미와 같은 문장을 고르시오.

> If I had much money, I could buy a new car.

① As I don't have much money, I will buy a new car.
② As I have much money, I can buy a new car.
③ As I don't have much money, I can not buy a new car.
④ As I have much money, I can not buy a new car.
⑤ As I didn't have much money, I didn't buy a new car.

20 다음 중 어법상 옳은 문장을 고르시오.

① This is the place where I found the key.
② The house where he lived in was not large.
③ Look at the house which roof is blue.
④ Saturday is the day when comes after Friday.
⑤ We'll never forget the day how we won the game.

5점
21 다음 빈칸에 알맞은 말을 쓰시오.

> A: _____ city is bigger, Seoul or Busan?
> B: Seoul is bigger than Busan.

16 다음 중 빈칸에 which를 쓸 수 있는 것을 고르시오.

① I like girls _____ help other people.
② There were many students _____ study hard.
③ She wants someone _____ is honest.
④ I need a stove _____ has a good design.
⑤ There are some people _____ live in Korea.

17 다음 문장을 직접화법으로 바르게 옮긴 것을 고르시오.

> The doctor asked me if I coughed a lot.

① The doctor asked me, "Do I cough a lot?"
② The doctor said to me, "Do I cough a lot?"
③ The doctor said to me, "Did he cough a lot?"
④ The doctor said to me, "Do you cough a lot?"
⑤ The doctor said to me "If I cough a lot?"

18 다음 두 문장을 한 문장으로 바르게 연결한 것을 고르시오.

> Do you think? + Where does she live?

① Do you think where does she live?
② Do you think where does she live?
③ Do you think where she does live?
④ Where do you think she does live?
⑤ Where do you think she lives?

22 다음 빈칸에 공통으로 들어갈 말을 쓰시오.

- _____ greedy!
- _____ big the animal is!

23 다음 빈칸에 알맞은 관계 대명사를 쓰시오.

> Look at the boys _____ are dancing on the street.

24 다음 우리말과 일치하도록 빈칸에 알맞은 말을 쓰시오.

> 내가 키가 좀 더 크다면 좋을 텐데.
> → I _____ _____ taller.

25 다음 두 문장을 연결할 때 빈칸에 알맞은 말을 쓰시오.

> I don't know. + Can she play the piano?
> → I don't know _____ she can play the piano.

2-2

3점

Let's take a walk, ______________.

① will you ② do we ③ don't you
④ don't we ⑤ shall we

5 3점

______________ kind she is!

① What ② When ③ Where
④ Why ⑤ How

[6-7] 다음 두 문장의 의미가 같도록 빈칸에 알맞은 말을 고르시오.

6

I wish I could celebrate your birthday.
= I am sorry that I __________ celebrate your birthday.

① could ② couldn't ③ can
④ can't ⑤ will

7

A: __________ hours a day do you surf on the Internet?
B: More than 2-3 hours.

① How many ② How much ③ How long
④ How tall ⑤ How deep

- I don't know ________ he isn't here.
- Sam didn't explain the reason ________ he didn't come to the party.

① what ② when ③ how
④ which ⑤ why

11 다음 두 문장을 한 문장으로 바르게 고친 것을 고르시오.
기출

- This is my son.
- His name is Jack.

① This is my son which is Jack.
② This is my son that is his Jack.
③ This is my son who name is Jack.
④ This is my son whose name is Jack.
⑤ This is my son of which name is Jack.

12 다음 중 빈칸에 알맞은 말을 고르시오.
기출

She said to him, "What are you doing?"
→ She asked him what ______________.

① she was doing ② he was doing
③ she is doing ④ he is doing
⑤ you were doing

Grammar Mentor
Joy Plus 4

실전모의고사 **2회**

- 3점: 5문항
- 4점: 15문항
- 5점: 5문항

이름 :

점수 :

[1~5] 다음 중 빈칸에 알맞은 말을 고르시오.

1
3점

If you practiced hard, you _____ the race.

① win   ② will win   ③ would win
④ had won   ⑤ won

2
3점

_____ a wonderful machine it is!

① What   ② How   ③ Who
④ There's   ⑤ Here's

3
3점

This is the hotel _____ she stayed last night.

① what   ② how   ③ who
④ when   ⑤ where

---

8 다음 중 빈칸에 들어갈 말이 바르게 짝지어진 것을 고르시오.
기출

- The watch _____ was stolen has been found.
- Jack is the man _____ Cathy is going to marry.

① who – that   ② which – whose
③ which – whom   ④ whose – whom
⑤ that – which

[9~10] 다음 중 빈칸에 공통으로 들어갈 말을 고르시오.

9

- If I _____ you, I wouldn't do it.
- If she _____ my teacher, she could help me with my math.

① am   ② is   ③ were
④ would be   ⑤ had been

13 다음 중 보기의 우리말을 영어로 바르게 쓴 것을 고르시오.

내 자신을 믿지 않았더라면 나는 성공하지 못했을 것이다.

① If I don't believe in myself, I couldn't succeed.
② If I didn't believe in myself, I couldn't have succeeded.
③ If I hadn't believe in myself, I couldn't succeed.
④ If I hadn't believed in myself, I could have succeeded.
⑤ If I hadn't believed in myself, I couldn't have succeeded.

14 다음 중 밑줄 친 부분이 생략할 수 없는 것을 고르시오.

① I know the man that you like.
② I like the girl that is dancing.
③ This is the book that he bought.
④ It's the same watch that she lost.
⑤ I like the dress that Ann is wearing.

15 다음 중 밑줄 친 부분이 어법상 바르지 않은 것을 고르시오.

① I thought that he can fix the broken door.
② My mom knows that Kevin is my best friend.
③ I believe that she didn't tell a lie.

19 다음 중 대화의 질문으로 알맞은 것을 고르시오.

A: _____?
B: There isn't any water in the tank.

① Is there any waters in the tank?
② Are there any water in the tank?
③ Was there any water in the tank?
④ How much water is there in the tank?
⑤ How many water is there in the tank?

20 다음 감탄문으로 바꾸어 쓴 것 중 바르지 않은 것을 고르시오.

기출
① She is a very nice teacher.
→ What a nice teacher she is!
② He is a very honest boy.
→ What a honest boy he is!
③ This has a very long tail.
→ What a long tail this has!
④ This man is very cheerful.
→ How cheerful this man is!
⑤ The river is very deep.
→ How deep the river is!

21 다음 빈칸에 알맞은 의문사를 쓰시오.

5점
주말 어떻게 지냈니?
_____ was your weekend?

① What wonderful it was!
② How a wonderful night!
③ How a night!
④ What a wonderful night it was!
⑤ Wonderful night what was!

17 다음 밑줄 친 부분 중 어법상 올바른 것을 고르시오.

① Your grandfather is healthy, <u>is he</u>?
② He will come to Korea, <u>will he</u>?
③ They were not cheap, <u>weren't they</u>?
④ John and you are brothers, <u>aren't we</u>?
⑤ The robot dog is smart, <u>isn't it</u>?

18 다음 중 대화가 어색한 것을 고르시오. [기출]

① A: What time do you get up?
   B: I get up at 7 o'clock.
② A: Why are you in a hurry?
   B: I'm late for school.
③ A: Where does she live?
   B: She lives next to my house.
④ A: When did he leave for the station?
   B: He left for the station ten minutes ago.
⑤ A: How did you go to the town?
   B: I visited my uncle there.

23 다음 밑줄 친 부분을 시제에 맞게 바르게 고치시오. [5점]

He said, "I will be busy tomorrow."

↓

24 다음 빈칸에 알맞은 부가의문문을 쓰시오. [5점]

I <u>can't</u> run fast when I was very young.

↓

25 다음 두 문장을 관계대명사를 사용하여 한 문장으로 쓰시오. [5점]

She and he like to ski, _____?

↓

• Tell me the story.
• You heard it from him.

↓

3점

have gone on a picnic.

① was　　② were　　③ has been

④ had been　　⑤ would have been

5

3점

We didn't know that he _____ Japanese.

① study　　② will study　　③ studies

④ studied　　⑤ is going to study

[6~7] 다음 중 대화의 빈칸에 알맞은 말을 고르시오. 기출

6

A: _____ do you go to City Park?

B: About twice a month.

① How long　　② How much　　③ How far

④ How many　　⑤ How often

7

A: What are you doing here.

B: I want to buy a cap.

A: _____ one do you want to buy?

B: That black one

① Who　　② Which　　③ How

④ What　　⑤ Why

---

house.

① had – could buy

② didn't have – couldn't buy

③ have – could buy

④ had had – could have bought

⑤ don't have – can't buy

11 다음 문장이 의미하는 것을 고르시오.

I wish my uncle lived in Seoul.

① My uncle lives in Seoul.

② My uncle lived in Seoul.

③ My uncle doesn't live in Seoul.

④ My uncle didn't live in Seoul.

⑤ My uncle hasn't lived in Seoul.

12 다음 문장을 감탄문으로 알맞게 바꾼 것을 고르시오.

The flowers are very beautiful.

① What beautiful the flowers are!

② How beautiful the flowers are!

③ What beautiful flowers are!

④ How a beautiful flowers they are!

⑤ How beautiful flowers it is!

Grammar Mentor Joy Plus 4

실전모의고사 3회

- 3점: 5문항
- 4점: 15문항
- 5점: 5문항

이름 :

점수 :

[1-5] 다음 중 빈칸에 알맞은 말을 고르시오.

1 3점

_____ touch an electric cord with a wet hand.

① Don't   ② No   ③ Do

④ Must   ⑤ Doesn't

2 3점

This is the cake _____ I bought for my sister.

① who   ② which   ③ how

④ what   ⑤ why

3 3점

I don't believe _____ you told me.

① who   ② which   ③ how

④ what   ⑤ why

8 기출

다음 중 두 문장을 하나로 연결할 때 빈칸에 알맞은 말을 고르시오.

The boy is my brother. He is playing the guitar.
→ The boy _____ playing the piano is my guitar.

① who   ② that are   ③ which is

④ whom was   ⑤ who is

9

다음 중 빈칸에 공통으로 들어갈 말을 고르시오.

- The book _____ is in my bag is not yours.
- I'm proud of my uncle _____ is a teacher.

① which   ② who   ③ that

④ whose   ⑤ whom

10 기출

다음 중 빈칸에 들어갈 말이 바르게 짝지어진 것을 고르시오.

As I don't have much money, I can't buy

다음 중 어법에 맞지 <u>않는</u> 문장을 고르시오.

① How greedy!　　② How a nice car is!

③ What a nice party!　　④ What beautiful roses!

⑤ How big the animal is!

다음 중 대화의 빈칸에 알맞은 말을 고르시오.

A: _____

B: Because it makes me feel good.

① Why do you listen to music?
② When do you want to listen to music?
③ Where do you want to listen to music?
④ How do you want to listen to music?
⑤ How ofter do you listen to music?

다음 중 보기의 문장을 바르게 연결한 것을 고르시오.

기출

• Do you know?
• What did she buy for me?

① Do you know what did she buy for me?
② Do you know what she bought for me?
③ Do you know what did she bought for me?
④ Do you know what she did buy for me?
⑤ Do you know what she does bought for me?

다음 중 빈칸에 알맞지 <u>않은</u> 것을 고르시오.

Do you know _____?

① where Ann is　　② how airplanes fly

③ where I put the key　　④ what does she want

⑤ why she went home

다음 문장을 간접화법으로 바르게 고친 것을 고르시오.

She said to me, "Where are you going?"

① She said to me where are you going.
② She asked me where you are going.
③ She asked me where I was going.
④ She asked me where I am going.
⑤ She told me where I was going.

다음 두 문장의 의미가 같도록 문장을 완성하시오.

5점

Why don't you take a rest for five minutes?

= How _____?

Longman

GRAMMAR
MENTOR
JOY

롱맨
그래머
멘토
조이
시리즈

최신개정판
400만부 돌파
롱맨 JOY
시리즈

Chapter 01. 가정법

Unit 01. 가정법 과거

Warm up

01 finish, finished　　02 taught, teach
03 leave, left　　04 meet, met
05 invite, invited　　06 is, were
07 hurried, hurry　　08 take, took

Start up

❶ 01 knew　　02 were　　03 had
04 were　　05 had　　06 were
07 snowed　　08 rains　　09 will
10 would　　11 won't　　12 would
13 could make　　14 would cook
15 would visit

[해석]

01 그의 전화를 번호를 알고 있다면 그에게 전화할 텐데.
02 내가 너라면 사실을 말할 텐데.
03 나에게 많은 돈이 있다면 나는 멋진 집을 살 텐데.
04 네가 여기 있다면 나는 행복할 텐데.
05 내게 시간이 있다면 나는 책을 더 많이 읽을 텐데.
06 그가 바쁘지 않다면 너와 같이 갈 텐데.
07 눈이 많이 내린다면 우리 형과 나는 눈사람을 만들 수 있을 텐데.
08 비가 오면 우리는 산책하러 가지 않을 거야.
09 네가 식탁을 치우면 내가 설거지를 할 게.
10 찰스가 농구를 좋아하면 그가 우리 클럽에 가입할 텐데.
11 네가 그 지하철을 타면 너는 늦지 않을 거야.
12 그가 내 이메일 주소를 안다면 나에게 이메일을 보낼 텐데.
13 그가 좀 더 친절하다면 많은 친구를 사귈 수 있을 텐데.
14 아빠가 집에 일찍 온다면 아빠가 저녁식사를 요리할 텐데.
15 내가 런던에 간다면 런던아이를 제일 먼저 갈 텐데.

❷ 01 knew　　02 were　　03 won
04 were not　　05 read　　06 asked

07 would visit　　08 had　　09 could watch
10 would, do　　11 could go　　12 would lend
13 would not feel　　14 would fly
15 could win

[해석]

01 내가 좋은 식당을 안다면 너를 데리고 갈 텐데.
02 오늘이 일요일이면 나는 학교에 가지 않을 텐데.
03 그 대회에서 일등을 한다면 너는 무엇을 할래?
04 내가 아프지 않다면 내 친구들과 캠핑을 갈 수 있었을 텐데.
05 Robin이 그 책을 읽으면 그는 문학 시험에 통과할 수 있을 텐데.
06 그가 너에게 그 질문을 하면 너는 뭐라고 얘기하겠니?
07 내가 파리를 여행한다면 나는 루브르 박물관에 갈 텐데.
08 그녀에게 용기가 있다면 그녀는 스스로 결정을 내릴 텐데.
09 내가 스무 살이면 그 영화를 볼 수 있을 텐데.
10 당신이 제 입장이라면 어떻게 하시겠어요?
11 내가 피곤하지 않다면 너와 쇼핑하러 갈 텐데.
12 그녀에게 사진기가 있다면 그녀가 너에게 그것을 빌려줄 텐데.
13 Jamie가 두꺼운 외투를 입고 있다면 춥지 않을 텐데.
14 바람이 분다면 연이 높게 날 텐데.
15 그들이 열심히 연습한다면 그 경기에서 이길 수 있을 텐데.

Check up & Writing

❶ 01 am sick　　02 doesn't rain
03 hurts　　04 doesn't buy it
05 doesn't help the needy
06 can't get good grades
07 felt better　　08 came to see us
09 finished your homework
10 would come to watch the game with me
11 would play in nature more often
12 could drive you home

❷ 01 sold my car, could get
02 would be happy, came
03 used, would not[wouldn't] get

04 were you, would accept
05 were rich, could buy
06 heard the truth, would be surprised
07 were not snowy, would drive to work
08 had a lot of friends, would not[wouldn't]
   feel
09 stayed longer, would cook dinner
10 knew, would travel
11 spoke English, could pass
12 knew Jason, would introduce

Unit 02. 가정법 과거완료

Warm up

01 had left, left
02 came, had come
03 had, had had
04 knew, had known
05 stay, have stayed
06 have bought, buy
07 be, have been
08 have gone, go

Start up

❶ 01 had been
02 had been
03 had spoken
04 had known
05 had taken
06 had believed
07 have been
08 have taken
09 have failed
10 have answered
11 have gone
12 have finished
13 have told
14 have bought
15 have had

[해석]
01 화창했다면 우리는 소풍 갔을 텐데.
02 내가 그녀였다면 Jason을 믿지 않았을 텐데.
03 네가 또렷하게 말했다면 우리는 너의 말을 이해할
   수 있었을 텐데.
04 내가 그 사실을 알았다면 나는 너를 용서했을 텐데.
05 네가 내 충고를 들었다면 더 잘 할 수 있었을 텐데.
06 네가 네 자신을 믿었다면, 너는 성공했을 것이다.
07 기차가 제 시간에 도착했다면 나는 회사에 늦지 않
   았을 텐데.
08 Tim이 너를 좋아하지 않았다면 너에게 점심을 사
   주지 않았을 텐데.

09 Sam이 부정행위를 하지 않았다면 기말 시험에서
   낙제하지 않았을 텐데.
10 내가 전화벨 소리를 들었다면 전화를 받았을 텐데.
11 내가 아프지 않았더라면 네 파티에 갔을 텐데.
12 그에게 시간이 더 있었다면 숙제를 끝마칠 수 있었
   을 텐데.
13 네가 나에게 물어봤더라면 내가 너에게 그에 관해서
   얘기해줬을 텐데.
14 내가 좋은 성적을 받았다면 아빠가 새 컴퓨터를 사
   주셨을 텐데.
15 네가 조심해서 운전했다면 너는 차 사고를 당하지
   않았을 텐데.

❷ 01 had taken
02 had known
03 had heard
04 had been
05 had hurried
06 hadn't told
07 had listened
08 could have played
09 would have caught
10 wouldn't have waken
11 could have taken
12 could have made

[해석]
01 내가 지하철을 탔다면 늦지 않았을 텐데.
02 그가 모든 것을 알았다면 너에게 화를 내지 않았
   을 텐데,
03 엄마가 그 소식을 들었더라면 매우 기뻐했을 텐데.
04 네가 현명했다면 너는 그런 행동을 하지 않았을 텐데.
05 그들이 서둘렀다면 버스를 탈 수 있었을 텐데.
06 내 여동생이 얘기해주지 않았다면 나는 아빠 생신
   을 잊었을 텐데.
07 내가 선생님 말을 주의해서 들었다면 실험을 망치
   지 않았을 텐데.
08 비가 오지 않았더라면 우리는 밖에서 놀 수 있었
   을 텐데.
09 경찰이 더 일찍 도착했다면 도둑을 잡았을 텐데.
10 네가 조용히 했다면 아기는 깨지 않았을 텐데.
11 Beck이 카메라를 가지고 왔다면 멋진 사진을 찍을
   수 있었을 텐데.
12 네가 신선한 채소를 샀다면 샐러드를 만들 수 있었
   을 텐데.

Check up & Writing

❶ 01 didn't rain
02 knew what to do
03 didn't buy the book
04 had been interesting
05 had gone to the doctor
06 had worked hard
07 couldn't go to the movies with you
08 wasn't in trouble
09 failed it
10 could have left on time
11 would have been alive
12 wouldn't have broken into our house

❷ 01 had known, would have called
02 had met Eric, would have liked
03 had had, wouldn't have been lost
04 hadn't scored, couldn't have won
05 had told, wouldn't have gotten[got] angry
06 had sung, would have been more popular
07 had been, wouldn't have been rude
08 had studied hard, could have passed
09 hadn't cried, wouldn't have accepted
10 had been, could have joined
11 hadn't worn, wouldn't have fought
12 hadn't been busy, would have visited

Unit 03. I wish 가정법

Warm up

01 had snowed, snowed 02 had, had had
03 sold, had sold 04 were, had been
05 had taken, took 06 went, had gone
07 had been, were

Start up

❶ 01 had 02 could go 03 hadn't hurt
04 had worked 05 had taken
06 liked 07 hadn't eaten 08 had
09 knew 10 had visited 11 were
12 could ski 13 had gone
14 had followed 15 had watched

[해석]
01 지금 나를 도와줄 누군가가 있으면 좋을 텐데.
02 내가 너와 함께 갈 수 있으면 좋을 텐데.
03 내가 어젯밤에 그녀의 감정을 상하게 하지 않았다면 좋을 텐데.
04 내가 젊었을 때 일을 열심히 했다면 좋을 텐데.
05 작년에 발레 수업을 받았으면 좋았을 텐데.
06 Jim이 하이킹을 좋아하면 좋겠지만 그는 좋아하지 않는다.
07 나 지금 배가 아파. 내가 그렇게 많이 먹지 않았으면 좋았을 텐데.
08 비가 많이 와. 지금 나에게 우산이 있으면 좋을 텐데.
09 우리 길을 잃은 것 같아. 우리가 어디 있는지 알면 좋을 텐데.
10 나 지금 출장 중이야. 네가 어제 나를 방문했었다면 좋을 텐데.
11 나는 농구 팀에 지원하기엔 너무 키가 작아. 내가 키가 더 크다면 좋을 텐데.
12 내 모든 친구가 스키를 잘 타서 나는 그들이 부러워. 나는 스키를 잘 탈 수 있으면 좋을 텐데.
13 Emma와 Rachel이 어제 몰에서 영화배우를 봤어. 나도 거기에 갔으면 좋을 텐데.
14 이 닭고기 수프가 정말 맛이 없어. 네가 요리할 때 요리법을 따랐으면 좋을 텐데.
15 그 영화 정말 재미있어. 네가 어젯밤 우리와 같이 그 영화를 봤으면 좋을 텐데.

❷ 01 liked 02 earned
03 spoke 04 were
05 could dance 06 had thought
07 had
08 hadn't[had not] told 09 knew
10 had finished
11 hadn't[had not] broken down
12 had enjoyed 13 had listened
14 hadn't[had not] had

Check up & Writing

❶ 01 work late
02 likes him
03 don't wear warmer clothes
04 changed her mind

05 don't call me often
06 don't have more free time
07 didn't hear the news earlier
08 forgot my mom's birthday
09 spent all of my pocket money
10 didn't catch a big fish in the lake
11 asked that rude question to her
12 are not[aren't] here with me now

[해석]
01 내가 일을 늦게까지 하지 않으면 좋을 텐데.
02 그녀가 그를 좋아하지 않으면 좋을 텐데.
03 내가 좀 더 따뜻한 옷을 입으면 좋을 텐데.
04 그녀가 마음을 바꾸지 않았다면 좋을 텐데.
05 네가 자주 내게 전화하면 좋을 텐데.
06 내가 좀 더 자유시간이 많으면 좋을 텐데.
07 내가 그 소식을 좀더 빨리 들었다면 좋을 텐데.
08 엄마 생일을 잊지 않았다면 좋을 텐데.
09 내 용돈을 모두 사용하지 않았다면 좋을 텐데.
10 내가 호수에서 큰 물고기를 잡았다면 좋을 텐데.
11 내가 그녀에게 그 무례한 질문을 하지 않았다면 좋을 텐데.
12 내 부모님이 지금 이곳에 나와 함께 있으면 좋을 텐데.

❷ 01 it were not hot
02 there were a lot of parks
03 I had kept the promise
04 I had bought the house
05 the movie were not[weren't] boring
06 I could do something
07 I had a brother or a sister
08 I hadn't left my smartphone
09 my parents had been proud
10 Susan hadn't given up her dream
11 She had lent me some money
12 my mother bought me a computer

Level up

❶ 01 had
02 could, have, slept
03 would, travel
04 would, not, talk
05 had, not, told
06 had, not, asked
07 could, do
08 could, enjoy
09 were
10 had, won
11 would, not, have, happened

❷ 01 I wish Brian were my boyfriend.
02 If he married her, he would be very happy.
03 I wish I had lived in Paris when I was young.
04 If I were young, I would work hard.
05 If I had a car, I would drive you home.
06 If I spoke English fluently, I could get the job.
07 I wish I hadn't[had not] lost my smartphone yesterday.
08 If I made more mistakes, Dad would be angry.
09 If I had had a ladder, I could have fixed the roof.
10 If it were not so late, I could go grocery shopping.
11 I miss my friend, Carrie. I wish she came to see me now.
12 If the weather had been better, we would/could have gone hiking.

[해석]
01 Brian이 내 남자친구라면 좋을 텐데.
02 그가 그녀와 결혼한다면 그는 매우 행복할 텐데.
03 내가 어렸을 때 파리에 살았다면 좋을 텐데.
04 내가 젊으면 열심히 일 할 텐데.
05 네가 자동차가 있으면 너를 집에 데려다 줄 텐데.
06 내가 영어를 유창하게 한다면 그 직업을 구할 수 있을 텐데.
07 내가 어제 스마트폰을 잃어버리지 않았다면 좋을 텐데.
08 내가 실수를 더하면 아버지가 화를 낼 텐데.
09 내가 사다리가 있었다면 지붕을 고쳤을 텐데.
10 늦지 않았으면 식료품점에 갈 텐데.
11 내 친구 Carrie가 보고 싶다. 그녀가 지금 나를 보러 오면 좋을 텐데.
12 날씨가 좋았다면 우리는 하이킹을 했을 텐데.

❸ 01 I had eaten breakfast
02 I would refuse the offer
03 she would have won the race
04 he got up early
05 could take a break now

06 he had apologized to me

07 I were a superhero

08 you hadn't[had not] drunk the milk

09 he had been more careful

10 they had spent more time with me

❹ 01 had money, could buy the cake

02 wish my grandmother were alive

03 wish my brother were more polite

04 wish I hadn't stayed up all night

05 wish I had gone on a vacation

06 hadn't helped me, couldn't have succeeded

07 would you do, found

08 were taller, could play

09 had starred, would have been famous

10 it were sunny, would walk

11 had had more time, would[could] have completed

12 had studied hard, could have gotten/got better grades

Actual Test

01 ⑤	02 ③	03 ②	04 ④	05 ④
06 ⑤	07 ②	08 ④	09 ⑤	10 ③
11 ①	12 ②	13 ②	14 ④	

15 had asked   16 will have

17 I had helped you

18 would introduce him

19 hadn't been sick, wouldn't have stayed

20 wish I had bought a new car

[해석 및 해설]

01 내가 너라면 그에게 진실을 말할 텐데.

  *if절의 동사가 과거이다.

02 만약 내가 집에 일찍 왔다면 삼촌을 만날 수 있었을 텐데.

03 나는 기말고사 준비로 무척 바쁘다. 나는 쉴 수 있으면 좋을 텐데.

04 내가 어렸을 때 수영하는 법을 배웠더라면 좋았을 텐데.

05 A: 지갑을 집에 두고 왔어. 돈을 좀 빌려 줄 수 있니?

  B: 내가 돈이 있으면 네게 좀 빌려 줄 텐데.

  *가정법 과거의 문장이 되어야 하므로 had와 would lend가 들어가야 한다.

06 A: 어젯밤 파티에 왜 오지 않았니?

B: 동생을 돌봐야했어. 부모님이 집에 일찍 계셨으면 갈 수 있었을 텐데.

  *과거의 일에 대한 소망을 나타내므로 가정법 과거 완료 문장이 와야 한다.

08 *과거의 사실에 반대되는 상황·사실을 가정하고 있다.

09 내 전화가 고장 나서 어젯밤 너에게 전화할 수 없었다.

10 그녀가 그 소문을 들어서 유감이다.

11 ① 그가 영어를 하면 많은 외국친구를 만들 텐데.

  ② 우리가 최선을 다했다면 그 경기를 이겼을 텐데.

  ③ 나의 조부모님들이 나와 함께 살면 좋을 텐데.

  ④ 내가 그 바보 같은 실수를 하지 않았다면 좋을 텐데.

  ⑤ 내가 자동차가 있으면 공항으로 너를 데리러 갈 수 있을 텐데.

12 ① 그가 더 건강하면 좋을 텐데.

  ② 내가 어제 카메라를 잃어버리지 않았다면 좋을 텐데.

  ③ 비가 오지 않으면 소풍을 갈 텐데.

  ④ 내가 나의 상황이었다면 너는 무엇을 말했을 것 같니?

  ⑤ 깨진 유리 위를 걸었다면 너는 다쳤을 것이다.

13 *① is → were ③ will → would ④ called → had called ⑤ finished → had finished

14 ① A: Jeniffer 생일 아니?

  B: 알면 네게 알려줄 텐데.

  ② A: 우리는 지난주 눈 축제에서 좋은 시간을 보냈어.

  B: 정말? 나도 너와 함께 했으면 좋을 텐데.

  ③ A: Sam과 Tom은 자전거 타러 갈 거야. 너도 갈래?

  B: 내 자전거는 고장 났어. 새 자전거가 있으면 좋을 텐데.

  ④ A: 나는 운전면허시험에 또 떨어졌어.

  B: 유감이구나. 열심히 연습했다면 합격 할 수 있었을 텐데.

  ⑤ A: 최근에 Jane 봤니?

  B: 그래. 네가 어젯밤 파티에 왔다면 그녀를 볼 수 있었을 텐데.

15 만약 그가 나에게 저 질문을 했더라면 나는 무척 당황했을 텐데.

16 만약 네가 나에게 음료를 제공한다면 나는 커피를 마시겠다. *조건의 if

19 나는 아파서 하루 종일 침대에 있었다.

20 나는 새 차를 사지 않아서 유감이다.

Chapter 02. 관계사 I

Unit 01. 관계대명사

Warm up

01 which	02 which	03 who
04 which	05 lives	06 changed
07 who	08 who	09 invented
10 who	11 which	12 is
13 who	14 which	15 who

[해석 및 해설]

01 이곳은 유명한 그림이 많이 있는 미술관이다.
*선행사가 사물(the museum)이므로 which가 어울린다.

02 그녀는 장미가 많은 정원을 가지고 있다.
*선행사가 사물(a garden)이므로 which가 어울린다.

03 나는 매우 강한 남자를 만났다.

04 내 삼촌은 춤을 출 수 있는 고양이가 있다.
*선행사가 사물(a cat)이므로 which가 어울린다.

05 그는 옆집에 사는 소년이다.
*선행사가 3인칭 단수(the boy)이므로 lives가 와야 한다.

06 그녀는 세상을 바꾼 위대한 과학자들 중 한 명이다.

07 그는 모든 한국인에게 사랑받는 가수이다.
*선행사가 the singer이므로 who가 어울린다.

08 Cathy하고 얘기하고 있는 소년은 나의 친구다.

09 Graham Bell은 전화를 발명한 과학자이다.
*과거에 일어난 일이므로 invented가 와야 한다.

10 나는 너를 아는 소녀를 만났다.
*선행사가 a girl이므로 who가 어울린다.

11 이 개가 어제 나에게 짖은 개다.
*선행사가 사물(a dog)이므로 which가 어울린다.

12 나는 빨간색 셔츠를 입고 있는 소녀를 안다.
*선행사가 3인칭 단수(the girl)이므로 is가 와야 한다.

13 그는 종종 가난한 어린들을 돕는 의사이다.

14 그녀는 매우 낡은 컴퓨터가 있다.
*선행사가 사물(a computer)이므로 which가 어울린다.

15 나는 키가 매우 큰 어린이들을 만났다.
*선행사가 some children이므로 who가 어울린다.

Start up

❶
01 who	02 who	03 which
04 which	05 who	06 who
07 which	08 which	09 which
10 who	11 who	12 who

❷
01 who	02 which	03 who
04 which	05 which	06 which
07 who	08 who	09 which
10 which	11 which	12 who

Check up & Writing

❶
01 who	02 works / worked	03 who
04 was	05 which	06 which
07 who	08 who	09 gave
10 study	11 who	12 who
13 has	14 who	15 which

[해설]

01 *선행사가 사람(swimmer)이므로 who가 와야 한다.

02 *선행사 a lady가 3인칭 단수이므로 works가 와야 한다.

03 *선행사가 사람이므로 who가 와야 한다.

04 *선행사(the cake)가 단수이므로 was가 와야 한다.

05 *선행사가 사물(a room)이므로 which가 와야 한다.

06 *선행사가 사물(the cat)이므로 which가 와야 한다.

07 *선행사가 사람이므로 who가 와야 한다.

08 *선행사가 사람이므로 who가 와야 한다.

09 *시제가 과거(this morning)이므로 gave가 되어야 한다.

10 *선행사 students가 복수이므로 study가 와야 한다.

11 *선행사가 사람이므로 who가 와야 한다.

12 *선행사가 사람이므로 who가 와야 한다.

13 *선행사 a bike가 3인칭 단수이므로 has가 와야 한다.

14 *선행사가 사람이므로 who가 와야 한다.

15 *선행사가 사물(the car)이므로 which가 와야 한다.

❷ 01 who are interested in biology
02 which is located in the center of
03 who is loved by teenagers
04 which is bigger than mine
05 who made this food
06 which is hung on the wall
07 who is running on the ground
08 which goes to the airport
09 which can understand my words
10 who sings well
11 which are on the table
12 which was very hot

Unit 02. 관계대명사 – 목적격, 소유격

Warm up

01 whose	02 whose	03 who
04 whose	05 whose	06 which
07 which	08 whose	09 whom
10 whom	11 who	12 of which
13 whose	14 whose	15 which

[해석 및 해설]

01 나는 피아노 치는 것을 취미로 가진 남동생이 있다.
02 그녀는 색상이 하얀 스마트폰을 가지고 있다.
   *소유격 대명사 whose 다음에 명사가 온다.
03 그녀는 내가 매일 만나는 소녀이다.
   *meet의 목적어가 필요하므로 who(m)이 와야 한다.
04 너는 이름이 Andrew인 소년을 알고 있니?
05 정상이 눈으로 덮인 산을 보아라.
   *소유격 대명사 다음에 명사가 온다.
06 내가 어젯밤에 본 영화는 지루했다.
   *saw의 목적어가 필요하므로 which가 와야 한다. 선행사가 the movie이다.
07 이것들이 그녀가 사기를 원하는 신발이다. buy의 목적어가 필요하므로 which가 와야 한다. 선행사가 the shoes이다.
08 그는 유리창들이 깨진 문을 조심스럽게 열었다.
09 그녀는 내 동생이 좋아하는 선생님이다.
   *likes의 목적어가 필요하므로 whom이 와야 한다. 선행사가 the teacher이다.
10 내가 지난 밤에 본 남자는 Johnson 씨 이다.
   *saw의 목적어가 필요하므로 whom이 와야 한다. 선

행사가 the man이다.
11 내가 만나고 싶은 소녀는 여기에 없다.
12 그는 이름이 Bill인 개를 가지고 있다.
   *of which+the+명사
13 부모님이 돌아가신 아이를 고아라고 부른다.
   *소유격 대명사 whose 다음에 명사가 온다.
14 나는 책 표지가 노란색인 책을 발견했다.
   *소유격 대명사 whose 다음에 명사가 온다.
15 그녀는 그가 추천한 책을 읽었다.
   *recommended의 목적어가 필요하므로 which가 와야 한다. 선행사가 the book이다.

Start up

❶
01 whose	02 which	03 whose
04 whose	05 who(m)	06 which
07 whose	08 which	09 who(m)
10 whose[of which the]	11 which	
12 whose		

❷
01 whose	02 which	03 whose
04 whose	05 which	
06 whose(of which the)		07 which
08 whose	09 whose	10 who(m)
11 who(m)	12 whose	

Check up & Writing

❶
01 whose	02 who(m)	03 which
04 which	05 whose	06 whose
07 who(m)	08 who(m)	09 which
10 whose	11 of which	12 whose
13 who(m)	14 which	15 which

[해설]

01 그녀는 좋아하는 과목이 음악인 그 소녀이다.
   *소유격 대명사 whose 바로 다음에는 명사가 온다.
02 그는 엄마가 가장 좋아하는 가수 이다.
   *선행사가 a singer이고 동사 likes의 목적어가 필요하므로 who(m)가 온다.
03 이것이 내가 지난달에 수리한 자동차이다.
   *선행사가 the car이고 동사 fixed의 목적어가 필요하므로 which가 온다.
04 그녀가 어제 산 사전은 조금 비쌌다.
   *선행사가 the dictionary이고 동사 bought의 목

05 나는 택시 운전사가 직업인 친구들이 몇 명 있다.
*소유격 대명사 whose 바로 다음에는 명사가 온다.

06 나는 아버지가 음악가인 소녀를 만났다.
*선행사는 the girl이며, 소유격 대명사 whose 바로 다음에는 명사가 온다.

07 나는 네가 지난번에 언급한 남자를 알고 있다.
*선행사가 the man이고 동사 mentioned의 목적어가 필요하므로 who(m)가 온다.

08 그는 내가 신뢰할 수 있는 친구이다.
*선행사가 my friend이고 동사 trust의 목적어가 필요하므로 who(m)가 온다.

09 우리가 산 복사기는 수리가 필요하다.
*선행사가 the copy machine이고 동사 bought의 목적어가 필요하므로 which가 온다.

10 아내가 병원에 입원 중인 그 남자는 일을 구하고 있다.

11 Jack은 색상이 하얀 접시를 구매했다.
'of which+the 명사'가 되어야 한다.

12 Kevin은 아들이 두통으로 고생하는 남자를 알고 있다.

13 그녀가 오늘 만난 남자는 매우 잘생겼다.
동사 met의 목적어가 필요하므로 who(m)가 온다.

14 그는 누구도 열수 없었던 문을 열었다.

15 엄마는 내가 파티에 필요한 과일들을 사고 있다.
*선행사가 fruits이다.

❷ 01 whose roof is covered with snow
02 whose hobby is dancing
03 which I bought last month
04 who(m) Jack introduced
05 whose house is near the beach
06 whose hair is blond
07 whose[of which the] smell is fantastic
08 which I left last night
09 whose[of which the] tail is long
10 which he has just told me
11 who(m) I met at the market
12 who(m) we found in the cave

Unit 03. 관계대명사 that, what

Warm up

01 what	02 that	03 that
04 that	05 What	06 that
07 what	08 that	09 what
10 that	11 What	12 that
13 what	14 whose	15 that

[해석 및 해설]

01 그것이 바로 내가 말하려는 것이다.
*선행사가 없으므로 관계대명사 what이 와야 한다.

02 너는 네가 원하는 것을 모두 살 수 있다.
*선행사에 something, anything 등이 있으면 관계대명사 that이 온다.

03 John은 내가 믿을 수 있는 유일한 사람이다.
*선행사에 the only가 있으면 관계대명사 that이 온다.

04 나는 너에게 내가 아는 것을 모두 말할 것이다.

05 그가 말한 것은 사실이 아니다.
*선행사가 없으므로 관계대명사 what이 와야 한다.

06 그녀는 일본어를 할 수 있는 소녀이다.
*who 대신 that이 올 수 있다.

07 네가 저녁식사로 원하는 것을 선택해라.
*선행사가 없으므로 관계대명사 what이 와야 한다.

08 그는 내가 아는 유일한 야구 선수이다.
*선행사에 the only가 있으면 관계대명사 that이 온다.

09 이것이 내가 사기를 원했던 거니?

10 저기 뛰고 있는 소년과 그의 개를 봐라.
*선행사가 「사람+동물」일 때 관계대명사 that이 온다.

11 네가 해야 할 것은 열심히 공부하는 것이다.

12 그녀는 이곳에 첫 번째 온 학생이다.
*선행사에 the first, the second 등의 서수가 올 때 관계대명사 that이 온다.

13 그는 그가 계획한 것을 포기해야 할 것이다.

14 너는 아버지가 유명한 가수인 Jim을 알고 있니?

15 그녀는 내가 지하철에서 본 여성이다.
*who 대신 that이 올 수 있다.

Start up

❶ 01 that	02 that	03 what
04 that	05 what	06 What
07 that	08 what	09 that
10 that	11 that	12 that
13 what	14 that	15 what

[해석]

01 그녀는 내가 만난 가장 정직한 소녀이다.

02 그녀가 보고 있던 사진은 매우 아름다웠다.

03 그가 말한 것을 믿지 마라.

　*선행사가 없으므로 what이 온다.

04 그는 와인으로 유명한 작은 마을에 산다.

05 그는 내가 정말로 원했던 것을 내게 줬다.

06 나를 행복하게 하는 것은 아이들의 미소이다.

07 그녀는 내가 어제 파티에서 만났던 여자이다.

08 Sara는 내가 요리한 것을 먹지 않았다.

　*선행사가 없으므로 what이 온다.

09 그녀는 내가 진심으로 사랑한 첫 번째 여성이었다.

10 이것은 내가 지난주에 그녀에게 준 책이다.

11 내가 너에게 묻고 싶은 것이 있다.

12 그는 그 아이를 구할 수 있는 유일한 사람이다.

13 나는 그가 나에게 한 말을 이해할 수 없다.

14 프랑스에서 오신 선생님은 매우 잘생겼다.

15 Wilson은 내게 무엇을 해야 하는지 말했다.

　*선행사가 없으므로 what이 온다.

❷ 01 What　　02 that　　03 what
04 that　　05 what　　06 that
07 that　　08 what　　09 that
10 that　　11 that　　12 that
13 what　　14 that　　15 what

[해석]

01 그녀가 내게 말한 것은 매우 지루했다.

　*선행사가 없으므로 what이 온다.

02 이것은 우리가 원하는 것이 아니다.

03 John은 네가 한 것에 만족할 것이다.

04 이해 못한 것이 있니?

05 그들은 내가 내 동생을 위해 만든 것을 먹었다.

06 그녀는 내가 본 가장 아름다운 소녀이다.

07 그녀는 그가 사준 반지를 잃어버렸다.

08 그와 나는 그녀가 제안한 것을 받아들이기로 결심했다.

09 나는 그가 지난주에 보낸 편지를 막 받았다.

10 이것들은 한국에서 만든 스마트폰들이다.

11 분실물 센터는 내가 어제 잃어버린 가방을 보관하고 있다.

12 그 쓰나미는 해변가의 사람들과 건물들을 휩쓸어버렸다.

13 저것은 그녀가 오랫동안 원했던 것이다.

　*선행사가 없으므로 what이 온다.

14 그는 에베레스트산에 오른 첫 번째 사람이다.

15 그녀에게 내가 네게 말한 것을 말하지 마라.

　*선행사가 없으므로 what이 온다.

Check up & Writing

❶ 01 what　　　　02 that
03 that/which　　04 that/who(m)
05 that　　　　06 What
07 that　　　　08 that
09 what　　　　10 which/that
11 which/that　　12 that
13 that　　　　14 that
15 which/that

[해석]

01 이것은 내 아내가 구매하기를 원하는 것이다.

02 그녀는 내가 의지할 수 있는 유일한 친구다.

03 이것이 그녀가 찾고 있는 시계이다.

04 나와 얘기한 여성은 매우 친절했다.

05 책상 위에 있는 것은 아무거나 가질 수 있다.

06 내가 정말 원하는 것은 직업을 갖는 것이다.

07 그녀는 내가 만난 여성 중 가장 부유하다.

08 침대 위에 있는 소녀와 그녀의 인형을 보아라.

09 샤워는 그가 저녁식사 후 하는 것이다.

10 그는 나에게 사실 같은 이야기를 했다.

11 내가 사기를 원하는 책이 다 팔렸다.

12 그것은 내가 보아온 경기 중 가장 흥미로운 경기이다.

13 닐 암스트롱은 달을 걸은 최초의 남자다.

14 그는 너를 행복하게 할 뭔가를 네게 말할 것이다.

15 그들은 그의 어머니가 그들을 위해 만든 음식을 좋아했다.

❷ 01 what she is saying

02 what you want for your birthday

03 who[that] could cure her daughter

04 What I really need

05 what she does

06 whose roof is red

07 that flows through this area

08 that[which] were hard to answer

09 that[which] happened last night

10 what she knew about the project

11 what he did last night

12 that used the cellular phone

Level Up

❶
01 who	02 what	03 that
04 which	05 who	06 who
07 which	08 what	09 that
10 what	11 who	12 what
13 that	14 What	15 which

[해설]

01 *선행사가 사람이고, 관계대명사 뒤에 동사가 왔으므로 주격 관계대명사 who가 필요하다.

02 *관계대명사 what이 이끄는 절은 주어, 목적어, 보어 역할을 합니다.

03 *선행사에 최상급이 왔으므로 관계대명사 that이 필요하다.

04 *선행사가 사물이므로 관계대명사 which가 필요하다.

05 *선행사가 사람이고 관계대명사 다음 동사가 왔으므로 who가 필요하다.

06 *선행사가 사람이고 관계대명사 다음 동사가 왔으므로 who가 필요하다.

07 *선행사가 동물이고 관계대명사 다음 동사가 왔으므로 which가 필요하다.

08 *관계대명사 what이 이끄는 절은 주어, 목적어, 보어 역할을 합니다.

09 *선행사가 everything이므로 that이 와야 한다.

10 *what은 선행사가 필요 없는 관계대명사이다.

11 *선행사가 사람이고 관계대명사 다음 동사가 왔으므로 who가 필요하다.

12 *what은 선행사가 필요 없는 관계대명사이다.

13 *관계대명사 that은 who, whom, which 대신 사용할 수 있다.

14 *what은 선행사가 필요 없는 관계대명사이다.

15 *선행사가 the advice이고 목적어 역할을 하는 which가 필요하다.

❷ 01 너는 호주에서 사는 동물들을 알고 있니?

02 그녀가 어제 잃어버린 가방은 비싸지 않다.

03 내가 생각하는 것과 그녀가 생각하는 것이 다르다.

04 Jane은 빨간색 치마를 샀다.

05 우리가 TV로 봤던 야구경기가 재미있었다.

06 캐나다는 내년에 내가 방문하고 싶은 나라이다.

07 Susan은 영어로 쓰인 책을 읽고 있다.

08 너는 이름이 Jackson인 소년을 아니?

09 체육관에 온 첫 번째 학생은 Mike이다.

10 이것이 우리가 가지고 있는 유일한 물이다.

11 나는 그녀에게 내가 중국에서 본 것을 말할 것이다.

12 그가 내 동생에게 영어를 가르치는 선생님이다.

❸
01 which[that] I	02 who[that] is
03 who[that] lives	04 who[that] is
05 who[that] fell	06 whose wife
07 which[that] had	
08 which[that] my mother	
09 who[that] broke	10 whose name
11 which[that] is	12 what he

[해석]

01 나는 어제 잃어버린 책을 찾았다.

02 Cathy하고 얘기하는 남자는 내 아버지이다.

03 그 뉴욕에 사는 의사는 매우 바쁘다.

04 바이올린을 연주하고 있는 소녀는 내 동생이다.

05 그와 사랑에 빠진 여자는 작가였다.

06 옛날에 아내가 아픈 나무꾼이 있었습니다.

07 나는 내비게이션이 없는 자동차를 샀다.

08 나는 엄마가 두고 간 반지를 끼고 있다.

09 창문을 깨트린 소년은 도망갔다.

10 그녀는 이름이 Black인 개가 있다.

11 나는 봄에 매우 아름다운 제주도를 방문하고 싶다.

12 이것은 그가 지난주에 산 것이다.

❹
01 who(m)[that]	02 that
03 which[that]	04 which[that]
05 which[that]	06 whose
07 who(m)[that]	08 what
09 what	10 that
11 which[that]	12 What
13 whose	14 which[that]
15 that	

[해설]

01 *선행사가 사람이고 관계대명사 다음 「주어+동사」가 왔으므로 목적격 관계대명사 who(m)[that]가 필요하다.

02 *선행사가 최상급이므로 that이 필요하다.

03 *선행사가 사물이고 관계대명사 다음 「주어+동사」가 왔으므로 which[that]가 필요하다.

04 *선행사가 사물이고 관계대명사 다음 「주어+동사」가 왔으므로 which[that]가 필요하다.

05 *선행사가 사물이고 관계대명사 다음 「주어+동사」가 왔으므로 which[that]가 필요하다.

06 *관계대명사 다음 명사가 왔으므로 소유격 관계대명사가 필요하다.

07 *선행사가 사람이고 관계대명사 다음 「주어+동사」가 왔으므로 who(m)[that]가 필요하다.

08 *선행사가 없으므로 what이 와야 한다.

09 *선행사가 없으므로 what이 와야 한다.

10 *선행사에 the only가 이므로 that이 와야 한다.

11 *목적격 관계대명사 which[that]가 필요하다.

12 *선행사가 없으므로 what이 와야 한다.

13 *of which 다음에는 정관사 the가 필요하다.

14 *선행사가 사물(the books)이고 관계대명사 다음 동사가 왔으므로 which[that]가 필요하다.

15 *선행사가 anything이므로 that이 와야 한다.

Actual Test

01 ⑤	02 ③	03 ②	04 ①	05 ③
06 ④	07 ④	08 ②	09 ①	10 ③
11 ⑤	12 ①	13 ①	14 ③	15 ②

16 1) that[who] 2) that

17 These are the gifts that[which] I got from him.

18 This is the boy who[that] showed me the way to the park.

19 The building whose[of which the] roof is red is my office.

20 whose[of which the]

[해석 및 해설]

01 우리는 그가 부르는 노래를 듣는 것을 좋아한다.
*선행사가 the song이고 목적격 관계대명사가 필요하므로 that이 와야한다.

02 이것은 그녀가 원하는 것이 아니다.
*선행사가 없으므로 what이 온다.

03 그는 폭풍으로 자동차가 손상된 남자를 알았다.
*소유격 관계대명사 다음에 명사가 온다.

04 내가 믿을 수 있는 유일한 사람이 Jane이다.
*선행사에 the only가 있으므로 that이 필요하다.

05 책상 위에 있는 컴퓨터는 내 것이다.

내가 너를 도울 수 있는 유일한 사람이다.

06 이 소녀가 Linda라는 이름을 가진 소녀.
타이어가 터진 저 자동차를 보아라.
*소유격 관계대명사 다음에 명사가 온다.

07 *선행사(the cookies)가 복수이므로 are가 온다.

08 *선행사가 something이므로 that이 필요하다.
*선행사가 사람이고 관계대명사 다음 동사가 오므로 주격 관계대명사 who가 온다.

09 *①은 의문사 나머지는 관계대명사이다.

10 *목적격 관계대명사가 필요하다.

12 *관계대명사 that은 주격, 목적격을 대신해서 사용할 수 있다.

13 *주어가 복수 The men이므로 was 대신 were가 와야 한다.

14 *that of 대신 of which가 와야 한다.

15 ① who → that[which]
③ do - does *선행사가 3인칭 단수이므로 does가 와야 한다.
④ what → that[which]
⑤ whom → who[that]

16 1) 도서관에서 일하는 그 남자는 폴란드에서 왔다.
2) Jackson은 그가 가진 모든 것을 내게 줬다.
*선행사가 everything이므로 that이 필요하다.

17 이것들은 내가 그에게 받은 선물들이다.
*목적격 관계대명사가 필요하다.

18 이 소년이 나에게 공원 가는 길을 알려준 소년이다.
*주격 관계대명사가 필요하다.

19 *소유격 관계대명사가 필요하다.
지붕이 빨간 건물이 내 사무실이다.

Chapter 03. 관계사 II

Unit 01. 관계대명사 생략과 계속적 용법

Warm up

01 O	02 O	03 X	04 O	05 O
06 O	07 O	08 O	09 X	10 X
11 O	12 X	13 O	14 X	15 X

[해석 및 해설]

01 나 네가 나한테 준 우산을 잃어버렸다.

02 냉장고에 있던 피자 네가 먹었니?

03 난 뉴욕에 사는 친구가 한 명 있다.

04 나는 무대 위에서 춤을 추는 소녀를 사랑한다.

05 이것이 그녀가 구독하기 원하는 잡지이다.
  *that은 목적격 관계대명사로 생략할 수 있다.

06 이것이 남편이 결혼기념일 선물로 나에게 준 반지이다.

07 Sam한테 받은 향수 사용했니?

08 안경을 낀 여성이 우리 이모이시다.

09 나는 아들이 배우인 남자를 만났다.
  *소유격 관계대명사는 생략할 수 없다.

10 그녀는 배구를 하고 있는데 배구는 그녀가 좋아하는 운동이다. *계속적 용법의 관계대명사는 생략할 수 없다.

11 로비에 있는 자동판매기가 지금 수리되었다.

12 Ben은 냉장고를 만드는 회사에 다닌다.
  *주격 관계대명사는 생략할 수 없다.

13 이 소년이 내가 기차에서 본 소년이다.

14 Tony는 털이 긴 고양이를 가지고 있다.
  *소유격 관계대명사는 생략할 수 없다.

15 파리에 있는 에펠 타워가 유럽에서 제일 높은 타워이다.
  *계속적 용법의 관계대명사는 생략할 수 없다.

Start up

❶ 01 Do you know the girl under the tree?

02 Jina likes that tall guy dancing on the stage.

03 You can eat anything you want.

04 Sara is the smartest student I've ever taught.

05 This is the machine James is looking for.

06 Do you know the man talking to Susan?

07 My mom likes the cookies I make.

08 Look at the boy and his dog swimming in the river.

09 Bobby spent all the money he had.

10 This is the bike my brother wants to buy.

11 My son took the coins I put on the table.

12 The man delivering pizza is my cousin.

[해설]

01 *「관계대명사+be동사」는 생략가능하다.

03 *목적격 관계대명사는 생략할 수 있다.

04 *목적격 관계대명사는 생략할 수 있다.

05 *목적격 관계대명사는 생략할 수 있다.

06 *「관계대명사+be동사」는 생략가능하다.

07 *목적격관계대명사는 생략할 수 있다.

08 *「관계대명사+be동사」는 생략가능하다.

10 *목적격 관계대명사는 생략할 수 있다.

11 *목적격 관계대명사는 생략할 수 있다.

12 *「관계대명사+be동사」는 생략가능하다.

❷ 01 The man drinking coffee is my father.

02 I will do anything I can do for you.

03 This is the most interesting novel I have ever read.

04 There is nothing you can do.

05 She found the book I lost yesterday.

06 The dress she is wearing looks great on her.

07 The man you invited to the party is my friend.

08 He is living in the house overlooking the river.

09 The picture drawn by Samuel was beautiful.

10 The pizza I ordered two hours ago is not delivered yet.

11 The shirt he bought needs to be washed.

12 She wants to buy a bag made in France.

[해석]

01 커피를 마시고 있는 사람은 내 아버지이다.

02 나는 너를 위해 할 수 있는 것은 무엇이든 할 것이다.

03 이것은 내가 읽은 가장 흥미있는 소설이다.

04 네가 할 수 있는 것은 아무것도 없다.

05 그녀는 어제 내가 잃어버린 책을 발견했다.

06 그녀가 입고 있는 드레스는 그녀에게 잘 어울린다.

07 네가 파티에 초대한 그 사람은 내 친구다.

08 그는 강이 내려다보이는 집에 살고 있다.

09 Samuel이 그린 그림은 매우 아름답다.

10 두 시간 전에 주문한 피자가 아직 배달되지 않았다.

11 그가 구입한 셔츠는 세탁이 필요하다.

12 그녀는 프랑스에서 만들어진 가방을 구입하기를 원한다.

Check up & Writing

❶ 01 나는 내가 가졌던 모든 것을 그녀에게 줬다.

02 1879년에 태어난 Albert Einstein은 가장 위대한 과학자 중 한 사람이다.

03 나는 Sam을 만났는데, 그는 나의 직장 동료이다.

04 그녀는 딸이 둘 있는데, 둘 다 간호사가 되었다.

05 그녀가 운반하고 있는 짐은 매우 무겁다.

06 스페인에서 어떤 언어가 사용되니?

07 내 선생님은 캐나다에서 왔는데, 곧 영어를 가르칠 것이다.

08 너는 Susan이 쓴 편지를 읽었니?

09 이것이 내 아버지가 지난 달에 산 자동차이다.

10 Jeff는 내가 본 소년 중 가장 강인한 소년이다.

11 손을 들고 있는 저 소녀는 영어를 배우고 있다.

12 과학은 그들이 가장 좋아하는 과목이다.

❷ 01 the shirt she bought

02 the man standing on the roof

03 the movie I don't want to see

04 the teacher she respects a lot

05 a chair made of steel

06 Those books on the table

07 The woman sleeping on the couch

08 The book she is reading

09 the man crossing the street

10 The people getting off the train

11 anything we can drink

12 the man sleeping under the tree

Unit 02. 관계부사

Warm up

01 where	02 why	03 when
04 when	05 how	06 where
07 when	08 where	09 how
10 where	11 when	12 for which

Start up

❶
01 when	02 why	03 when
04 where	05 where	06 when
07 how	08 why	09 when
10 how	11 how	12 when

[해설]

01 *선행사 day는 시간을 나타내므로 when이 필요하다.

02 *이유를 나타내는 관계부사는 why이다.

03 *선행사 year는 시간을 나타내므로 when이 필요하다.

04 *선행사 a restaurant는 장소를 나타내므로 where이 필요하다.

05 *선행사 the place는 장소를 나타내므로 where이 필요하다.

07 *방법을 나타내는 관계부사는 how이다.

08 *이유를 나타내는 관계부사는 why이다.

10 *방법을 나타내는 관계부사는 how이다.

11 *방법을 나타내는 관계부사는 how이다.

❷
01 where	02 why	03 why
04 where	05 when	06 when
07 how	08 how	09 why
10 where	11 when	12 how

[해설]

01 *선행사 place는 장소이므로 where이 필요하다.

02 *이유를 나타내는 관계부사는 why이다.

03 *이유를 나타내는 관계부사는 why이다.

04 *선행사 library는 장소이므로 where이 필요하다.

05 *시간을 나타내는 관계부사는 when이다.

06 *선행사 day는 시간을 나타내므로 when이 필요하다.

07 *방법을 나타내는 관계부사는 how이다.

10 *선행사 bank는 장소이므로 where이 필요하다.

11 *선행사 season은 시간을 나타내므로 when이 필요하다.

❶ 01 That is the company where they worked five years ago.
02 Wilson showed me how he made spaghetti.
03 I will drop by the office where my mom works.
04 He explained the reason why the car broke down.
05 Sunday is the day when we can play computer games.
06 Do you know the hotel where the next conference will be held.
07 Do you know how he made the cake?
08 We didn't know the reason why Sally failed the driver's test.
09 Spring is the season when we go on a picnic.
10 The cafe is the place where he meets his friends every day.
11 I will show you the point where you can start.
12 2010 was the year when we received a bonus.

[해석]
01 저곳이 그들이 5년 전에 일했던 회사이다.
02 Wilson은 내게 스파게티 만드는 방법을 보여줬다.
03 나는 엄마가 일하는 사무실에 방문할 것이다.
04 그는 그 자동차가 고장 난 이유를 설명했다.
05 일요일은 우리가 컴퓨터 게임을 할 수 있는 날이다.
06 너는 다음 번 회의가 열리는 호텔을 알고 있니?
07 너는 그가 케이크를 만드는 방법을 알고 있니?
08 우리는 Sally가 운전면허시험을 떨어진 이유를 모른다.
09 봄은 우리가 소풍을 가는 계절이다.
10 그 카페는 그가 매일 친구를 만나는 장소이다.
11 네게 출발할 수 있는 장소를 보여줄 것이다.
12 2010년은 우리가 보너스를 받은 해이다.

❷ 01 where I was born
02 where Sam lived for five years
03 when she is going to graduate from high school
04 where we could see the whole town
05 when she first saw him
06 why the company went bankrupt
07 how he spends his free time
08 why she canceled her performance
09 when we have to make a decision
10 when he arrived there
11 why I lied to you
12 where he bought his coat

❶ 01 Kevin is using the laptop computer which[that] he bought last week.
02 The doctor who(m)[that] you want to see is very busy now.
03 He is the student who(m)[that] I taught English last year.
04 This is the drawer which[that] my mom ordered on the Internet.
05 The boys who[that] are playing baseball are my friedns.
06 Do you know the language which[that] is spoken in Thailand?
07 This is the book that[which] I gave to Sam.
08 This is the dog that[which] my sister wants to keep.
09 Look at the car which[that] is covered with snow.
10 The man who(m)[that] I met yesterday was my father.
11 The palace which[that] we want to visit is currently under renovation.
12 Do you know the man who[that] is[was] sleeping on the sofa?

❷ 01 그가 살던 집은 매우 작았다.
02 나는 Jeniffer를 처음 만난 날을 기억하지 못한다.
03 그 위대한 음악가가 태어난 나라는 독일이다.
04 그녀가 항상 저녁식사를 거르는 이유를 말해줘요.
05 9월은 캐나다에서 새로운 학기가 시작하는 달이다.
06 이곳이 그들이 방과 후 농구를 하는 체육관이다.

07 우리는 그가 어떻게 목적지에 도착했는지 알았다.
08 일요일은 그녀가 미술관에 가는 날이다.
09 나는 그에게 우리가 만나기로 한 장소를 말 할 것이다.
10 그녀가 지난주 묵은 호텔은 매우 좋았다.
11 그녀는 그녀가 그와 헤어진 이유를 내게 말했다.
12 그 비디오는 펑크난 타이어를 바꾸는 방법을 보여주고 있다.

③ 01 how, in which   02 where, in[at] which
   03 when, on which   04 why, for which
   05 where, in[at] which 06 when, in which
   07 why, for which   08 in which
   09 when, in which   10 where, at which

[해석]
01 그는 며칠 만에 그것을 완성한 방법을 설명했다.
02 이곳이 아버지가 지갑을 잃어버린 상점이다.
03 성탄절은 예수의 탄생을 사람들이 기념하는 날이다.
04 왜 그런 결정을 하셨는지 물어봐도 될까요?
05 그녀는 남편을 처음 만났던 공원에 갔다.
06 그는 Paul이 캐나다로 이민간 연도를 알고 있다.
07 그녀가 왜 학교에 결석했는지 이유를 말해주세요.
08 그들은 내가 말하는 방식을 좋아하지 않는다.
09 3월은 겨울이 봄으로 바뀌기 시작하는 달이다.
10 이곳이 내가 졸업 후 일하고 싶어 하는 회사이다.

④ 01 who is[was]   02 where / in which
   03 when / at which   04 when / on which
   05 the way / how   06 for which / why
   07 wearing   08 which is
   09 where / in[at] which 10 when / on which
   11 when / on which   12 the way / how
   13 who are   14 in which / when
   15 why / for which

[해설]
01 *who 다음에 is가 와야 한다.
02 *선행사가 장소를 나타내는 the apartment이므로 where이나 in which가 와야 한다.
03 *선행사가 시간을 나타내는 the time이므로 when이나 at which가 와야 한다.
04 *선행사가 시간을 나타내는 the day이므로 when이나 on which가 와야 한다.
05 *the way와 how는 함께 올 수 없다.
06 *the reason이 왔으므로 why나 for which가 와

07 *guy를 수식하는 현재분사이므로 wear를 wearing 으로 바꿔야한다.
08 *「관계대명사+be동사」는 생략할 수 있다.
09 *선행사가 장소를 나타내는 the market이므로 where 이나 in which가 와야 한다.
10 *선행사가 시간을 나타내는 the date 이므로 when이 나 on which가 와야 한다.
11 *선행사가 시간을 나타내는 the day이므로 when이 나 on which가 와야 한다.
12 네가 어떻게 영어를 숙달했는지 우리에게 가르쳐 줘.
   *관계부사 앞에는 전치사가 올 수 없다.
13 *주어 the children이 복수이므로 who are가 되어 야 한다.
14 *선행사가 시간을 나타내는 the summer이므로 when 이나 in which가 와야 한다.
15 *the reason이 왔으므로 why나 for which가 와 야 한다.

Actual Test

01 ②	02 ⑤	03 ③	04 ⑤	05 ②
06 ①	07 ①	08 ③	09 ⑤	10 ②
11 ④	12 ②	13 ⑤	14 ②	15 ②

16 where / in which
17 We climbed to the top of the mountain where we could see the whole city of Seoul.
18 1) Do you know the man washing a car?
   2) This is the book written by John Grisham.
19 1) who is / that is   2) that / which
20 in where → in which 또는 where

[해석 및 해설]
01 화요일은 그녀가 발레레슨을 받는 날이다.
   *선행사가 시간을 나타내는 the day이므로 when이 필요하다.
02 내 동생은 항상 책을 읽는다. 그것이 그가 과학에 대해 많이 알고 있는 이유이다.
   *선행사 the reason은 생략할 수 있다.
03 Tommy는 선생님이 얘기했던 뭔가를 기억했다.
   *목적격 관계대명사가 필요하다.
04 이 기계가 어떻게 작동하는지 설명할게.
05 이것은 James가 발명한 기계이다.
06 우리는 음식이 항상 신선한 식당을 방문할 것이다.

나는 그를 처음 본 날을 기억한다.

*when은 on which 로 바꿔 쓸 수 있다.

07 그는 희귀한 동물들을 볼 수 있는 정글로 갔다.

이곳이 엄마가 자란 마을이다.

*선행사가 장소를 나타내는 the jungle과 the town 이므로 where[in which]이 필요하다.

08 ① 저곳이 그녀가 일요일마다 John을 만나는 카페이다.

② 그녀는 옆집에 사는 의사이다.

③ Sam은 내가 본 소년 중에서 가장 영리한 소년이다.

④ 그녀는 컴퓨터를 가지고 있는 유일한 소녀이다.

⑤ 그는 아버지가 농부인 소년이다.

*③ 목적격 관계대명사는 생략할 수 있다.

09 *관계부사 where은 선행사로 장소가 와야 하므로 ⑤ the reason은 빈칸에 어울리지 않는다.

10 우리는 방학이 시작되는 날을 기다리고 있다.

*when은 on which로 바꿔 쓸 수 있다.

11 Susan과 얘기하는 남자를 아니?

12 ① 8월은 사람들이 휴가를 가는 달이다.

② 내가 책을 읽고 있었을 때 그는 저녁을 먹고 있었다.

③ 그들이 이곳에 도착한 시간을 기억하니?

④ 일요일은 우리가 쉴 수 있는 유일한 날이다.

⑤ 나의 모든 고통이 사라지는 날을 고대하고 있다.

*②의 when은 접속사이고 나머지는 관계부사이다.

13 ⑤ a house와 made 사이에 'which was'가 생략되었다.

14 *the way와 how는 함께 사용할 수 없다.

15 ① which → where

③ which → where

④ where → which

⑤ when → where

16 우리가 농구를 하기로 한 체육관이 닫혀있다.

*선행사가 장소를 나타내는 the gym이므로 where 「in which」가 필요하다.

17 우리는 서울시 전체를 볼 수 있는 산에 올랐다.

*선행사가 장소를 나타내는 the mountain이므로 where 가 필요하다.

18 1) 세차하고 있는 남자를 아니?

2) 이 책은 John Grisham이 썼다.

19 1) 테니스를 하고 있는 소녀를 보아라.

2) 야구는 내가 가장 좋아하는 운동이다.

20 나는 유명한 그림을 많이 볼 수 있는 박물관을 방문할 것이다.

Review Test

❶ 01 I were in Seoul

02 had a daughter

03 I were with my family

04 you practiced hard

05 could finish it today

06 Kevin were not sick

07 could have purchased the expensive furniture

08 would have arrived here on time

09 could have driven you home

10 I had had an umbrella

11 would have known about the story

12 you had called me

[해석]

01 내가 서울에 있으면 그녀 결혼식에 참석할 텐데.

02 딸이 있으면 좋을 텐데.

03 가족과 함께 있으면 행복할 텐데.

04 너가 열심히 연습하면 경주에서 승리할 텐데.

05 우리가 시간이 충분하면 그것을 오늘 마칠 수 있을 텐데.

06 Kevin이 아프지 않으면 저녁식사 하러 나갈 텐데.

07 내가 돈이 충분히 있었더라면 그 비싼 가구를 구매했었을 텐데.

08 그녀가 일찍 일어났더라면 정각에 이곳에 도착 했었을 텐데.

09 내가 차가 있었더라면 너를 집에 데려다 줄 수 있었을 텐데.

10 내가 우산이 있었더라면 젖지 않았었을 텐데.

11 Jeff가 책을 읽었더라면 그 이야기에 대해 알았을 텐데.

12 네가 나에게 전화해 줬으면 좋을 텐데.

❷ 01 I am not rich

02 I didn't pass the test

03 I can't speak Japanese

04 I had accepted her advice then

05 we had taken the taxi last night

06 I can't help you

07 I am not rich

08 I am not as tall as you

09 you had asked me, would have helped you

10 couldn't get there on time

11 Mike had been in the office, would have answered the phone

12 he had done well the the exam, would have been happy

[해석]

01 내가 부자면 좋을 텐데.

02 내가 시험에 합격했으면 좋을 텐데.

03 내가 일본어를 할 수 있으면 좋을 텐데.

04 그녀의 충고를 그때 받아들였으면 좋을 텐데.

05 어젯밤에 택시를 탔더라면 좋을 텐데.

06 내가 너를 도와줄 수 있다면 좋을 텐데.

07 나는 부자가 아니라서 자동차를 살 수 없다.

08 너만큼 키가 컸으면 좋을 텐데.

09 당신이 내게 요청했었다면 내가 도와주었을 텐데.

10 기차가 늦지 않았더라면 그곳에 제시간에 도착했었을 텐데.

11 Mike가 사무실에 있었으면 전화를 받았을 텐데.

12 그가 시험을 잘 보았으면 그의 어머니가 기뻐했을 텐데.

❸ 01 who(m)[that]　　02 whose

03 that[which]　　04 who[that]

05 what　　06 what

07 what　　08 whose

09 whose　　10 who[that]

11 which[that]　　12 which[that]

13 who[that]　　14 that

15 that

[해설]

02 *소유격 관계대명사 다음에 명사가 온다.

03 *선행사가 사물이고 목적격관계대명사가 필요하다.

04 *선행사가 a daughter이고, 주격 관계대명사 다음에 동사가 온다.

05 *선행사가 없으므로 what이 와야 한다.

06 *선행사가 없으므로 what이 와야 한다.

07 *선행사가 없으므로 what이 와야 한다.

08 *소유격 관계대명사 다음에 명사가 온다.

09 *소유격 관계대명사 다음에 명사가 온다.

10 *선행사가 old lady이고, 주격 관계대명사 다음에 동사가 온다.

11 *선행사가 사물이고 주격 관계대명사가 필요하다.

12 *목적격 관계대명사 다음에 주어+동사가 온다.

13 *선행사가 사람이고, 주격 관계대명사 다음에 동사가 온다.

14 *선행사에 anything이 있으므로 that이 어울린다.

15 *선행사에 서수가 있으므로 that이 어울린다.

❹ 01 나는 그에게 일본에서 온 작가를 소개 했다.

02 Amy는 어제 잃어버린 반지를 찾고 있다.

03 저쪽에서 울고 있는 소년은 내 동생이다.

04 내게 케이크를 보낸 남자는 도서관에서 일한다.

05 Mike는 네가 오랫동안 사용하고 있지 않은 컴퓨터를 수리 할 것이다.

06 나는 중국어를 할 수 있는 학생을 찾을 수가 없다.

❺ 01 This is the lamp I bought at the store yesterday.

02 I received a letter written in English.

03 There were a lot of students studying in the library.

04 The painting on the wall is very fantastic.

05 These are the books useful for students.

06 Look at the boy sleeping under the tree.

❻ 1 where　　02 for which　　03 in which

04 when　　05 in which　　06 when

07 on which　　08 when　　09 the way

10 why　　11 when　　12 where

[해석]

01 이곳이 내가 그를 만났던 카페이다.

02 그것이 그녀가 나를 떠난 이유이다.

03 이곳이 내가 어린 시절을 보낸 곳이다.

04 월요일은 그가 매우 바쁜 날이다.

05 이것이 그가 자동차를 훔친 방법이다.

06 2010년은 그녀가 피난민으로 캐나다에 온 해이다.

07 일요일은 그가 친구들과 낚시를 가는 날이다.

08 너는 그녀가 우리를 파티에 데려간 날을 기억하니?

09 너는 그들이 어떻게 함께 일하고 사는지 배울 것이다.

10 너는 게임이 왜 지체되었는지 이유를 아니?

11 11월은 입학시험 시즌이 시작되는 시기이다.

12 저곳이 그들이 보물을 숨겨둔 섬이다.

01 ⑤	02 ③	03 ①	04 ⑤	05 ④
06 ⑤	07 ①	08 ③	09 ①	10 ③
11 ②	12 ②	13 ⑤	14 ③	15 ②
16 ③	17 ⑤	18 ④	19 ⑤	20 ①
21 ②	22 ③	23 ①		

24 1) where 2) when   25 were a bird

26 would have missed

27 would not tell a lie

28 만약 내가 충분히 돈이 있다면 새로운 컴퓨터를 살 수 있을 텐데.   29 1) who → whose 2) whom → who

30 where

[해석 및 해설]

01 *I wish+가정법과거(주어+동사의 과거)

02 *가정법 과거완료는 「If+주어+had+과거분사~, 주어+조동사+have+과거분사」의 형태이다.

03 *선행사가 사물이고 동사 visit의 목적어 역할을 하는 관계대명사는 which나 that이다.

04 *소유격 관계대명사 다음에는 명사가 온다.

05 Tom은 나에게 그가 왜 화가 났는지 말했다.

06 *가정법 과거완료는 「If+주어+had+과거분사~, 주어+조동사+have+과거분사」의 형태이다.

08 *선행사가 사물이고 주어 역할을 하는 관계대명사는 which나 that이다.
*선행사가 사람이고 동사 marry의 목적어 역할을 하는 관계대명사는 who(m)나 that이다

10 *관계부사 where의 선행사는 장소여야 하므로 the moment가 이울리지 않는다. the moment는 when과 함께 해야 한다.

11 이것은 내가 사고 싶은 것이다.
*the thing which은 what으로 바꿔 쓸 수 있다.

12 일요일은 그가 한가한 날이다.
*when은 on which로 바꿔 쓸 수 있다.

14 *가정법 과거는 현재 사실을 가정한다.

15 *② Paul이 안전벨트를 하지 않아서 다리가 부러졌다.

16 *주격 관계대명사는 생략할 수 없다.

17 *⑤ whose가 필요하고 나머지는 what이 필요하다.

18 *「주격관계대명사+be동사」는 생략이 가능하다.

19 *⑤는 의문사 나머지는 관계대명사이다.

20 *① whom 대신 which[that]가 와야 한다.

21 *② 선행사가 the girl이므로 which 대신 who나 that이 와야 한다.

22 *③은 관계대명사 which보다 관계부사 where이 오거나 in which가 와야 한다.

23 *①은 접속사이고 나머지는 관계대명사이다.

26 *가정법 과거완료이므로 주절에는 「would[could]+have+과거분사」의 형태가 되어야 한다.

27 *가정법 과거이므로 「would[could]+동사원형」의 형태가 되어야 한다.

29 1) *소유격 관계대명사 다음에는 명사가 온다.
2) *관계대명사가 주어의 역할을 하고 있으므로 주격 관계대명사가 와야 한다.

30 선행사가 장소를 나태내고 있으므로 관계부사 where가 적당하다.

Chapter 04. 여러 가지 문장 I

Unit 01. 의문사가 있는 의문문 1

Warm up

01 Who is	02 What did	03 Whose is
04 What	05 Which do	06 What do
07 What did	08 Who will	09 What
10 What did	11 Which	12 Knows

Start up

❶
01 What is	02 What	03 What does
04 Which	05 Whose	06 Which
07 What is	08 Who	09 Whose
10 What	11 What did	12 Who

[해석]

08 누가 질문에 대답했나요?

12 누구를 가장 좋아하나요?

❷
01 Who is	02 What	03 Who
04 Whose	05 Who	06 Which
07 What do	08 Who	09 Whose
10 What	11 Who will	12 Which do

Check up & Writing

❶
01 take → takes	02 whose → what
03 who → whose	04 Whose → Who
05 Who → What	06 What → Who
07 do → does	08 What → Which

09 What → Whose   10 does → is

11 is → does   12 What → Who

[해설]

01 *who는 3인칭 단수 취급하므로 takes가 되어야 한다.

03 *whose는 '누구의 것'을 의미한다.

07 *he는 3인칭 단수이므로 does가 와야 한다.

08 *which는 둘 중 하나를 선택할 때 사용한다.

09 *whose는 '누구의 것'을 의미한다.

10 *문장에 일반 동사가 없으므로 dose를 is로 바꾼다.

11 *문장에 일반 동사 do가 있으므로 is를 does로 바꾼다.

❷ 01 Who is   02 What is

03 Who(m) do   04 Whose car

05 Which do   06 Which is

07 Who are   08 What are

09 What are   10 Which movie

11 Who cleans   12 What does

Unit 02. 의문사가 있는 의문문 II

Warm up

01 When   02 How   03 When is

04 Where did   05 When   06 When did

07 Where is   08 Where did   09 Why was

10 Where   11 What   12 How does

Start up

❶ 01 Why do   02 Where does

03 Where did   04 When

05 When do   06 Where can

07 How much   08 How many

09 How long   10 What time

11 How   12 How far

[해석]

01 Because로 답하고 있으므로 질문에 Why가 와야 한다.

02 대답에 swimming pool이라는 장소가 있으므로 Where이 와야 한다.

03 대답에 hotel이라는 장소가 있으므로 Where이 와야 하며 시제가 과거이므로 did가 되어야 한다.

04 next Tuesday라고 답하고 있으므로 When이 와야 한다.

05 after school이라는 시간을 나타내므로 When이 와야 한다.

06 장소를 나타내는 Where이 와야 하며, can으로 답하고 있으므로 can으로 실문해야 하나.

07 가격을 나타내는 How much가 와야 한다.

08 three languages라고 답하고 있으므로 How many가 와야 한다.

09 for three days라고 기간을 나타내므로 How long이 와야 한다.

10 시간을 나타내는 What time이 와야 한다.

11 날씨의 상태를 나타내므로 How가 와야 한다.

12 거리를 나타고 있으므로 How far가 와야 한다.

❷ 01 How old   02 How many

03 How often   04 How many

05 How long   06 How often

07 How deep   08 Where did

09 When can   10 How

11 When did   12 How tall

Check up & Writing

❶ 01 How often   02 How tall

03 How much   04 How much

05 How many   06 How far

07 How old   08 How long

09 How deep   10 Where does

11 Why were   12 When does

[해석]

01 A: 너는 얼마나 자주 기타를 치니?

   B: 일주일에 한번.

02 A: 네 아버지는 키가 얼마나 크니?

   B: 그는 키가 170cm입니다.

03 A: 이 코트는 얼마입니까?

   B: 300달러입니다.

04 A: 그녀는 설탕이 얼마나 필요하니?

   B: 두 자루 필요해.

05 A: 당신은 아이가 몇 명 있습니까?

   B: 셋 있습니다.

06 A: 네 학교가 집에서 얼마나 머니?

B: 약 3km 떨어져 있어.

07 A: 네 여동생은 몇 살이니?

B: 11살

08 A: 그 다리는 얼마나 기니?

B: 다리의 길이는 2km입니다.

09 A: 이 호수는 얼마나 깊니?

B: 깊이가 5피트입니다.

10 A: 그는 어디에 가기를 원하니?

B: 테마 파크에 가기를 원해.

11 A: 회의에 왜 늦었니?

B: 교통체증 때문에.

12 A: 부산가는 다음 기차는 언제 있습니까?

B: 오후 5시에 있습니다.

❷ 01 When[What time] do you usually have

02 How many books are there

03 How often do you go

04 How do you like your

05 How much flour do you

06 How many dogs does she

07 Why did they refuse my

08 How many classes do you have

09 How long are you going to stay

10 Where did you leave

11 Why is he so popular

12 How far is the subway station from

Unit 03. 명령문과 제안문

Warm up

01 go	02 buying	03 Don't
04 Let's not	05 watching	06 Don't
07 Shall	08 not	09 be
10 Why	11 talk	12 Don't
13 press	14 why	15 Don't

[해석]

01 강으로 수영하러 가자.

02 엄마를 위해 꽃을 사는 게 어때?

03 시간을 낭비 하지 마라.

04 그를 방해하지 마라.

05 점심 먹고 영화 보는 거 어때?

06 TV를 너무 많이 보지 마라.

07 오늘 축구 할래?

08 오늘은 컴퓨터 게임 하지 말자.

09 지각하지 마라.

10 지하철 타는 게 어때?

11 너의 문제에 대해 말해 보자.

12 네 부모님을 실망시키지 마.

13 빨간색 단추를 누르지 마라.

14 너 하얀색 드레스 입는 거 어때?

15 잔디 위에 앉지 마라.

Start up

❶ 01 Why	2 Let's	03 How about
04 buying	05 Shall	06 go to
07 Don't	08 turn off	09 or
10 Be	11 not	12 Don't be

[해석]

01 그를 음악회에 데려가는 게 어때?

02 그와 함께 외식하자.

03 그를 위해 파티를 여는 게 어때?

04 그녀에게 자전거를 사주는 게 어때?

05 그에게 쿠키를 구워주눈 거 어때?

06 우리 해변에 갈래?

07 과속하지 마세요.

08 램프를 사용하지 않을 때에는 끄자.

09 지하철을 타라, 그렇지 않으면 비행기를 놓칠 것이다.

10 도서관에서는 조용히 해라.

11 돈을 낭비하지 말자.

12 학교에 지각하지 마라.

❷ 01 Shall	02 meet	03 and
04 or	05 Be	06 recycle
07 Take	08 unplug	09 Don't be
10 Why don't	11 Let's not	12 drinking

[해석 및 해설]

01 우리 점심 식사하러 나갈래?

02 10시에 우리 공원에서 만날래?

03 일찍 일어나라, 그러면 기분이 더 좋아질 것이다.
   *and 다음에는 긍정의 결과가 온다.

04 열심히 공부해라, 그렇지 않으면 기말고사를 망칠 것이다.

05 다른 사람들에게 친절해라.
   *형용사 앞에 be동사가 와야 한다.

06 병과 신문을 재활용하자.

07 이 약을 먹어라, 그러면 고통이 사라질 것이다.

08 전자 장비를 사용한 후에는 전원을 뽑아라.

09 실망하지 마라. 기운 내!

    *be disappointed는 '실망하다'라는 의미이다.

10 너 방과 후에 독서 모임에 가입하는 거 어때?

11 그 용감한 군인들을 잊지 말자.

12 우유를 좀 마시는 거 어때?

    *how about+동명사

Check up & Writing

❶ 01 and → or   02 coming → come

  03 throws → throw   04 order → ordering

  05 making → make   06 doesn't → don't

  07 go → going   08 carrying → carry

  09 Do → Be   10 stay → staying

  11 gave up → give up   12 doesn't – don't

  13 or → and   14 going → go

  15 and → or

[해석 및 해설]

01 열심히 공부해라 그렇지 않으면 좋은 점수를 받지 못할 것이다.

    *and대신 or가 와야 한다.

02 와서 나랑 노는 거 어때?

    *coming 대신 동사원형의 come이 와야 한다.

03 재활용할 수 있는 것을 버리지 마라.

    *"Don't+동사원형"이 되어야 하므로 throws대신 throw가 와야 한다.

04 그녀를 위해 피자를 주문 하는거 어때?

    *"What+about+동명사"가 되어야 하므로 order 대신 ordering이 와야 한다.

05 그녀를 위해 아침식사를 만들자.

    *making을 make로 바꿔야 한다.

06 소란 피우지 마세요.

    *부정명령문은 "Don't+동사원형"이 되어야 한다.

07 다음 주 등산 가는 거 어때?

    *"What+about+동명사"가 되어야 하므로 go대신 going이 와야 한다.

08 나를 위해 이 가방 좀 들어줄래?

    *"why don't you+동사원형"의 형태가 되어야 하므로 carrying 대신 carry가 와야 한다.

09 정직하라 그러면 사람들이 너를 믿을 것이다.

    *honest가 형용사이므로 Do 대신 Be가 와야 한다.

10 오늘 호텔에 머무는 거 어때?

    *"How+about+동명사"가 되어야 하므로 stay대신 staying이 와야 한다.

11 지금 포기하자 마라.

12 우리 10분간 휴식하는 거 어때?

    *"why don't we+동사원형"

13 창문을 열면 신선한 공기를 마실 수 있다.

    *긍정의 결과가 있으므로 and가 와야 한다.

14 간단히 뭐 좀 먹으러 나갈래?

    *"Shall we+동사원형"의 형태가 되어야 하므로 going 대신 go가 온다.

15 숙제를 마쳐라 그렇지 않으면 너는 TV를 볼 수 없다.

❷ 01 Shall, eat dinner before

  02 Let's not talk about

  03 don't we ask for

  04 don't you change

  05 about going out for

  06 about staying at home

  07 Don't eat the cookies

  08 and you will meet her

  09 Don't spend too much

  10 or you will miss the school bus

  11 Be nice to

  12 Don't be rude to

Level up

❶ 01 Who is   02 What does   03 Whose

  04 Which   05 What   06 Who is

  07 What is   08 Who is   09 What are

  10 Who can   11 Which   12 Who do

[해석]

03 이것은 누구의 우산이니?

04 이 케이크와 저 케이크 중 어느 것이 저렴하니?

05 무슨 동물을 좋아하니?

❷ 01 much → many   02 What → Why

  03 long → often   04 many → much

  05 Who → Whose   06 deep → long

  07 long → tall   08 tall → far

  09 deep → long   10 Who → What

  11 Where → When   12 What → How

01 *many+복수명사, much+셀 수 없는 명사

02 *because로 대답하므로 why로 질문해야 한다.

03 *빈도를 묻는 대답이 와야 하므로 long 대신 often
이 와야 한다.

04 *many+복수명사, much+셀 수 없는 명사

05 *소유를 나타내는 의문사 whose가 와야 한다.

06 *기간을 나타내는 how long이 와야 한다.

07 *높이를 나타내는 tall이 와야 한다.

08 *거리를 나타내는 far가 와야 한다.

09 *길이를 나타내는 long이 와야 한다.

10 *직업을 묻는 질문으로 what이 와야 한다.

11 *where 대신 시간을 나타내는 when이 와야 한다.

12 *what 대신 방법을 나타내는 how가 와야 한다.

❸ 01 Why don't we go for a bike ride this
Sunday?

02 How about getting together next week?

03 Shall we go to the movies?

04 Clean up the meeting room after using it.

05 Don't buy such a book.

06 Let's help poor people.

07 Why don't you drink lots of water every
day?

08 Let's not talk about this problem next time.

09 Follow the traffic rules when you drive.

10 Be careful when you use a knife.

11 Shall we play soccer together?

12 Don't be late for school.

❹ 01 당신이 없는 동안 누가 정원에 물을 줄 거니?

02 우리 좋아하는 색상에 대해서 말해 보자.

03 너는 언제 도서관에 가니?

04 너는 얼마나 많은 과목을 배우니?

05 너는 얼마나 오래 영어를 배우고 있니?

06 그는 보통 어디에 주차를 하니?

07 공항에서 그 호텔에 어떻게 가니?

08 네가 가난한 나라의 사람들을 도와주는 거 어때?

09 스마트폰을 너무 많이 사용하지 말자.

10 부모님과 얼마나 자주 대화하니?

11 친구야, 제발 슬퍼하지 마.

12 진열 중인 신발은 얼마입니까?

Actual Test

01 ③　02 ④　03 ①　04 ④　05 ①
06 ①　07 ⑤　08 ②　09 ④　10 ①
11 ④　12 ⑤　13 ②　14 ②　15 ①
16 What　17 playing
18 1) Whose　2) Why　3) Which
19 Don't be nervous
20 1) making → make　2) apple – apples

[해석 및 해설]

01 오늘 오후에 영화 보러 가는 거 어때?
　*제안문이므로 Why가 와야 한다.

02 오늘 놀라지 마.
　*surprised가 형용사이므로 be가 와야 한다.

03 피자와 스파게티 중 어느 것을 좋아하니?

04 체육관에 얼마나 많은 사람이 있니?

05 이곳은 내가 태어난 집이다.
　도서관이 어디니?

07 *기간을 묻고 있으므로 How long 와야 한다.

08 너 피곤해 보인다. 쉬는 게 어떠니?

09 이것은 누구의 사전이니?
　스마트폰을 언제 잃어버렸니?

10 *'일주일에 두세 번'이라고 대답하므로 빈도를 묻는 질
문이 와야 한다.

11 *직업을 묻고 있으므로 ④가 정답이다.

12 *'2시간 동안'이라고 대답하므로 기간을 묻는 질문이
와야 한다.

13 *②는 '내가 방과 후 축구 모임에 가입해도 되니?'라
는 뜻으로 상대방에게 허락을 묻는 의미이며, 나머지
는 제안문이다.

14 *②는 whom 대신 Who가 와야 한다.

16 A: 가장 좋아하는 음식이 뭐니?
　B: 피자를 좋아해. 너는?
　A: 나는 국수를 좋아해.

17 *How about+동명사

19 *nervous가 형용사이므로 be가 와야 한다.

20 1) 오늘 새로운 습관을 만드는 거 어때?
　2) 몇 개의 사과가 필요하니?

Unit 01. 부가의문문

Warm up

01 is she   02 were they   03 will you
04 didn't you   05 won't   06 can't
07 doesn't he   08 Is   09 can she
10 shall we

[해석]

01 그 여성은 너의 엄마가 아니야, 그렇지?
02 그것들은 무겁지 않아, 그렇지?
03 학교에 지각하지 마, 알았지?
04 너는 계획을 바꿨지, 그렇지 않니?
05 그는 시험에서 부정행위를 하지 않을 것이다, 그렇지?
06 그는 부러진 손으로 야구를 할 수 없어, 그렇지?
07 네 아버지는 야구경기 보는 것을 좋아하셔, 그렇지 않니?
08 Andrew는 영국에서 왔어, 그렇지 않니?
09 내 여동생은 매운 음식을 못 먹어, 그렇지?
10 오늘 야구하자, 그럴래?

Start up

❶ 01 will you   02 won't she   03 doesn't she
04 doesn't she   05 don't they   06 does it
07 do they   08 will you   09 didn't you
10 didn't she   11 didn't he   12 can't they
13 didn't she   14 isn't it   15 will you

[해설]

01 *명령문은 부가의문문으로 will you가 온다.
02 *Sara는 여성이므로 she로 받는다.
03 *My younger sister는 여성이므로 she로 받고, 시제가 현재이고 3인칭 단수이므로 doesn't가 온다.
04 *시제가 현재이고 3인칭 단수이므로 doesn't가 온다.
05 *Brown and James은 3인칭 복수이므로 they가 온다.
06 *The shopping mall은 it으로 받는다.
07 *앞문장이 부정이므로 부가의문문은 긍정이 온다.
08 *명령문은 부가의문문으로 will you가 온다.
09 *stayed가 과거이므로 did가 온다.
10 *found가 과거이므로 did가 온다.

11 *His younger brother는 남성이므로 he로 받고, 시제가 과거이므로 didn't가 와야 한다.
12 *Your friends가 복수이므로 they가 온다.
13 *시제가 과거이므로 didn't가 쓰였다
14 *that은 it으로 받는다.

❷ 01 doesn't he   02 isn't it   03 isn't it
04 shall we   05 did I   06 aren't they
07 isn't she   08 will you   09 didn't you
10 aren't they   11 will he   12 doesn't she
13 can't they   14 shall we   15 is it

[해설]

01 *시제가 현재이고 주어가 3인칭 단수이므로 doesn't가 온다.
02 *this는 it으로 받는다.
03 *The new copy machine은 it으로 받는다.
04 *Let's ~로 시작하는 제안문에는 shall we가 온다.
06 *주어 the stairs가 복수이므로 they가 온다.
08 *명령문은 부가의문문으로 will you가 온다.
09 *You and Mike는 2인칭 복수이므로 부가의문문에 you가 온다.
10 *주어 those boxes가 복수이므로 they가 온다.
11 *앞문장의 조동사가 부정이므로 긍정의 will이 와야 한다.
13 *앞문장의 조동사가 긍정이므로 부정의 can't가 와야 한다.
14 *Let's ~로 시작하는 제안문에는 shall we가 온다.
15 *that은 it으로 받는다.

Check up & Writing

❶ 01 don't they   02 isn't it   03 do they
04 shall we   05 doesn't it   06 didn't they
07 will you   08 can't they   09 is it
10 won't he   11 will you   12 doesn't she
13 didn't it   14 do you   15 wasn't it

[해설]

01 *like는 일반동사 현재형이므로 don't가 온다.
02 *This movie는 it으로 받는다.
03 *앞문장이 부정이고 시제가 현재이므로 do they가 온다.
04 *Let's ~로 시작하는 제안문에는 shall we가 온다.
05 *tastes는 3인칭 단수 현재형이므로 doesn't가 온다.

06 *시제가 일반동사 과거이므로 didn't they가 되어야 한다.

07 *명령문은 모두 will you가 와야 한다.

08 *The birds 복수이므로 they로 받는다.

09 *Your favorite sport는 it으로 받으며, isn't의 긍정인 is가 온다.

10 *앞 문장에 will이 왔으므로 won't가 나와야 한다.

11 *명령문은 모두 will you가 와야 한다.

12 *His mom은 she로 받는다.

13 *His face는 it으로 받는다.

14 *You and your sister는 2인칭 복수이므로 you로 받는다.

15 *시제가 과거이므로 wasn't it이 되어야 한다.

❷ 01 are good at math, aren't they

02 worry about the test result, will you

03 drives carefully, doesn't he

04 doesn't help her friends, does she

05 didn't listen to classical music, did they

06 goes down in the west, doesn't it

07 go for a walk, shall we

08 don't have any water, do you

09 will be free this weekend, won't he

10 are very useful for children, aren't they

11 not take a taxi today, shall we

12 caught the thief yesterday, didn't he

Unit 02. 간접의문문 / 선택의문문

Warm up

01 What do you think   **02** his name is

03 if   **04** why he was

05 he will   **06** Do you know where

07 or   **08** Where do you think

09 think   **10** where she lives

[해석]

01 그가 무엇을 원한다고 생각하니?

02 너는 그의 이름이 무엇인지 아니?

03 나는 그녀가 시험에 통과할지 확신하지 못한다.

04 왜 그가 회의에 늦었는지 말해주세요.

05 그가 언제 파티에 올 거라고 믿니?

06 Mike가 어디에 있는지 아니?

07 너와 Jake 중 누가 창문을 닫았니?

08 그가 어디에 살고 있다고 생각하니?

09 그녀가 왜 직업을 그만두었다고 생각하니?

10 그녀가 어디에 사는지 궁금하다.

Start up

❶ 01 Who, is a doctor

02 what his favorite color is

03 if[whether] he can play the flute

04 if[whether] he was at the shopping mall yesterday

05 she ate dinner

06 how tall the tree is

07 where she had lunch

08 Why, they go to the beach

09 Where, lost your cell phone

10 if[whether] he has a laptop computer

11 why you learn English

12 if[whether] there is a bookstore near your house

❷ 01 what his phone number is

02 what that means

03 if[whether] she is a math teacher

04 Who, won the race

05 how I can get to the airport

06 if[whether] she can ride a bike

07 What, she is making

08 When, he took the pill

09 if[whether] there is a shopping mall near here

10 where she is going now

11 how old her uncle is

12 Why, Susan got up early today?

Check up & Writing

❶ 01 Do you know what Mike's hobby is?

02 Do you know if[whether] she likes apples?

03 Do you know where she bought the camera?

04 Do you know how he got his job?

05 Do you know who she likes?

06 Why do you think she cried?
07 What do you think his job is?
08 When do you think she arrived at the station?
09 Why do you think she came here?
10 Who do you think he likes?
11 How do you think she opened the door?
12 What time do you think she came back here?

❷ 01 where he found his wallet
02 how deep the river is
03 why she wants to meet him
04 How do you think she went
05 what time she left
06 if she washed her car yesterday
07 his favorite sport is
08 made him angry
09 if Jane can stay a little longer
10 what Amy bought for me
11 who stole the pictures
12 how he is going to solve the problem

Unit 03. 감탄문

Warm up

01 How
02 What
03 What
04 What
05 What
06 it is
07 a kind
08 How
09 nice
10 How
11 What
12 What
13 beautiful
14 How
15 present

[해설]

01 *부사 high를 강조하므로 「How+형용사/부사(+주어+동사)!」 어순이 되어야 한다.

02 *명사 train를 강조하므로 「What+a/an+형용사+명사(+주어+동사)!」 어순이 되어야 한다.

03 *명사 day를 강조하므로 「What+a/an+형용사+명사(+주어+동사)!」 어순이 되어야 한다.

04 *명사 car를 강조하므로 「What+a/an+형용사+명사(+주어+동사)!」 어순이 되어야 한다.

05 *명사 idea를 강조하므로 「What+a/an+형용사+명사(+주어+동사)!」 어순이 되어야 한다.

06 *a trip이 단수이므로 it is가 와야 한다.

07 *명사 boy를 강조하므로 「What+a/an+형용사+명사(+주어+동사)!」 어순이 되어야 한다.

08 *형용사 kind를 강조하므로 「How+형용사/부사(+주어+동사)!」 어순이 되어야 한다.

09 *명사 girls가 복수이므로 a가 오지 않는다.

10 *형용사 greedy를 강조하므로 「How+형용사/부사(+주어+동사)!」 어순이 되어야 한다.

11 *명사 mountain를 강조하므로 「What+a/an+형용사+명사(+주어+동사)!」 어순이 되어야 한다.

12 *명사 party를 강조하므로 「What+a/an+형용사+명사(+주어+동사)!」 어순이 되어야 한다. it is가 생략되었다.

13 *명사 roses가 복수이므로 a가 오지 않는다. they are가 생략되었다.

14 *형용사 big을 강조하므로 「How+형용사/부사(+주어+동사)!」 어순이 되어야 한다.

15 *부정관사 a가 있으므로 단수형 명사가 와야 한다.

Start up

❶ 01 What
02 How
03 How
04 What
05 What
06 How
07 What
08 How
09 How
10 What
11 How
12 What
13 What
14 How
15 How

[해석 및 해설]

01 정원이 매우 아름답구나!
*명사 garden을 강조하므로 What으로 시작한다.

02 그는 정말 잘생겼구나!
*형용사 handsome을 강조하므로 How로 시작한다.

03 그 개는 정말 빨리 달릴 수 있구나!
*부사 fast를 강조하므로 How로 시작한다.

04 너는 정말 작은 차를 가지고 있구나!
*명사 car를 강조하므로 What으로 시작한다.

05 이것들은 정말 멋진 그림들이구나!
*명사 paintings을 강조하므로 What으로 시작한다.

06 그녀는 얼마나 천천히 걷는지!
*부사 slowly를 강조하므로 How로 시작한다.

07 Tom은 얼마나 운이 좋은 사람인지!
*명사 man을 강조하므로 What으로 시작한다.

08 그 아기는 매우 귀엽구나!

*형용사 cute를 강조하므로 How로 시작한다.

09 그 영화는 정말 슬프구나!

*형용사 sad를 강조하므로 How로 시작한다.

10 그는 정말 이기적인 사람이구나!

11 그것들은 정말 맛있구나!

*형용사 delicious를 강조하므로 How로 시작한다.

12 그녀는 정말 사랑스러운 소녀이구나!

*명사 girl을 강조하므로 What으로 시작한다.

13 그들은 정말 영리한 학생들이구나!

*명사 students를 강조하므로 What으로 시작한다.

14 Jane은 영어를 정말 잘하는구나!

*부사 well을 강조하므로 How로 시작한다.

15 그녀는 정말 바쁘구나!

*형용사 busy를 강조하므로 How로 시작한다.

❷ 01 How　　02 How　　03 What
04 How　　05 How　　06 What
07 How　　08 What　　09 What
10 How　　11 What　　12 How
13 What　　14 What　　15 How

[해석]

01 저 보름달은 정말 아름답구나!

02 그 컴퓨터 게임은 정말 재미있구나!

03 Mary는 정말 키 큰 소녀이구나!

04 얼마나 비가 많이 내리는지!

05 그녀는 질투심이 매우 많구나!

06 그녀는 매우 좋은 의자를 가지고 있구나!

07 그 꽃들은 매우 아름답구나!

08 그녀는 매우 아름다운 드레스를 가지고 있구나!

09 그는 매우 정직한 소년이구나!

10 저 소년들은 매우 쾌활하구나!

11 이것들은 정말로 비싼 신발들이구나!

12 David는 정말 열심히 일하는구나!

13 그것은 매우 놀라운 기록이구나!

14 그들은 매우 친절한 간호사들이구나!

15 매우 깊은 강이구나!

Check up & Writing

❶ 01 How small your room is!

02 What big pants they are! / How big the pants are!

03 What an exciting game it was!

04 What a brave policeman he is!

05 What a long bridge this is! / How long this bridge is!

06 What an old watch this is! / How old this watch is!

07 What a good time we had!

08 How hot it is!

09 How heavy the traffic is!

10 What a wise man he is! / How wise he is!

11 How carefully he drives!

12 How difficult the test was!

❷ 01 What a large house

02 dirty your room is

03 What a strong man

04 What a nice gift

05 How fast he

06 What cheap clothes they

07 What an expensive car

08 How useful this machine

09 How cute

10 What an ugly dog

11 How terrible the accident

12 What an excellent idea

Level up

❶ 01 don't you　02 don't you　03 aren't we
04 is it　　　05 wasn't she　06 isn't it
07 didn't they　08 doesn't it　09 do they
10 will you　11 isn't it　　12 did he
13 didn't she　14 will you　15 shall we

[해설]

03 *My brother and I는 1인칭 복수 we로 받는다.

04 *This computer는 it으로 받는다.

05 *Your mother는 she로 받는다.

06 *That은 it으로 받는다.

07 *Tom and Jack은 they로 받는다.

09 *His parents는 복수이므로 they가 온다.

11 *Your favorite food은 it으로 받는다.

12 *시제가 과거이므로 did he가 온다.

14 *명령문은 will you가 온다.

15 *let's로 시작하는 문장의 부가의문문은 shall we로 한다.

❷ 01 Do you know where she was last night?
02 Can you tell me how I can get to the beach?
03 I wonder if[whether] she likes Korean food.
04 Do you know why Mike met Jenny yesterday?
05 When do you think they are going to have dinner?
06 What do you think she is doing now?
07 Do you know who will take her to the hospital?
08 I wonder how old his father is.
09 I can't remember where I put my glasses.
10 Please tell me what you want.
11 Who do you believe is responsible for the accident?
12 Do you know how long it takes to Seoul?

❸ 01 How funny the movie is!
02 How curious she is!
03 What fresh vegetables she grows!
04 How comfortable this chair is!
05 How fast Kelly speaks!
06 What a wonderful story it is!
/ How wonderful the story is!
07 What a pretty doll she has!
08 What scary movies they are!
/ How scary the movies are!
09 How fantastic the music is!
10 How cold it is today!
11 What a creative idea Jack has!
12 What an old truck this is!
/ How old this truck is!

[해석]
01 그 영화는 매우 재미있구나!
02 그녀는 호기심이 많구나!
03 그녀는 매우 신선한 채소를 재배하는 구나!
04 이 의자는 정말 편안하구나!
05 Kelly는 정말 빠르게 말하는 구나!
06 그것은 정말 아름다운 이야기이구나!
07 그녀는 정말 예쁜 인형을 가지고 있구나!
08 그것들은 매우 무서운 영화들이구나!

09 그 음악이 매우 좋구나!
10 오늘은 매우 춥구나!
11 Jack은 매우 창의적인 생각을 가지고 있구나!
12 이것은 정말 오래된 트럭이구나!

❹ 01 will you → shall we 02 How → What
03 does she → doesn't she
04 How → What   05 will who → who will
06 what → if[whether] 07 and → or
08 a kind → kind   09 a → an
10 What → How   11 and → or
12 what is your dream → what your dream is
13 Do you think who → Who do you think
14 do you → will you
15 aren't they → are they

[해설]
01 *let's로 시작하는 문장의 부가의문문은 shall we 로 한다.
02 *명사 car를 강조하므로 what으로 시작해야 한다.
03 *앞이 긍정이므로 부정의 부가의문문이 와야 한다.
04 *명사 roses를 강조하므로 what으로 시작해야 한다.
05 *will who를 who will로 바꿔야 한다.
06 *what을 if[whether]로 바꿔야 한다.
07 *선택의문문은 or를 사용한다.
08 *teachers가 복수이므로 a를 생략한다.
09 *단수 명사를 수식하는 모음으로 시작하는 형용사 앞에는 an이 와야 한다.
10 *형용사 beautiful를 강조하므로 how로 시작해야 한다.
11 *선택의문문은 or를 사용한다.
12 *간접의문문은 「의문사+주어+동사」의 어순이다.
13 *think가 오면 의문사는 문장 앞으로 이동한다.
14 *명령문에는 부가의문문으로 will you가 온다.
15 *앞이 부정이므로 are they가 와야 한다.

Actual Test

01 ②	02 ⑤	03 ④	04 ①	05 ⑤
06 ④	07 ④	08 ③	09 ③	10 ①
11 ④	12 ③	13 ②	14 ①	15 ②

16 1) What good cheese this is!
/ How good this cheese is!
2) How delicious the food is!

17 We don't know where he is.
18 1) did you 2) will you 3) didn't they
19 1) What 2) How
20 너는 어젯밤 TV를 보지 않았어, 그렇지?

[해석 및 해설]

01 *앞 문장이 긍정이고 시제가 현재이므로 don't you 가 와야 한다.

02 *형용사 pretty를 강조하므로 how가 와야 한다.

03 *앞 문장이 부정이고 시제가 현재이므로 does he가 와야 한다.

04 나는 그가 나를 도울 수 있을지 확신하지 못한다.
   *if는 간접의문문을 이끌어 '…인지 어떤지'의 의미를 가지고 있다.

05 여기서 수영하지 마라, 알았지?
   음악회에 가자, 그럴래?

06 *간접의문문은 「의문사+주어+동사」의 어순이어야 한다.

07 *시제가 과거이므로 ④가 정답이다.

08 *③은 명사 나머지는 형용사이다.

09 *간접의문문은 「의문사+주어+동사」의 어순이어야 한다.

10 *동사 think, believe와 오면 의문사는 문장 앞에 온다.

11 ① can she ② aren't you ③ isn't it ⑤ can't they

12 ① will you ② didn't you ④ can you ⑤ shall we

13 *명사 boy를 강조해야 하므로 what으로 해야 한다.

14 A: 따라오세요. 박물관 가는 길을 가르쳐줄게요.
   B: 친절하시군요.
   A: 별 말씀을.

16 1) 이것은 정말 좋은 치즈이구나!
   2) 음식이 매우 맛있구나!

17 우리는 그가 어디에 있는지 모른다.

18 He and Tony는 they로 받는다.

19 1) 매우 영리한 개구나!
   2) 너는 정말 아름답구나!

Chapter 06. 시제 일치와 화법

Unit 01. 수의 일치

Warm up

01 are	02 is	03 looks	04 has
05 is	06 wears	07 go	08 are
09 is	10 has	11 has to	12 were
13 likes	14 eat	15 has been	

[해설]

01 *주어 the girls가 복수이므로 are가 온다.

02 *주어로 to부정사, 동명사, 절이 올 때 단수 취급한다.

03 *주어가 3인칭 단수이므로 looks가 와야 한다.

04 *주어가 「every+단수명사」 또는 「each+단수명사」일 때, 동사는 단수형으로 쓴다.

05 *주어로 to부정사, 동명사, 절이 올 때 단수 취급한다.

06 *주어가 「every+단수명사」 또는 「each+단수명사」일 때, 동사는 단수형으로 쓴다.

07 *주어가 both A and B(A, B 둘 다)일 때, 동사는 복수형으로 쓴다.

08 *「A number of[많은~]+복수명사」일 때, 동사는 복수형으로 쓴다.

09 *주어가 이름(학문, 국가, 질병)일 때, 동사는 단수형으로 쓴다.

10 *주어가 「each+단수명사」일 때, 동사는 단수형으로 쓴다.

12 *관계대명사가 이끄는 절은 선행사의 수에 동사를 일치시킨다. 선행사 pies가 복수이다.

13 *상관접속사 구문이 주어일 때 동사는 B에 수를 일치시킨다.

14 *상관접속사 구문이 주어일 때 동사는 B에 수를 일치시킨다.

15 *주어가 「the number+복수명사」일 때, 동사는 단수형으로 쓴다.

Start up

❶
01 is	02 is	03 work	04 have
05 do	06 is	07 looks	08 is
09 is	10 are	11 like	12 is
13 is	14 go	15 are	

[해설]

01 *주어로 to부정사, 동명사, 절이 올 때 단수취 급한다.

02 *주어로 to부정사, 동명사, 절이 올 때 단수 취급한다.

03 *상관접속사 구문이 주어일 때 동사는 B(his brothers)에 수를 일치시킨다.

04 *상관접속사 구문이 주어일 때 동사는 B(I)에 수를 일치시킨다.

05 *주어가 both A and B(A, B 둘 다)일 때, 동사는 복수형으로 쓴다.

06 셀 수 없는 명사는 단수취급 한다.

07 *주어가 「every+단수명사」 또는 「each+단수명사」일 때, 동사는 단수형으로 쓴다.

08 *주어가 「every+단수명사」 또는 「each+단수명사」일 때, 동사는 단수형으로 쓴다.

12 *주어로 to부정사, 동명사, 절이 올 때 단수 취급한다.

14 *주어가 복수이거나 「A and B」일 때 동사는 복수형으로 쓴다.

15 *「A number of[많은~]+복수명사」일 때, 동사는 복수형으로 쓴다.

❷ 01 get up   **02** keeps   **03** is
   04 are   **05** plan   **06** are
   07 is   **08** is   **09** has
   10 wants   **11** is   **12** is
   13 is   **14** has   **15** have

Check up & Writing

❶ 01 are   **02** learns   **03** are
   04 is   **05** have   **06** consists
   07 is   **08** visit   **09** is
   10 has   **11** were   **12** bring
   13 is   **14** has   **15** is

[해석 및 해설]

01 서랍의 양말들은 아버지 것이다.

02 잭의 친구들뿐만 아니라 잭도 영어를 배운다.
   *A as well B는 A에 수를 일치시킨다.

03 그녀에 대한 많은 소문들이 전국에 퍼지고 있다.

04 울타리에 앉아있는 고양이가 보이니?

05 Amy뿐만 아니라 그 소년들도 캐나다에 가보지 못했다.

06 미국은 50개의 주로 구성되어 있다.

07 물리학은 십대들 사이에서 인기가 없다.

08 Cathy와 Richard는 종종 절을 방문한다.

09 내가 어젯밤에 본 것은 그의 개다.

10 교통사고 수가 빠르게 감소했다.

11 소파뿐만 아니라 의자들도 이태리에서 수입되었다.

12 백화점의 모든 직원들이 점심을 싸온다.

13 모든 학생들이 회의에 참여할 예정이다.

14 각각의 사람들은 다른 목소리를 가지고 있다.

15 초상화를 그리는 것이 내 아버지의 직업이다.

❷ 01 To go to the theme park is
   02 Swimming in the sea is
   03 Every parent thinks that
   04 A number of students are
   05 Either she or I am
   06 What I want to study at college is
   07 Both Jane and Jessie are
   08 Neither Sam nor his friends want
   09 The number of cars in Seoul has
   10 Each person has the right
   11 Something is wrong with
   12 were renovated last year

Unit 02. 시제의 일치

Warm up

01 rained   **02** takes   **03** had
04 could   **05** is, was   **06** ended
07 is   **08** could   **09** washes
10 had been   **11** would not   **12** is
13 practices   **14** moves   **15** was

[해석]

01 나는 어젯밤에 심하게 비가 왔던 것을 안다.

02 Jane은 매일 아침에 샤워한다고 말했다.

03 나는 그에게 내가 소방서에서 자원봉사를 했었다고 말했다.

04 그는 이곳에 제시간에 올 수 있다고 확신했다.

05 Jane은 그것은 훌륭한 영화였다(영화라)고 말했다.

06 그 책은 세계 2차 대전이 1945년에 끝났다고 한다.

07 나의 아들은 기름이 물보다 무겁다는 것을 알고 있었다.

08 그녀는 Mike는 파티에 올 수 없다고 말했다.

09 그녀는 Tom에게 그녀는 매일 머리를 감는다고 말했다.

10 그녀는 그 영화가 지루했었다고 말했다.

11 Alice는 그녀의 엄마가 그녀를 도와주지 않을 것이라는 것을 알았다.

12 우리는 서울이 부산보다 크다는 것을 배웠다.

13 그녀는 매주 토요일 바이올린을 연습한다고 말했다.

14 그들은 내게 달이 지구 주위를 돈다는 것을 말했다.

15 그 아이는 한국이 1592년 일본에게 침략당했다는 것을 알고 있었다.

❶ 01 loved 02 would take 03 could drive
04 had been 05 had been 06 discovered
07 rises 08 had agreed 09 had had
10 was 11 had tried 12 had cut

[해설]

01 *현재는 과거시제로 바꾼다.
04 *과거는 과거완료시제로 바꾼다.
05 *현재완료는 과거완료로 바꾼다.
06 *역사적 사실은 과거시제로 그대로 쓴다.
07 *불변의 진리는 현재시제로 그대로 쓴다.
08 *과거시제는 과거완료로 바꾼다.
10 *역사적 사실은 과거시제로 그대로 쓴다.
11 *과거시제는 과거완료로 바꾼다.
12 *현재완료는 과거완료로 바꾼다.

❷ 01 would 02 worked 03 had been
04 had made 05 closed 06 invented
07 could 08 had bought 09 would
10 was born 11 had gone 12 had been

[해설]

01 *현재는 과거시제로 바꾼다.
02 *현재는 과거시제로 바꾼다.
03 *과거시제는 과거완료로 바꾼다.
04 *과거시제는 과거완료로 바꾼다.
05 *현재는 과거시제로 바꾼다.
06 *역사적 사실은 과거시제로 그대로 쓴다.
07 *현재는 과거시제로 바꾼다.
08 *과거시제는 과거완료로 바꾼다.
10 *역사적 사실은 과거시제로 그대로 쓴다.
11 *현재완료는 과거완료로 바꾼다.
12 *현재완료는 과거완료로 바꾼다.

Check up & Writing

❶ 01 sets 02 would 03 boils
04 had seen 05 broke out 06 composed
07 invented 08 goes 09 was
10 goes 11 was / had been
12 had been

❷ 01 was built in 1931
02 he had given a ring to her
03 they are satisfied with their jobs
04 worked for a computer company last year
05 she goes to bed at 10 p.m.
06 Germany invaded Poland in 1939
07 the Apollo landed on the moon
08 the earth is larger than the moon
09 she has worked at the bank
10 she had met me before
11 they solved the pollution problem
12 would get good grades

Unit 03. 간접화법

Warm up

❶ 01 was 02 she 03 then
04 had seen 05 told, had 06 she
07 would 08 his 09 had bought
10 I 11 was 12 his

❷ 01 she 02 had eaten 03 if
04 could 05 my
06 asked / had got 07 I
08 had stolen 09 she
10 the next day 11 had
12 how

Start up

❶ 01 said that he 02 told me, I
03 she would leave 04 he had done
05 asked him, he 06 told him, he
07 asked, if 08 he had eaten
09 would call me 10 she had broken
11 asked, I 12 asked, if I

❷ 01 he was, then 02 she respected me

03 told, she had met　04 he would go
05 asked, when I could
06 told, she needed　07 asked, if I was
08 he didn't like to
09 he had visited, the day before
10 said, he could　　　11 he was there
12 he would, my

Check up & Writing

❶ 01 My mom told me that she had good news for me.
02 Bill told me that he loved my sister.
03 I told him that I would help him.
04 Sam told me that he would go swimming the next day.
05 He asked me if[whether] I liked Tom.
06 He told me that he agreed with me.
07 She asked her brother if[whether] he wanted some milk.
08 Paul asked me how I was doing at school.
09 He told me that he had done his best the day before.
10 He asked her where she had found the bag.
11 The doctor asked him if[whether] he coughed a lot.
12 He asked me if[whether] I had a cat.

❷ 01 He asked her who she was.
02 She told me that she had lost her dog the day before.
03 He asked me why she was crying.
04 The man asked her when the next train would arrive.
05 My mom told me that I made her happy.
06 He asked her if[whether] he could borrow her computer.
07 My teacher asked me if[whether] I had been in the shopping mall the day before.
08 James said that he had a fever and a runny nose.
09 The weather said[that] it would be windy the next day.
10 Joe asked her where she had bought that sofa.
11 John asked me if[whether] I had seen the game.
12 She asked me where I was going.

Level up

❶ 01 are　　　02 are　　　03 look
04 are　　　05 is　　　06 participate
07 is　　　08 want　　　09 has
10 are　　　11 goes　　　12 is
13 is　　　14 is　　　15 has

[해석]
01 공원에 있는 나무들이 매우 크다.
02 새장에 있는 새들은 매우 작다.
03 사무실에 있는 모든 사람들이 바쁘게 보인다.
04 무대 위에 있는 소녀들을 아니?
05 TV로 축구경기를 시청하는 것은 매우 재미있다.
06 많은 영화배우들이 매년 그 영화제에 참여하고 있다.
07 독신 여성의 수가 증가하고 있다.
08 Steve와 Susan은 패션디자이너가 되고 싶어한다.
09 Steve나 그의 엄마가 둘 중 한 명이 상자를 옮겨야 한다.
10 Mike뿐만 아니라 그의 부모님도 내 건강을 걱정하신다.
11 그녀와 Sam은 일요일에 교회에 가지 않는다.
12 일찍 일어나는 것이 건강에 좋다.
13 중고차를 판매하는 것이 삼촌의 직업이다.
14 내가 원하는 것은 집에 가서 자는 것이다.
15 냉장고의 모든 고기가 상했다.

❷ 01 are　　　02 is　　　03 is
04 has　　　05 has　　　06 is
07 are　　　08 has　　　09 are
10 visits　　　11 is　　　12 is
13 are　　　14 is　　　15 work

[해석]
01 내 모든 친구들이 개회식에 초대된다.
02 모든 가구가 프랑스에서 만들어 진다.

03 물리학을 공부하는 것은 그녀가 원하는 것이 아니다.

04 모든 사람은 사회에서 그들의 역할이 있다.

05 외국학생들의 수가 증가하고 있다.

06 균형 잡힌 식사를 하는 것이 매우 중요하다.

07 그 나라에서는 많은 언어들이 사용된다.

08 각 팀은 골키퍼를 포함해 6명의 선수가 있다.

09 Jane의 반 친구들과 Jane은 탁아소에서 자원봉사를 할 것이다.

10 Joe와 그의 친구는 모두 박물관에 가지 않는다.

11 네덜란드는 풍차로 유명하다.

12 기자로 일하는 것은 매우 어렵다.

13 버스의 모든 승객들이 학생이다.

14 필리핀은 7000개 이상의 섬들로 구성되어 있다.

15 이들은 나와 함께 일하는 사람들이다.

❸ 01 She asked me if[whether] I liked apples.

02 She told me that she had met Mike the day before.

03 He told me that he had loved her.

04 I asked her what her father had said about it.

05 He asked me which movie I would see.

06 John told me that he didn't like to listen to the radio that day.

07 My mom asked me if[whether] I had used her computer.

08 She asked me if[whether] I had seen John.

09 She asked me if[whether] I was hungry then.

10 She told me that she would meet him the next day.

11 Joe asked her where she had bought that bike.

12 My father told me that he didn't understand what I said.

❹ 01 said to, Do   02 I, now
03 I have, tomorrow   04 When, your
05 I will, tomorrow   06 Where did
07 Do you like
08 Why were you, yesterday
09 are you   10 do you, do
11 said to, "I will, tomorrow

[해석 및 해설]

01 *역사적 사실은 과거시제로 한다.

02 *접속사 if는 "~인지 아닌지"의 의미이다.
그녀는 내가 한국음식을 좋아하는지 물었다.

03 *⑤의 「Both A and B」는 복수취급을 하고 나머지는 단수취급을 한다.

04 *like는 현재형 일반 동사로 주어가 복수여야 합니다. 주어가 단수이면 likes가 와야 한다.
*"Not only A but also B"는 B에 동사의 수를 일치시킨다.

08 *직접화법의 시제가 과거이면 간접화법으로 전환 시 과거완료가 된다.

09 주절의 시제가 과거이므로 현재완료가 올 수 없다.

10 *직접화법의 시제가 과거이면 간접화법으로 전환 시 과거완료가 된다.

12 *역사적 사실은 과거시제로 한다.
나는 2002년에 월드컵이 한국과 일본에서 열렸다는 것을 알았다.

13 ① 그 또는 그녀의 엄마 중 한 사람은 그녀가 어디에 있는지 안다.
② 그녀와 너는 둘 다 거짓말쟁이가 아니다.
③ 그들 뿐 만 아니라 그녀도 일찍 일어난다.
④ 그와 그의 아내 둘다 의사이다.
⑤ 모든 학생은 말하기대회에 참여해야 한다.
*「every+단수명사」는 단수 취급 한다. 따라서 have to를 has to로 바꿔야 한다.

14 ① 그녀는 미국에 가 본 적이 있다고 말한다.
② Jessie는 Tim이 산책을 규칙적으로 했다고 한다.
③ 그는 콜럼버스가 미 대륙을 1492년에 발견했다고 말했다.
④ 그들은 내가 저녁으로 피자를 먹었다고 생각했다.
⑤ 나는 금연할 거라고 약속한다.

*③ 역사적 사실은 과거시제로 한다.

15 *② I was kind to my brother를 I was kind to her brother로 바꿔야 한다.

18 *직접화법의 시제가 과거이면 간접화법으로 전환 시 과거완료가 된다.

19 1) Sam 또는 그의 엄마 둘 중 한 명이 설거지를 해야 한다.

2) Mike뿐만 아니라 그의 부모님도 내 안전을 걱정하신다.

Review Test

❶ 01 What　　02 Who　　03 How
04 Why　　05 When　　06 Why
07 What　　08 Who　　09 Why
10 When　　11 Whose　　12 Where

❷ 01 How many　02 How often　03 How many
04 How much　05 How long

❸ 01 Why don't we go for a walk after dinner?
02 How about meeting at 4:00 tomorrow?
03 Shall we have a surprise birthday party for her?
04 Don't drive at the park.
05 Let's save the money for a rainy day.
06 Why don't you eat lots of vegetables.

❹ 01 do they　02 didn't they　03 can't you
04 isn't it　05 doesn't she　06 didn't he
07 is it

❺ 01 Do you know what she bought?
02 Why do you think she is so busy?
03 What do you think his favorite sport is?
04 How much do you think the shoes are?
05 Can you tell me what he looks like?
06 Do you know how big the museum is?

❻ 01 How　　02 What　　03 How
04 What　　05 How　　06 What
07 How　　08 What

❼ 01 How big the museum is!
02 How cheap these sneakers are!
03 What kind nurses they are!

04 How hard they work!
05 What sweet mangos these are! / How sweet these mangos are!
06 What a windy day (it is)!

❽ 01 has to　02 x　03 are　04 x
05 has　06 x　07 was　08 use

[해설]
01 *주어가 「every+단수명사」 또는 「each+단수명사」일 때, 동사는 단수형으로 쓴다.
02 *주어가 both A and B (A, B 둘 다) 일 때, 동사는 복수형으로 쓴다.
03 *「A number of 「많은~」+복수명사」일 때, 동사는 복수형으로 쓴다.
04 *주어가 이름(학문, 국가, 질병)일 때, 동사는 단수형으로 쓴다.
05 *주어가 「each+단수명사」일 때, 동사는 단수형으로 쓴다.
06 *상관접속사 구문이 주어일 때 동사는 B에 수를 일치시킨다.
07 *관계대명사가 이끄는 절은 선행사의 수에 동사를 일치시킨다. 선행사 cake가 단수이다.
08 *상관접속사 구문이 주어일 때 동사는 B에 수를 일치시킨다.

❾ 01 The boy told me he didn't want to eat pizza.
02 She told us that we looked very young.
03 He told her that he liked her daughter.
04 She asked him where he was.
05 She asked me where I had parked my car.
06 He asked her who she had met the day before.

Achievement test 4~6

01 ④　02 ④　03 ②　04 ③　05 ①
06 ④　07 ④　08 ③　09 ①　10 ④
11 ④　12 ⑤　13 ②　14 ②　15 ⑤
16 ⑤　17 ⑤　18 ②　19 ④　20 ①
21 ③　22 ③　23 learning
24 오늘은 긴장하지 마라.
25 Do you know what he is going to buy?
26 about reading a book tonight

27 Shall / Why don't

28 She asked him where he had got that?

29 She told me that I was kind to her.

30 get up – gets up

[해석 및 해설]

01 신발 사는 데 얼마를 썼니?

02 *앞의 동사시제가 과거이고 긍정이므로 didn't you 가 정답이다.

03 *접속사 if는 "~인지 아닌지"의 의미이다.

04 *for 6 months라고 기간을 대답하고 있으므로 How long으로 물어야 한다.

05 *which 다음에는 명사[대명사]가 올 수 있다.

07 *① can't she ② aren't you ③ didn't she ⑤ didn't he

08 *③은 산책을 했는지 물어보는 문장이고 나머지는 산책하자고 제안하는 문장이다.

10 *현재 완료는 간접화법에서 과거완료로 바꿔야 한다.

11 *간접의문문의 어순은 「의문사+주어+동사」이다. 따라서 ④의 what did he want는 what he wanted 로 바꿔야 한다.

12 *동사 know를 사용할 때 의문사는 know 다음에 위치한다.

13 *What+(a)+명사+주어+동사

14 그녀를 위해 아침식사를 만드는 거 어때?

15 *How often은 빈도를 묻는 질문으로 ⑤번이 가장 적합하다.

16 *next month라고 시간을 답하고 있으므로 ⑤번이 가장 적합하다.

17 *동사 know를 사용할 때 의문시는 know 다음에 위치한다. → Do you know when she fixed the door?

18 *Neither A or B는 B에 동사의 수를 일치시켜야 하므로 like를 likes로 바꿔야 한다.

19 *동사 think를 사용한 간접의문문은 의문사가 문두에 위치한다.

20 *Why don't you+동사원형은 '~하는 게 어때'라는 의미로 상대방에게 권유할 때 사용한다.

23 *How about+~ing는 '~하는 게 어때?'라는 제안 문이다.

28 *직접화법의 시제가 과거일 때 간접화법으로 전환하면 과거완료가 되어야 합니다.

30 *A as well as B는 A에 수를 일치시켜야 한다. 따라서 get up을 gets up으로 바꿔야 한다.

실전모의고사 ❶

01 ③	02 ⑤	03 ①	04 ④	05 ④
06 ③	07 ③	08 ④	09 ⑤	10 ①
11 ④	12 ②	13 ⑤	14 ②	15 ①
16 ⑤	17 ③	18 ①	19 ③	20 ①

21 Which   22 1) didn't you 2) does she

23 we were rich

24 she would leave the next day

25 Don't be nervous.

[해석 및 해설]

01 Twice a week. (일주일에 두 번)라고 빈도를 나타내고 있으므로 빈칸에는 often이 와야 한다.

03 빈칸 다음에 동사가 왔으며 선행사는 the man이므로 who가 와야 한다.

04 주절의 시제가 과거(didn't)이므로 빈칸에는 would be가 와야 한다.

05 선행사가 books이므로 관계대명사 which가 어울린다.

06 관계대명사 that은 선행사가 사람과 사물 일 때 모두 사용할 수 있다.

08 did를 한 시제 앞선 had done으로 바꿔야 한다.

12 ② He asked me who he was.를 He asked me who I was.로 고쳐야 한다.

14 우리는 전쟁이 끝날 날을 기다리고 있다.
관계부사 when은 on which로 바꿔 쓸 수 있다.

15 ①은 의문사이고 나머지는 관계대명사이다.
① 너는 누구를 가장 존경하니?
② 그녀가 저 기계를 발명한 과학자이다.
③ 나는 너를 아는 소녀를 만났다.
④ 이 사람이 너를 만나고 싶어하는 사람이다.
⑤ 나는 치마를 입은 소녀를 의미하는 거다.

16 ⑤에는 관계대명사 whose가 필요하고 나머지는 who 가 필요하다.
① 옆집에 사는 여성은 작가이다.
② 그에게 책을 준 사람을 아니?
③ 나래이터는 연극에서 벌어지는 일을 설명하는 사람이다.
④ 누가 음악회에 갔는지 아니?
⑤ 옛날에 이름이 Pride인 어리석은 왕자가 살았다.

17 주격 관계대명사는 생략할 수 없다.

18 ①의 which를 where로 바꿔야 한다.

20 ② where → which ③ which → whose
④ when → which[that] ⑤ how → when
21 둘 중 하나를 비교하는 것이므로 which가 필요하다.
24 tomorrow는 the next day가 되어야 한다.

실전모의고사 ❷

01 ③	**02** ①	**03** ⑤	**04** ⑤	**05** ⑤
06 ④	**07** ①	**08** ③	**09** ③	**10** ⑤
11 ④	**12** ②	**13** ⑤	**14** ②	**15** ①
16 ④	**17** ④	**18** ⑤	**19** ④	**20** ②

21 How **22** How **23** who[that]
24 wish I were **25** if[whether]

[해석 및 해설]
01 가정법과거 문장이므로 would win을 고른다.
02 「What+a+형용사+명사+주어+동사!」
03 선행사가 the hotel이므로 where가 적당하다.
04 Let's로 시작하는 문장의 부가의문문에는 shall we 가 온다.
05 How+형용사[부사]+주어+동사!
07 How many+복수 명사
08 선행사가 The watch이고 주격 관계대명사가 필요하 므로 which가 와야 한다.
동사 marry 목적어가 필요하므로 관계대명사 whom 이 와야 한다.
13 시제가 과거이므로 가정법 과거완료의 문장이 와야 한 다.
14 주격 관계대명사는 생략 할 수 없다.
① 나는 네가 좋아하는 남자를 알고 있다.
② 나는 춤을 추고 있는 소녀를 좋아한다.
③ 이것이 그가 구매한 책이다.
④ 그것은 그녀가 잃어버린 시계와 같은 종류이다.
⑤ 나는 Ann이 입고 있는 드레스가 마음에 든다.
15 ① I thought that he can fix the broken door에 서 주절의 시제가 과거이므로 종속절의 can을 could 로 바꿔야 한다.
① 나는 그가 부서진 문을 고칠 수 있다고 생각했다.
② 엄마는 Kevin이 나와 가장 친한 친구라는 것을 안 다.
③ 나는 그녀가 거짓말을 하지 않았다고 믿고 있다.

④ 그는 당근을 싫어한다고 말한다.
⑤ 우리는 축제가 성공적이었다는 것을 알았다.
16 ④의 stove는 사물이므로 which가 필요하고 나머지 는 who가 필요하다.
18 think가 있으면 의문사 where이 문장 앞에 위치한다.
20 What a honest boy he is! → What an honest boy he is!
21 How+형용사[부사]+주어+동사!

실전모의고사 ❸

01 ①	**02** ②	**03** ④	**04** ④	**05** ④
06 ⑤	**07** ②	**08** ⑤	**09** ③	**10** ①
11 ③	**12** ②	**13** ②	**14** ①	**15** ②
16 ④	**17** ⑤	**18** ⑤	**19** ④	**20** ③

21 about taking a rest for five minutes
22 He said that he would be busy the next day.
23 couldn't **24** don't they
25 Tell me the story that [which] you heard from him.

[해석 및 해설]
01 부정 명령문이므로 Don't이 필요하다.
젖은 손으로 전기 코드를 만지지 마라.
02 동사 bought의 목적어가 필요하므로 which가 와야 한다.
03 관계대명사 what은 선행사가 필요하지 않습니다.
04 가정법과거완료는 'If+주어+had+p.p~, 주어+would /could+have+p.p~'
05 주절의 시제가 과거이므로 빈칸에는 과거시제인 studied 가 와야 한다.
06 빈도를 나타내는 의문사는 How often이다.
07 Which 다음에는 명사나 부정대명사가 올 수 있다.
09 관계대명사 that은 선행사가 사물이나 사람 모두에 사 용된다.
내 가방에 있는 책은 너의 것이 아니다.
나는 선생님인 나의 삼촌이 자랑스럽다.
12 How+형용사[부사]+주어+동사!
13 ② How a nice car is! → What a nice car it is!

14 Because로 답하고 있으므로 Why로 질문해야 한다.

　　A: 너는 왜 음악을 듣니?

　　B: 왜냐하면 음악은 나를 기분 좋게 해.

15 간접의문문은 '의문사+주어+동사'의 어순이 되어야 한다.

17 ① is he → isn't he

　　② will he → won't he

　　③ weren't they → were they

　　④ aren't we? → aren't you

19 ④ what does she want → what she wants

21 Why don't you ~? = How about+동명사 ~?

22 tomorrow를 the next day로 바꿔야 한다.

23 과거의 일이므로 can't을 couldn't로 바꿔야 한다.

24 She and he는 they로 받는다.

Longman

그래머
멘토
조이
플러스
넷

MENTOR

정답
및
해설

GRAMMAR

JOY

pluS 4

Longman

그래머
멘토
조이
플러스
넷

MENTOR

Vocabulary
미니북

GRAMMAR

JOY

pluS

4

PEARSON

GRAMMAR MENTOR JOY

Vocabulary 미니북

plus 4

01	accept 받아들이다 [əksépt]	He decided to accept what she offered. 그는 그녀가 제안한 것을 받아들이기로 결심했다.
02	address 주소 [ədrés]	They knew my e-mail address. 그들은 내 이메일 주소를 알고 있었다.
03	alive 살아 있는 [əláiv]	I wish my grandmother were alive. 할머니가 살아계시면 좋을 텐데.
04	apologize 사과하다 [əpálədʒàiz]	He had to apologize to me. 그는 나에게 사과를 했어야 했다.
05	awful 끔찍한, 지독한 [ɔ́:fəl]	This chicken soup tastes awful. 닭고기 수프가 정말 맛이 없다.
06	comfortable 편안한, [kʌ́mfərtəbl] 편한	I wish my shoes were more comfortable. 내 신발이 좀 더 편하다면 좋을 텐데.
07	complete 완성하다 [kəmplí:t]	The painter completed the wonderful painting. 그 화가는 그 멋진 그림을 완성했다.
08	courage 용기 [kə́:ridʒ]	If she had courage, she would make a decision by herself. 그녀에게 용기가 있다면 그녀는 스스로 결정을 내릴 텐데.
09	crop 농작물 [krɑp]	If it had rained, the crops wouldn't have died. 비가 왔더라면 그 농작물은 죽지 않았을 텐데.
10	during ~동안 [djú(:)əriŋ]	I listened to the teacher during the class. 나는 수업 시간에 선생님 말에 귀를 기울였다.
11	envy 부러워하다 [énvi]	I envy him because he is good at skiing. 나는 그가 스키를 잘 타서 부럽다.
12	experiment 실험 [ikspérəmənt]	I am sorry that I spoiled the experiment. 그 실험을 망쳐서 미안하다.
13	feeling 느낌, 기분 [fí:liŋ]	I hurt her feelings last night. 내가 어젯밤에 그녀의 감정을 상하게 했다.
14	flight 비행기; 비행 [flait]	They will not miss the flight. 그들은 그 비행기를 놓치지 않을 것이다.
15	fluently 유창하게 [flú(:)əntli]	I can speak English fluently. 나는 영어를 유창하게 말할 수 있다.

16	forget 잊다 [fərgét]	Don't forget the advice which I gave you. 내가 너에게 했던 그 충고를 잊지 마라.
17	forgive 용서하다 [fərgív]	I'll never forgive him for what he did. 난 그가 한 일을 결코 용서하지 않을 것이다.
18	happen 일어나다, 발생하다 [hǽpən]	The car accident happened last night. 그 자동차 사고가 어젯밤 발생했다.
19	hesitation 주저, 망설임 [hèzitéiʃən]	He took the opportunity without hesitation. 그가 망설임 없이 그 기회를 잡았다.
20	interview 면접, 인터뷰 [íntərvjù:]	He has a job interview today. 그는 오늘 직장 면접이 있다.
21	introduce 소개하다 [ìntrədjú:s]	I am happy to introduce him to you. 나는 너에게 그를 소개해서 기쁘다.
22	ladder 사다리 [lǽdər]	He is climbing up the ladder. 그는 사다리를 타고 올라가고 있다.
23	literature 문학 [lítərətʃùər]	Robin is sad not to pass the literature test. Robin은 그 문학 시험에 통과하지 못해서 슬프다.
24	millionaire 백만장자 [mìljənɛ́ər]	If he were a millionaire, he would help the needy. 그가 백만장자라면 빈곤한 사람들을 도울 수 있을 텐데.
25	nature 자연 [néitʃər]	Children who play in nature have more positive feelings. 자연에서 노는 어린이들은 더욱 긍정적인 마음을 갖는다.
26	opportunity 기회 [àpərtjú:nəti]	It sounds like a great opportunity for me. 그것은 나에게는 아주 좋은 기회인 것 같다.
27	polite 예의 바른 [pəláit]	I wish my brother were more polite. 내 남동생이 더 예의 바르면 좋을 텐데.
28	recipe 요리법 [résəpì:]	You had to follow the recipe when you cooked. 너는 요리할 때 요리법을 따라야 했다.
29	stomach ache 복통 [stʌ́məkeik]	I have a stomachache now. 나 지금 배가 아파.
30	sunscreen 자외선 차단제 [sʌnskri:n]	If you used sunscreen, you would not get sunburned. 네가 자외선 차단제를 사용하면 햇볕에 타지 않을 텐데.

Check Up

1 다음 우리말 뜻에 해당하는 영어 단어를 쓰세요.

01 사과하다

02 느낌, 기분

03 요리법

04 살아 있는

05 일어나다, 발생하다

06 끔찍한, 지독한

07 완성하다

08 편안한, 편한

09 부러워하다

10 비행기; 비행

11 유창하게

12 면접, 인터뷰

13 문학

14 자연

15 자외선 차단제

2 다음 영어 단어에 해당하는 우리말 뜻을 쓰세요.

01 address

02 courage

03 crop

04 experiment

05 forgive

06 introduce

07 ladder

08 millionaire

09 opportunity

10 stomachache

3 다음 빈칸에 우리말과 일치하도록 알맞은 단어를 쓰세요.

01 He decided to _____ what she offered.
내가 그녀가 제안한 것을 받아들이기로 결심했다

02 I listened to the teacher _____ the class.
내가 수업 시간에 선생님 말에 귀를 기울였다.

03 Don't _____ the advice which I gave you.
내가 너에게 했던 그 충고를 잊지 마라.

04 It sounds like a great _____ for me.
그것은 나에게는 아주 좋은 기회인 것 같다.

05 I wish my brother were more _____.
내 남동생이 더 예의 바르면 좋을 텐데.

01	advice 충고, 조언 [ədváis]	I didn't accept her advice then. 나는 그때 그녀의 충고를 받아들이지 않았다.
02	astronaut 우주비행사 [金strənɔːt]	Their dream is to become astronauts. 그들의 꿈은 우주비행사가 되는 것이다.
03	bill 청구서 [bil]	This is an electric bill. 이것은 전기요금 고지서이다.
04	bark 짖다 [bark]	The dog barked at me yesterday. 그 개가 어제 나에게 짖었다.
05	biology 생물학 [baiɑ́lədʒi]	I am teaching the students who are interested in biology. 나는 생물학에 관심 있어 하는 학생들을 가르치고 있다.
06	blond 금발 [blɑnd]	I met the woman with blond hair. 나는 금발 머리 여성을 만났다.
07	boring 지루한 [bɔ́ːriŋ]	What she told me was very boring. 그녀가 내게 말한 것은 매우 지루했다.
08	choose 선택하다 [tʃuːz]	Choose what you want for dinner. 네가 저녁식사로 원하는 것을 선택해라
09	conductor 지휘자 [kəndʌ́ktər]	Simon became a conductor. Simon은 지휘자가 되었다.
10	cover 표지 [kʌ́vər]	I found the book whose cover is yellow. 나는 책 표지가 노란색인 책을 발견했다
11	cure 치료하다 [kjuər]	She wanted to meet someone who could cure her daughter. 그녀는 자신의 딸을 치료할 수 있는 누군가를 만나기를 바랐다.
12	damage 손상을 주다, [dǽmidʒ] 피해, 손상	His house was damaged by the storm. 그의 집은 폭풍으로 손상되었다.
13	difficulty 어려움 [dífəkʌ̀lti]	He got over many difficulties. 그는 많은 어려움들을 극복했다.
14	expel 추방하다, 쫓아내다 [ikspél]	His brother was expelled from the school. 그의 형은 그 학교에서 추방되었다.
15	expensive 비싼 [ikspénsiv]	The dictionary was a little expensive. 그 사전은 조금 비쌌다.

16	feather 깃털 [féðər]	Look at the birds whose feathers are colorful. 깃털이 화려한 새들을 봐라.
17	flow 흐르다 [flou]	The river flows through this area. 그 강은 이 지역을 흐르고 있다.
18	mention 언급하다 [ménʃən]	I know the man who you mentioned. 나는 네가 언급한 남자를 알고 있다.
19	navigation 항해, [nævəɡéiʃən] 항법	My car has no navigation system. 내 차는 항법 시스템이 없다.
20	ocean 바다, 해양 [óuʃən]	I want a room which has an ocean view. 나는 바다가 보이는 방을 원한다.
21	orphan 고아 [ɔ́ːrfən]	A child whose parents are dead is called an orphan. 부모님이 돌아가신 아이를 고아라고 부른다.
22	record 기록 [rékərd]	What an amazing record it is! 그것은 매우 놀라운 기록이구나!
23	repair 수리하다 [ripέər]	The copy machine needs to be repaired. 그 복사기는 수리가 필요하다.
24	seem ~처럼 보이다 [siːm]	He told me a story which seemed real. 그는 나에게 사실 같은 이야기를 했다.
25	several 몇 개의 [sévərəl]	I have several friends whose jobs are taxi drivers. 나는 택시운전이 직업인 친구들이 몇 명 있다.
26	steal 훔치다 [stiːl]	This man stole my car. 이 남자가 내 차를 훔쳤다.
27	suffer 고생하다 [sʌ́fər]	Kevin knows the man who suffers from a headache. Kevin은 두통으로 고생하는 남자를 알고 있다.
28	system 시스템 [sístəm]	Stress can weaken our immune system. 스트레스는 우리의 면역 체계를 악화시킬 수 있다.
29	teenager 십대 [tíːnèidʒər]	Physics is not popular among teenagers. 물리학은 십대들 사이에서 인기가 없다.
30	translate 번역하다 [trænsléit]	His job is to translate English into Korean. 그의 직업은 영어를 한국어로 번역하는 것이다.

Check Up

1 다음 우리말 뜻에 해당하는 영어 단어를 쓰세요.

01 충고, 조언

02 짖다

03 몇 개의

04 번역하다

05 선택하다

06 언급하다

07 추방하다, 쫓아내다

08 손상을 주다, 피해, 손상

09 깃털

10 흐르다

11 항해, 항법

12 수리하다

13 ~처럼 보이다

14 고생하다

15 십대

2 다음 영어 단어에 해당하는 우리말 뜻을 쓰세요.

01 astronaut

02 bill

03 blond

04 conductor

05 cure

06 difficulty

07 orphan

08 record

09 steal

10 system

3 다음 빈칸에 우리말과 일치하도록 알맞은 단어를 쓰세요.

01 I am teaching the students who are interested in _____.
나는 생물학에 관심 있어 하는 학생들을 가르치고 있다.

02 What she told me was very _____.
그녀가 내게 말한 것은 매우 지루했다.

03 I found the book whose _____ is yellow.
나는 책 표지가 노란색인 책을 발견했다

04 The dictionary was a little _____.
그 사전은 조금 비쌌다.

05 I want a room which has an _____ view.
그는 바다가 보이는 전망의 방을 원한다.

Chapter 3

관계사 II

01	absent 결석한 [ǽbsənt]	Why is John absent today? John이 왜 오늘 결석했니?
02	anniversary 기념일 [ænəvə́:rsəri]	My husband gave me this ring for our wedding anniversary. 남편이 결혼기념일 선물로 이 반지를 줬다.
03	bankrupt 파산한 [bǽŋkrʌpt]	The company went bankrupt last year. 그 회사가 작년에 망했다.
04	bloom 꽃이 피다 [blu:m]	A lot of flowers bloom in spring. 봄에 많은 꽃들이 핀다.
05	celebrate 기념하다 [sélәbrèit]	People celebrate the birth of Jesus Christ at Christmas. 성탄절에 사람들은 예수의 탄생을 기념한다.
06	company 회사 [kʌ́mpəni]	They started to work for this company five years ago. 그들이 이 회사에서 5년 전에 일하기 시작했다.
07	couch 긴 의자, 소파 [kautʃ]	He asked me where I got the couch. 그는 내가 그 긴 의자를 어디서 얻었는지 나에게 물었다.
08	coworker 직장동료 [kouwə́:rkər]	I met Sam, who is my coworker. 나는 Sam을 만났는데, 그는 나의 직장 동료이다.
09	crash (자동차 충돌· [kræʃ] 항공기 추락) 사고	This is how he survived that crash. 이것이 그가 자동차 사고에서 살아남은 방법이다.
10	currently 현재 [kə́:rəntli]	The palace is currently under renovation. 그 궁전은 현재 수리 중이다.
11	decision 결정 [disíʒən]	Now is the time to make a decision. 지금이야 말로 결정을 내려야 할 때다.
12	deliver 배달하다 [dilívər]	When can you deliver the furniture? 언제 가구를 배달해 주실 수 있나요?
13	destination 목적지 [dèstənéiʃən]	We found the way he got to the destination. 우리는 그가 어떻게 목적지에 도착했는지 알았다.
14	explain 설명하다 [ikspléin]	He explained the reason why the car broke down. 그는 그 자동차가 고장 난 이유를 설명했다.
15	favor 부탁, 찬성, 친절 [féivər]	I'm calling you to ask you a favor. 내가 너에게 부탁 좀 하려고 전화했어.

16	flat 평평한; 김빠진, 맥 빠진 [flæt]	The video shows how we change a flat tire.
		그 비디오는 펑크난 타이어를 바꾸는 방법을 보여주고 있다.
17	fur 털 [fəːr]	Tony has a cat whose fur is long.
		Tony는 털이 긴 고양이를 가지고 있다.
18	graduation 졸업 [græ̀dʒəwéiʃən]	I want to work at this company after graduation.
		나는 졸업 후 이 회사에서 일하고 싶다.
19	immigrate 이민가다 [íməgrèit]	Paul immigrated to Canada last year.
		Paul은 작년에 캐나다로 이민갔다.
20	invent 발명하다 [invént]	Who invented a telephone?
		누가 전화를 발명했니?
21	lawyer 변호사 [lɔ́ːjər]	This is how she became a lawyer.
		이것이 그녀가 변호사가 된 방법이다
22	luggage 짐 [lʌ́gidʒ]	The luggage she is carrying is very heavy.
		그녀가 운반하고 있는 짐은 매우 무겁다.
23	overlook (건물 등이) [óuvərlùk] 내려다보다	He is living in the house overlooking the river.
		그는 강이 내려다보이는 집에 살고 있다.
24	performance 공연, [pərfɔ́ːrməns] 연주회	That's why she canceled her performance.
		그것이 그녀가 자신의 공연을 취소한 이유이다.
25	perfume 향수 [pə́ːrfjùːm]	Did you use this perfume?
		너는 이 향수를 사용했니?
26	recommend 추천하다 [rèkəménd]	She read the book which he recommended.
		그녀는 그가 추천한 책을 읽었다.
27	renovation 수선, 수리 [rinouvéiʃən]	The library has been closed for renovation.
		그 도서관은 수리를 위해 문을 닫았다.
28	respect 존경하다 [rispékt]	She respects the teacher a lot.
		그녀는 그 선생님을 많이 존경한다.
29	subscribe 구독하다 [səbskráib]	She wants to subscribe to this magazine.
		그녀는 이 잡지를 구독하고 싶다.
30	survive 살아남다, [sərváiv] 생존하다	He survived the terrible crash.
		그는 끔찍한 자동차 사고에서 살아남았다

Check Up

1 다음 우리말 뜻에 해당하는 영어 단어를 쓰세요.

01 결석한

02 파산한

03 꽃이 피다

04 기념하다

05 부탁, 찬성, 친절

06 긴 의자, 소파

07 직장동료

08 살아남다, 생존하다

09 설명하다

10 공연, 연주회

11 평평한; 김빠진, 맥 빠진

12 이민가다

13 변호사

14 (건물 등이) 내려다보다

15 구독하다

2 다음 영어 단어에 해당하는 우리말 뜻을 쓰세요.

01 anniversary

02 company

03 decision

04 deliver

05 destination

06 fur

07 invent

08 perfume

09 recommend

10 respect

3 다음 빈칸에 우리말과 일치하도록 알맞은 단어를 쓰세요.

01 This is how he survived that _____.
이것이 그가 자동차 사고에서 살아남은 방법이다.

02 The palace is _____ under renovation.
그 궁전은 현재 수선 중이다.

03 I want to work at this company after _____.
나는 졸업 후 이 회사에서 일하고 싶다.

04 The _____ she is carrying is very heavy.
그녀가 운반하고 있는 짐은 매우 무겁다.

05 The library has been closed for _____.
그 도서관은 수리를 위해 문을 닫았다.

Chapter 4

여러 가지 문장 I

01	about 대략 [əbáut]	She knows a lot about different cultures. 그녀는 다른 문화에 대해 많이 알고 있다.
02	answer 대답하다 [ǽnsər]	The questions were hard to answer. 그 질문들은 대답하기 어려웠다.
03	architect 건축가 [á:rkitèkt]	He is a very famous architect. 그는 매우 유명한 건축가다.
04	bite 소량의 음식[식사], [bait] 요기	Shall we go out for a bite? 간단히 뭐 좀 먹으러 나갈래?
05	bother 괴롭히다 [báðər]	Let's not bother him. 그를 방해하지 마라.
06	diplomat 외교관 [dípləmæt]	I want to be a diplomat. 나는 외교관이 되고 싶다.
07	disappointed 실망한 [dìsəpɔ́intid]	Don't be disappointed. 실망하지 마라.
08	display 진열 [displéi]	I want to buy the shoes on display. 난 진열 중인 그 신발을 사고 싶다.
09	election 선거 [ilékʃən]	Who did you support in the election? 너는 선거에서 누구를 지지했니?
10	electrical 전자의 [iléktrikəl]	Let's unplug electrical equipments after we use them. 전자 장비를 사용한 후에는 전원을 뽑아라.
11	equipment 장비 [ikwípmənt]	They are replacing some office equipment. 그들은 사무 장비를 교체하고 있다.
12	favorite 좋아하는 [féivərit]	What do you think his favorite sport is ? 그가 좋아하는 운동이 뭐라고 생각하니?
13	furniture 기구 [fɔ́:rnitʃər]	All the furniture is made in France. 모든 가구가 프랑스에서 만들어 진다.
14	subject 과목 [sʌ́bdʒikt]	Science is the subject they like most. 과학은 그들이 가장 좋아하는 과목이다.
15	language 언어 [lǽŋgwidʒ]	What is the language spoken in Spain? 스페인에서 어떤 언어가 사용되니?

16	leave 떠나다; 두고 오다 [liːv]	Where did you leave your umbrella? 너는 우산을 어디에 두고 왔니?
17	nervous 긴장한 [nə́ːrvəs]	My brother is so nervous now. 남동생은 지금 무척 긴장하고 있다.
18	noise 소음 [nɔiz]	Please, don't make a noise. 소란 피우지 마세요.
19	recycle 재활용하다 [riːsáikl]	Let's recycle bottles and newspapers. 병과 신문을 재활용하자.
20	refuse 거절하다 [réfjuːs]	If I were Steve, I would refuse the offer. 내가 Steve라면 그 제안을 거절할 텐데.
21	request 요청, 요구 [rikwést]	Why did they refuse my request? 그들은 왜 나의 요구를 거절했니?
22	return 돌아오다 [ritə́ːrn]	He will return to school next Tuesday. 그는 다음주 화요일에 학교에 돌아올 것이다.
23	statue 동상 [stǽtʃuː]	How tall is the statue over there? 저기 있는 동상은 얼마나 높니?
24	such 그러한 [sətʃ; sʌtʃ]	You should not buy such a book. 너는 그런 책은 사지 말아야 한다.
25	support 지지하다, 지원하다 [səpɔ́ːrt]	I supported Mr. Clerk in the election. 나는 선거에서 Clerk 씨를 지지했다.
26	surf 인터넷을 서핑[검색] 하다 [səːrf]	How many hours a day do you surf on the Internet? 너는 하루에 얼마나 많은 시간을 인터넷을 서핑하니?
27	trust 신뢰하다 [trʌst]	Be honest, and people will trust you. 정직하라 그러면 사람들이 너를 믿을 것이다
28	unplug ~에서 전원을 끊다 [ʌnplʌ́g]	I have to unplug the power cable later. 난 나중에 전원 케이블을 빼야 한다.
29	usually 보통, 대개 [júːʒuəli]	I usually get up at 7 a.m. 나는 보통 아침 7시에 일어난다.
30	waste 낭비하다 [weist]	Don't waste your money. 너의 돈을 낭비하지 마라.

Check Up

1 다음 우리말 뜻에 해당하는 영어 단어를 쓰세요.

01 대답하다

02 떠나다; 두고 오다

03 괴롭히다

04 보통, 대개

05 진열

06 전자의

07 좋아하는

08 지지하다, 지원하다

09 실망한

10 언어

11 긴장한

12 거절하다

13 요청, 요구

14 인터넷을 서핑[검색]하다

15 ~에서 전원을 끊다

2 다음 영어 단어에 해당하는 우리말 뜻을 쓰세요.

01 about

02 architect

03 diplomat

04 equipment

05 subject

06 noise

07 return

08 statue

09 trust

10 waste

3 다음 빈칸에 우리말과 일치하도록 알맞은 단어를 쓰세요.

01 Shall we go out for a _____?
간단히 뭐 좀 먹으러 나갈래?

02 Who did you support in the _____?
너는 선거에서 누구를 지지했니?

03 All the _____ is made in France.
모든 가구가 프랑스에서 만들어 진다.

04 Let's _____ bottles and newspapers.
병과 신문을 재활용하자.

05 You should not buy _____ a book.
너는 그런 책은 사지 말아야 한다.

Chapter 5

여러 가지 문장 II

01	abroad 해외에서 [əbrɔ́ːd]	**Mike studied** abroad. Mike는 해외에서 공부했다.
02	accident 사고 [ǽksidənt]	**The car** accident **happened yesterday.** 어제 자동차 사고가 발생했다.
03	amazing 놀라 [əméiziŋ]	**What an** amazing **record it is!** 그것은 매우 놀라운 기록이구나!
04	anger 노여움, 화 [ǽŋgər]	**His face turned red with** anger. 그의 얼굴은 노여움으로 붉게 변했다.
05	borrow 빌리다 [bárou]	**You can** borrow **the books in the library.** 너는 도서관에서 책들은 빌릴 수 있다.
06	breathe 숨 쉬다 [briːð]	**They can** breathe **under the water.** 그것들은 바다 아래서 숨을 쉴 수 있다.
07	cheat 속이다, 부정행위를 하다 [tʃiːt]	**He won't** cheat **on the test.** 그는 시험에서 부정행위를 하지 않을 것이다.
08	cheerful 발랄한, 쾌활한 [tʃíərfəl]	**How** cheerful **those boys are!** 저 소년들은 매우 쾌활하구나!
09	creative 창조적인 [kriéitiv]	**Jack has a really** creative **idea.** Jack은 매우 창의적인 생각을 가지고 있다.
10	curious 호기심이 있는 [kjú(ː)əriəs]	**She is very** curious. 그녀는 호기심이 많다.
11	efficient 효율적인 [ifíʃənt]	**The new copy machine is more** efficient. 그 새 복사기가 더 효율적이다.
12	excellent 훌륭한 [ǽksələnt]	**What an** excellent **idea it is!** 그것은 매우 훌륭한 생각이구나!
13	fantastic 환상적인 [fæntǽstik]	**The painting on the wall is very** fantastic. 벽에 걸린 그 그림은 매우 환상적이다.
14	film 영화 [film]	**Let's go to the** film **festival.** 영화제에 가자.
15	greedy 욕심 많은 [gríːdi]	**She is a very** greedy **student.** 그녀는 매우 욕심 많은 학생이다.

16	heavily 심하게, 아주 많이 [hévəli]	How heavily it rains! 얼마나 비가 많이 내리는지!
17	jealous 질투심이 있는 [dʒéləs]	They are jealous of Sue's success. 그들은 Sue의 성공을 질투한다.
18	pill 알약 [pil]	He takes the pill every morning. 그는 매일 아침 알약을 먹는다.
19	present 선물 [prézənt]	What a wonderful present it is! 그것은 매우 훌륭한 선물이구나!
20	promise 약속하다 [prámis]	I promise that I will stop smoking. 나는 금연할 거라고 약속한다.
21	purse (여성용) 지갑 [pəːrs]	She found the lost purse. 그녀는 잃어버린 지갑을 찾았다.
22	responsible 책임 있는 [rispánsəbl]	He is responsible for the accident. 그는 그 사고에 책임이 있다.
23	result 결과 [rizʌ́lt]	Don't worry about the test result. 시험 성적에 대해서 걱정하지 마라.
24	scary 무서운 [skέ(ː)əri]	They are very scary movies. 그것들은 매우 무서운 영화들이다.
25	selfish 이기적인 [sélfiʃ]	What a selfish man he is! 그는 정말 이기적인 사람이구나!
26	solve 해결하다 [sɑlv]	Sam solved the math problem. Sam이 그 수학 문제를 풀었다.
27	steep 가파른 [stiːp]	The stairs on the third floor are too steep. 3층 계단은 너무 가파르다.
28	terrible 끔찍한 [térəbl]	How terrible the accident is! 사고가 매우 끔찍하구나!
29	wallet 지갑[남성용] [wálit]	I left my wallet at home. 나는 지갑을 집에 두고 왔다.
30	wonder 궁금해 하다 [wʌ́ndər]	I wonder where she lives. 나는 그녀가 어디에 사는지 궁금하다.

Check Up

1 다음 우리말 뜻에 해당하는 영어 단어를 쓰세요.

01 빌리다

02 해외에서

03 발랄한, 쾌활한

04 호기심이 있는

05 궁금해 하다

06 환상적인

07 욕심 많은

08 책임 있는

09 심하게, 아주 많이

10 질투심이 있는

11 (여성용) 지갑

12 무서운

13 이기적인

14 해결하다

15 끔찍한

2 다음 영어 단어에 해당하는 우리말 뜻을 쓰세요.

01 accident

02 amazing

03 excellent

04 film

05 pill

06 present

07 promise

08 result

09 steep

10 wallet

3 다음 빈칸에 우리말과 일치하도록 알맞은 단어를 쓰세요.

01 His face turned red with _____.
그의 얼굴은 노여움으로 붉게 변했다.

02 They can _____ under the water.
그것들은 바다 아래서 숨을 쉴 수 있다.

03 He won't _____ on the test.
그는 시험에서 부정행위를 하지 않을 것이다.

04 Jack has a really _____ idea.
Jack은 매우 창의적인 생각을 가지고 있다.

05 The new copy machine is more _____.
그 새 복사기가 더 효율적이다.

Chapter 6

일치와 화법

01	accurate 정확한 [ǽkjərit]	The information in his books is accurate. 그의 책들에 있는 정보는 정확하다.
02	ceremony 의식 [sérəmòuni]	All my friends are invited to the opening ceremony. 내 모든 친구들이 개회식에 초대된다.
03	college 대학 [kálidʒ]	What I want to study at college is economics. 내가 대학에서 공부하려고 하는 것은 경제학이다.
04	complain 불평하다 [kəmpléin]	She complained that the movie had been boring. 그녀는 그 영화가 지루했었다고 불평했다.
05	compose 작곡하다 [kəmpóuz]	Beethoven composed "Moonlight Sonata." 베토벤이 월광 소나타를 작곡했다.
06	consist 구성하다 [kənsíst]	The United States consists of 50 states. 미국은 50개의 주로 구성되어 있다.
07	cooperate 협력하다 [kouápərèit]	You agreed to cooperate with each other. 너희들은 서로 협력하겠다고 동의했다.
08	decrease 줄어들다 [díːkriːs]	The number of traffic accidents has decreased rapidly. 교통사고 수가 빠르게 감소했다.
09	discover 발견하다 [diskávər]	Columbus discovered America in 1492. 콜럼버스가 미 대륙을 1492년에 발견했다.
10	foreign 외국의 [fɔ́ːrin]	Studying foreign languages is very useful. 외국어를 공부하는 것은 매우 유용하다.
11	embassy 대사관 [émbəsi]	How can I get to the embassy? 대사관에는 어떻게 가죠?
12	emigrant 이민자 [éməgrənt]	The number of emigrants is decreasing. 이민자들의 수가 감소하고 있다.
13	employee 종업원 [implɔiíː]	All the employees at the department bring their lunch. 백화점의 모든 직원들이 점심을 싸온다.
14	exhausted 지친 [igzɔ́ːstid]	Every person in the office looks exhausted. 이 사무실의 모든 사람이 지쳐 보인다.
15	gravity 중력 [grǽvəti]	Isaac Newton discovered the law of gravity. Isaac Newton이 중력의 법칙을 발견했다.

16	import 수입하다 [ímpɔ́ːrt]	The chairs were imported from Italy. 그 의자들은 이태리에서 수입되었다.
17	increase 증가하다 [ínkrìːs]	The number of cars in Seoul has increased lately. 최근에 서울의 자동차 수가 증가했다.
18	invade 침입하다 [invéid]	He knows that Germany invaded Poland in 1939. 그는 독일이 폴란드를 1939년 침공했다는 것을 알고 있다.
19	obese 비만의, 뚱뚱한 [oubíːs]	A number of obese children are going to join the camp. 다수 비만의 학생들이 그 캠프에 합류할 것이다.
20	participate 참여하다 [pɑːrtísəpèit]	Many movie stars participate in the film festival. 많은 영화배우들이 그 영화제에 참여한다.
21	passenger 승객 [pǽsəndʒər]	All the passengers on the bus are students. 버스의 모든 승객들이 학생이다.
22	physics 물리학 [fíziks]	Studying physics is not what she wants. 물리학을 공부하는 것은 그녀가 원하는 것이 아니다.
23	politician 정치인 [pàlitíʃən]	The news about the politician is not true. 그 정치가에 대한 뉴스는 사실이 아니다.
24	pollution 공해, 오염 [pəljúːʃən]	They solved the pollution problem last month. 그들은 지난달 공해 문제를 해결했다.
25	portrait 초상화 [pɔ́ːrtrit]	Drawing portraits is my father's job. 초상화를 그리는 것이 내 아버지의 직업이다.
26	renovate 보수하다 [rénəvèit]	All the rooms in this hotel were renovated last year. 이 호텔의 모든 객실이 지난 해 보수되었다.
27	responsibility 책임 [rispànsəbíləti]	Either she or I am going to take the responsibility. 그녀 또는 내가 책임을 질 것이다.
28	spread 퍼지다 [spred]	A number of rumors about her are spreading over the country. 그녀에 대한 많은 소문들이 전국에 퍼지고 있다
29	traditional 전통적인 [trədíʃənəl]	Each country has its own traditional culture. 나라마다 그만의 전통 문화가 있다.
30	volunteer 자원하다 [vàləntíər]	I volunteered at the fire station. 나는 소방서에서 자원봉사를 했다.

Check Up

1 다음 우리말 뜻에 해당하는 영어 단어를 쓰세요.

01 정확한

02 불평하다

03 퍼지다

04 구성하다

05 줄어들다

06 발견하다

07 이민자

08 참여하다

09 전통적인

10 수입하다

11 증가하다

12 침입하다

13 비만의, 뚱뚱한

14 공해, 오염

15 보수하다

2 다음 영어 단어에 해당하는 우리말 뜻을 쓰세요.

01 ceremony

02 college

03 compose

04 embassy

05 employee

06 passenger

07 physics

08 portrait

09 responsibility

10 volunteer

3 다음 빈칸에 우리말과 일치하도록 알맞은 단어를 쓰세요.

01 You agreed to _____ with each other.
너희들은 서로 협력하겠다고 동의했다.

02 Studying _____ languages is very useful.
외국어를 공부하는 것은 매우 유용하다.

03 Every person in the office looks _____.
이 사무실의 모든 사람이 지쳐 보인다.

04 Isaac Newton discovered the law of _____.
Isaac Newton이 중력의 법칙을 발견했다.

05 The news about the _____ is not true
그 정치가에 대한 뉴스는 사실이 아니다.

단어장 해답

Chapter 01. 가정법

❶ 01. apologize 02. feeling 03. recipe 04. alive
05. happen 06. awful 07. complete 08. comfortable
09. envy 10. flight 11. fluently 12. interview
13. literature 14. nature 15. sunscreen

❷ 01. 주소 02. 용기 03. 농작물 04. 실험
05. 용서하다 06. 소개하다 07. 사다리 08. 백만장자
09. 기회 10. 복통

❸ 01. accept 02. during 03. forget 04. opportunity
05. polite

Chapter 02. 관계사 Ⅰ

❶ 01. advice 02. bark 03. several 04. translate
05. choose 06. mention 07. expel 08. damage
09. feather 10. flow 11. navigation 12. repair
13. seem 14. suffer 15. teenager

❷ 01. 우주비행사 02. 청구서 03. 금발 04. 지휘자
05. 치료하다 06. 어려움 07. 고아 08. 기록
09. 훔치다 10. 시스템

❸ 01. biology 02. boring 03. cover 04. expensive
05. ocean

Chapter 03. 관계사 Ⅱ

❶ 01. absent 02. bankrupt 03. bloom 04. celebrate
05. favor 06. couch 07. coworker 08. survive
09. explain 10. performance 11. flat 12. immigrate

13. lawyer   14. overlook   15. subscribe

❷ 01. 기념일   02. 회사   03. 결정   04. 배달하다
05. 목적지   06. 털   07. 발명하다   08. 향수
09. 추천하다   10. 존경하다

❸ 01. crash   02. currently   03. graduation   04. luggage
05. renovation

Chapter 04. 여러 가지 문장 Ⅰ

❶ 01. answer   02. leave   03. bother   04. usually
05. display   06. electrical   07. favorite   08. support
09. disappointed   10. language   11. nervous   12. refuse
13. request   14. surf   15. unplug

❷ 01. 대략   02. 건축가   03. 외교관   04. 장비
05. 과목   06. 소음   07. 돌아오다   08. 동상
09. 신뢰하다   10. 낭비하다

❸ 01. bite   02. election   03. furniture   04. recycle
05. such

Chapter 05. 여러 가지 문장 Ⅱ

❶ 01. borrow   02. abroad   03. cheerful   04. curious
05. wonder   06. fantastic   07. greedy   08. responsible
09. heavily   10. jealous   11. purse   12. scary
13. selfish   14. solve   15. terrible

❷ 01. 사고   02. 놀라운   03. 훌륭한   04. 영화
05. 알약   06. 선물   07. 약속하다   08. 결과
09. 가파른   10. 지갑

❸ 01. anger   02. breathe   03. cheat   04. creative
05. efficient

Chapter 06. 일치와 화법

❶ 01. accurate   02. complain   03. spread   04. consist
   05. decrease   06. discover   07. emigrant   08. participate
   09. traditional   10. import   11. increase   12. invade
   13. obese   14. pollution   15. renovate

❷ 01. 의식   02. 대학   03. 작곡하다   04. 대사관
   05. 종업원   06. 승객   07. 물리학   08. 초상화
   09. 책임   10. 자원하다

❸ 01. cooperate   02. foreign   03. exhausted   04. gravity
   05. politician

Longman

GRAMMAR
MENTOR
JOY

롱맨
그래머
멘토
조이
시리즈

최신개정판
400만부 돌파
롱맨 JOY
시리즈